Trekking
in the
Himalayas

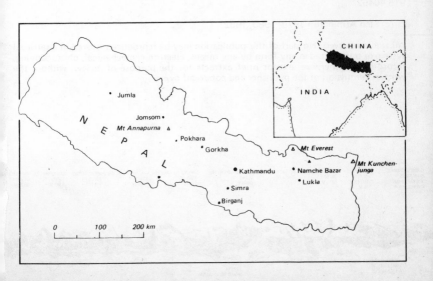

CHINA

INDIA

Jumla •

Jomsom •
Mt Annapurna △
Pokhara •
Gorkha •

△ Mt Everest

Kathmandu •   • Namche Bazar   △ Mt Kunchen-
                                        junga
• Simra   • Lukla
• Birganj

0   100   200 km

Trekking in the Himalayas

Published by:
Lonely Planet Publications, PO Box 88, South Yarra, Victoria 3141, Australia

Printed by:
Colorcraft, Hong Kong

Maps by:
Graphics Rachana, Kathmandu

Photographs by:
Dolf Reist (cover, page 4), Singh Photo, Kathmandu (11, 198/199), Marcus Brooke (56, 70, 100), Terry Walker (194, 195); all other photos by Stan Armington.

This Edition:
February 1982

**National Library of Australia
Cataloguing-in-Publication entry**

Armington, Stan.
Trekking in the Himalayas.

3rd rev. ed.
Previous ed.: South Yarra, Vic.: Lonely Planet, 1979.
ISBN 0 908086 29 6.

1. Himalaya Mountains — Description and travel —
Guidebooks. I. Title.

915.40452

GANESH HIMAL MANASLU ANNAPURNA DHAULAGIRI

LANGTANG -LIRUNG 23750 FT. 7246 M.

GOSAINTHAN 26150 FT. 8013 M.

DORJE-LAKPA 22870 FT. 6975 M.

PHURBI-GHYACHU 21840 FT. 6660 M.

CHHOBA-BHAMARE 19550 FT. 5970 M.

GAURI-SHANKAR 23442 FT. 7145 M.

MELUNGTSE 23560 FT. 7181 M.

CHUGIMAGO 20660 FT. 6297 M.

PIGFERAGO 21720 FT. 6620 M.

KATHMANDU 4423 FT. 1350 M.

KODARI 5800 FT. 1770 M. ROAD TO LHASSA

The Routes

Thyangboche	Dingboche	Pangboche
Pheriche	place place	the
map	is always right	

we don't	follow rivers	but climb
three thousand feet over	ridges to rejoin	the course
the rivers	get there first	but we've
been there twice		

Nuptse Lhotse	Phortse Kharte	
Khumbila Khunde	Khumjung	
place place	the map	is always right

we live upright	as the land	which
is never	level	the map says
the map	is not	mistaken

Pemba	Passang	
A Gelu	Ang Geljen	
	U Tsering	
of people	the	map
makes no mention		

from *Time by Distance*
by William A Fox

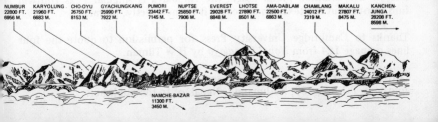

| NUMBUR 22800 FT. 6956 M. | KARYOLUNG 21960 FT. 6683 M. | CHO-OYU 26750 FT. 8153 M. | GYACHUNGKANG 25990 FT. 7922 M. | PUMORI 23442 FT. 7145 M. | NUPTSE 25850 FT. 7906 M. | EVEREST 29028 FT. 8848 M. | LHOTSE 27890 FT. 8501 M. | AMA-DABLAM 22500 FT. 6863 M. | CHAMLANG 24012 FT. 7319 M. | MAKALU 27807 FT. 8475 M. | KANCHEN-JUNGA 28208 FT. 8598 M. |

NAMCHE-BAZAR 11300 FT. 3450 M.

Stan Armington, the American managing director of Himalayan Journeys in Kathmandu, has been organising and leading treks in Nepal since 1971. A graduate engineer, he has also worked for the US National Park Service in the Yellowstone and Olympic parks, as well as serving as a guide on Mt Hood in Oregon. Stan is a fellow of the Royal Geographical Society, a member of the American Alpine Club, the Explorers' Club, and the Alpine Stomach Club. He is also the board of directors of the Chesley Donovan Foundation and Himalayan Journeys, Ltd. Stan is very enthusiastic about the country of Nepal and its people, with whom he works and lives.

A word of thanks to the many people who encouraged and assisted me with writing this material. In particular Terence Walker, Chuck McDougal, Lewis Underwood, Harka Gurung and Tek Pokharel provided information about places I have not been or things I did not understand. Hundreds of trekkers have helped me by asking questions that I would never have otherwise thought of; I have tried to answer most of them here. A trekking book could never be written without the help of the many Sherpas who led me up and down hills and patiently answered all my foolish questions about what we were seeing. Ang Geljen, Sona Hishi, Ila Tsering, Dawa Zangbu and Dawa Sundar helped the most. Mr B B Singh, of Singh Photo in Kathmandu, ran back and forth between his studio and my house trying to get all the pictures printed just the way I wanted them and the people at Graphics Rachan in Kathmandu laboriously transformed my crude sketches into first class maps. And most of all, thanks to Tony Wheeler who pushed me to tackle this project.

Despite the common plural usage, the Himalaya is singular — as you will find throughout the text. On the cover it is, incorrectly, plural!

Thanks to Cambridge University Press for permission to quote the four lines on page 124 from *Nepal Himalaya* by H W Tilman.

Corrections or suggestions can be sent to Stan Armington at Himalayan Journeys, PO Box 989, Kathmandu, Nepal, or to the publisher.

Contents

Preface

To travel in the remote areas of Nepal today offers much more than superb mountain scenery. It provides an opportunity to step back in time and meet people who, like our ancestors many centuries ago, lived free of complications, social, economic and political, which beset the developed countries. To the Nepal peasant, his life revolves around his homestead, his fields and, above all, his family and neighbours in the little village perched high on a Himalayan mountainside. Here we can see the meaning of community, free of the drive of competition. We see human happiness despite — or because of — the absence of amenities furnished by our modern civilisation.

Change will come to the Nepalese way of life, but it behoves travellers from the modernised countries to understand and respect the values and virtues of life today in rural Nepal. They have much to teach us about how to live.

John Hunt

Lord Hunt was the leader of the 1953 Mt Everest expedition when the peak was first scaled by Sir Edmund Hillary and Tenzing Norgay Sherpa.

Introduction

The Himalaya, the 'abode of snows', extends from Assam in eastern India, across Bhutan, Nepal and Pakistan, and west to Afghanistan. It is the chain of highest and youngest mountains on earth, a region of deep religious and cultural traditions and the home of an amazing diversity of people. Nowhere is this diversity more apparent and the culture more varied and interesting than in Nepal. This book concentrates on trekking in Nepal. Treks in the Himalaya of India, Pakistan, China and Afghanistan, while the traditions may be similar to those described here, are not quite the same sort of experience as a trek in Nepal.

This book is designed to help you prepare for a trek in Nepal organised through a trekking agency. The first section provides some background information about Nepal and trekking, and describes some alternate methods by which you may trek. The second part of this book provides detailed information about how to prepare yourself and your gear for a trek, and the third section describes the important trekking regions of Nepal and gives day-to-day descriptions of the best routes through these regions.

This book was not written to convince people to trek in Nepal, but instead provides those who are already considering a trek with some background about how and where to trek and makes some suggestions that may make a trek more worthwhile and enjoyable. Nepal has attracted trekkers, tourists and mountaineers ever since she opened her borders for the first time in 1950. It was a hippie mecca in the 1960's because of the availability of high quality marijuana and hashish. These drugs are now illegal in Nepal, but the remnants of that crowd still hang around Kathmandu and patronise a few black market dope dealers. Kathmandu's 'Freak Street' has become as much a tourist attraction as the temples of Durbar Square. A particularly important element of living this life style is an attempt to live as cheaply as possible. This, coupled with the tradition of 'getting back to the land', has resulted in many westerners trekking through Nepal on an artificially limited budget, continually striving to spend as little money as possible. Many of the problems in Nepal have resulted from this phenomenon and several books, articles and other publications have been written to exploit the idea that it is easy and cheap to trek through Nepal.

Another segment of writers, travel promoters and 'do'ers of professional good' are publicising the opportunities for visiting a primitive people and providing them with what we consider to be necessities of life in our western society.

It is important to recognise that tourism is Nepal's major industry, and one of the largest sources of the foreign exchange necessary for the continued economic development of the kingdom. Tourists are encouraged to visit Nepal because they spend money. While it is important that you spend this money wisely and in places where it may have a useful economic impact, it is important to Nepal's tourist industry that you do spend money. This book makes some suggestions on how you can arrange a trek in the most economically beneficial manner with a minimum of hassles.

I have sensed an increasing lack of mutual respect and understanding between Nepalese and westerners, a particularly distressing situation because both can learn so much from each other. If this learning is on a personal basis, not in schools, both peoples will be rewarded by a new understanding and insight, and in most cases can develop a new respect for their own culture and values. A well organised trek provides the opportunity for this learning and can lead to lasting friendships. Many suggestions are aimed at enhancing this opportunity for cultural exchange.

The information in this book is based on my own experiences in trekking, leading and organising treks, and living in Nepal for the past 11 years. Based on these experiences, I have included a lot of material that is my own opinion, but it is not unsubstantiated opinion. My conscious individual conclusions relate to two topics: trekking equipment and the personal relationship between westerners and Nepalese especially with the people of the hills.

If you have done a lot of hiking you will have certainly developed your own opinions, preferred equipment and techniques. Since my own opinions are the distillation of my own experiences on a particular type of outdoor trip, they may easily differ from yours. Please read over my suggestions about equipment — then make your own decisions.

My observations about the intermixing of two cultures — again, my opinion — are based on conditions as they now currently exist, not as they were in the immediate past. Even during the time I have spent in Nepal, there has been a dramatic change, just as in the west. Conditions in Nepal will continue to change. If you, the present-day trekker, are considerate, thoughtful and prepared (this book will help you in all three areas), these changes will be for the good of the hill people of Nepal and the trekkers who follow you.

A note on trekking that may help you understand this concept better at the outset: a trek in Nepal is many days long. A "long" trek is four or more weeks; a "short" one is at least a week or ten days. These terms conflict with our preconceptions of bush walking or hiking where a short hike may only be for a few hours and a long hike is a three-day weekend.

Part 1

Why Trek in Nepal?

Just as New York is not representative of the United States, so Kathmandu is not representative of Nepal. Those with the physical and personality qualifications should not miss the opportunity to leave Kathmandu and observe the spectacular beauty and the unique culture of Nepal. Fortunately for the visitor to Nepal there are few roads extending deeply into the hills, so the kingdom must be visited in the slowest and most intimate manner — by walking. The time and effort required for this mode of transportation certainly is greater than other ways, but then the rewards are correspondingly greater. Instead of zipping down a freeway, racing to the next "point of interest", each step provides new and intriguing viewpoints, and you will perceive your day as an entity, rather than a few highlights strung together by a ribbon of concrete. For the romanticist, each step is a step in the footsteps of Hillary, Tenzing and other Himalayan explorers. If you have neither the patience nor the physical stamina to visit the hills of Nepal on foot, aircraft and helicopters are available, providing an expensive and unsatisfactory substitute.

Trekking in Nepal will take you through a country that has captured the imagination of mountaineers and explorers for over a hundred years. You will encounter people in remote mountain villages whose life-style has not changed in generations, yet they will convey a trust of foreigners that is made possible by their secure position as the only country in the world that has never been ruled by a foreign power.

A trek also provides a glimpse into the ancient culture of Tibet. This culture has all but disappeared in its homeland, and is now rapidly being altered in Nepal by the influence of tourism and foreign-aid programmes.

On a trek you will see great diversity throughout Nepal. Villages embrace many ethnic groups and cultures, and the terrain changes from the tropical jungles to high glaciated peaks in only 150 km. From the start, the towering peaks of the Himalaya provide one of the highlights of a trek. Appearing first as many clouds on the horizon as your plane approaches Kathmandu, they become more definable and reach to seemingly impossible heights as you finally land at Kathmandu's Tribhuvan airport. During a trek the Himalaya disappears behind Nepal's continual hills, but dominates the northern skyline at each pass — Annapurna, Langtang, Gauri Shankar and Everest. Finally, after weeks of walking you will arrive at the foot of the mountains themselves — astonishing heights from which gigantic avalanches tumble earthwards in apparent slow motion, dwarfed by their surroundings. Your preconceptions of the Himalaya alter as you turn from peaks famed only for their height to gaze at far more picturesque summits you have never before heard of: Kantega, Ama Dablam, Machhapuchhare and Jannu.

A Trek is not a Wilderness Experience

The landscape of Nepal is almost continually inhabited. A population of several million people of various ethnic groups live in villages that seemingly blanket the hills. Even in the high mountains, small settlements of stone houses and yak pastures dot every possible flat space. Much of the fascination of a trek will be derived from the opportunity to observe life in these villages, where people truly live off the land, using only a few manufactured items such as soap, kerosene, paper and matches, all of which are imported in bamboo baskets carried by barefoot porters.

It is difficult for most westerners to comprehend this aspect of Nepal until they actually visit the kingdom. Our preconception of a roadless area is strongly influenced by the places we backpack or hike at home — true wilderness, usually protected as a National Park or forest. In the roadless areas of Nepal, there is little wilderness up to an elevation of 4000 metres. The average population density in the hills is more than 95 people per square km, and if this statistic is altered to eliminate all the mountainous places, the average rises to an incredible 500 or more persons per square km of cultivated land. The size and type of rural settlements varies widely, but most villages have from 15 to 75 houses, a population of 200 to 1000, and are spread out over an area of several square km.

Many of the values associated with a hiking trip at home do not have the same importance during a trek in Nepal. It is impossible to get completely away from people, except for short times or at extremely high elevations, though isolation is traditionally a crucial element of any wilderness experience. The concept of ecology must be expanded to include the effects of conservation measures on rural people and the economic effects of tourism on indigenous populations. Even national park management must be modified because there are significant population centres within Sagarmatha (Mt Everest) and Langtang National Parks.

Rather than detract from the enjoyment of a trek, the hill people, particularly their traditional hospitality and fascinating culture, make a trek in Nepal a special kind of mountain holiday unlike any other in the world.

Terraces

A Trek is not a Climbing Trip

A trek in Nepal spends most of its time in the middle hills region at elevations between 500 and 3000 metres. In this region, the trek is always on well-developed trails through villages and across mountain passes. Even at high altitudes there are intermittent settlements used in the summer by herders, so the trails, though often indistinct, are always there. All trails are easily traversed without the aid of ropes or any mountaineering skill. There are rare occasions when snow is encountered, and on some high passes it may be necessary to place a safety line for the porters if there is deep snow, but alpine techniques are almost never used on a traditional trek. Anyone who has walked extensively in the mountains has all the skills necessary for an extended trek in Nepal.

Though some treks venture near glaciers, and even cross the foot of them, most treks do not allow the fulfilment of any Himalayan mountaineering ambitions. A recent change in mountaineering regulations allows trekkers to climb 18 specified peaks with a minimum of formality, but advance arrangements must always be made for such climbs. Many agents are introducing 'climbing treks' which include the ascent of one of these peaks as a feature of the trek. This may be included as an option or, for more difficult

peaks, as a goal for the trip. This is discussed in greater detail in the section on climbing, later in this book.

Much of the beauty of the Nepal Himalaya is seen not only in the peaks themselves, but also in their surroundings: friendly people, picturesque villages and a great variety of cultures and traditions that seem to exemplify many of the attributes we have lost in our headlong rush for development and progress in the west. While the ascent of an Himalayan peak may be an attraction for some, it is not necessary to have such a goal to enjoy a trek. Throughout this book, trekking always refers to walking on trails.

Should you go on a Trek?

Not everyone should be encouraged to trek in Nepal. A number of people would be unhappy and uncomfortable, would give the Nepalese a poor impression of westerners, and would make things difficult and expensive for the trekkers who follow them. Some tour operators are now selling short treks as part of a deluxe package tour, and are attracting people who have never hiked before. Climbers are coming to Nepal in hopes of subverting the regulations for expeditions and making a Himalayan climb. Backpackers arrive in Nepal planning to carry a 30 kg load and trek in Nepal as they have hiked in their own country. These and many other misinformed people will usually be disappointed and often bitter after such an experience in Nepal.

Therefore you should evaluate yourself in at least two areas before undergoing a trek: are you in the proper physical condition for a trek and do you truly enjoy the outdoors? Do you have a disposition that will allow you to feel comfortable among the hill people of Nepal and accept a society with totally different motivations than your own for an extended period?

Physical Qualifications

A trek is physically demanding because of its length and the almost unbelievable changes in elevation. During the 550 km on a trek to and from the Everest base camp, for example, over 20,000 metres elevation are gained and lost during the many steep ascents and descents. On most treks, the daily gain is less than 800 metres in about 15 km, though ascents of as much as 1200 metres are typical of some days. There is plenty of time during the day to cover this distance, so the physical exertion, though quite strenuous at times, is not sustained. There will be plenty of time for rest. Probably the only physical problem that may make a trek impossible is a history of knee problems on descents. In Nepal the descents are long, steep and unrelenting. There is hardly a level stretch of trail in the entire kingdom. Therefore you should be in the best possible physical condition before beginning the trek. If you are an experienced bush walker and often hike 15 km a day with a pack, a trek should prove to be no difficulty. You will be pleasantly surprised at how easy the hiking can be when you only carry a light rucksack and all your meals are cooked and served for you.

Personality Qualifications

Because you must, of necessity, come into contact with other people, both Nepalese and western, you should consider how well you will fit in with them before committing yourself to a trek. Evaluate yourself in accordance with the following:

Previous experience in hiking and living outdoors. The first night of a month-long trip is too late to discover that you do not like to sleep in a sleeping bag. Mountaineering experience is not necessary, but you must enjoy walking.

The ability to adapt to unusual situations, to accept confusion, lack of certainty, and a flexible schedule — or even no schedule at all.

Acceptance of the fact that your values and the western way of life are not held throughout the universe. Accept the possibility that they just may not be the best standards for everyone.

The last two qualifications are perhaps the most important. In Nepal you will have assistance from many people who will do their best to provide you with whatever you ask for, in the manner to which you are accustomed. But since these people have never visited the west, they may not understand just what it is that you want, why you want it, or how you want it done. It's great fun to listen to western tourists demanding dry martinis, three-minute eggs, or a particular bottle of wine from a waiter who has never tasted these things and has no idea why anyone would pay such outrageous prices for them. Too often the tourist becomes angry and asks for "someone who speaks good English", never considering that he does not know a single word of Nepali. If you are able to accept confusion in situations or, better still forget the martini and head for a local shop patronised by Nepalese to enjoy *Chhang* or *rakshi* — the local brews — you are more likely to enjoy a trek. If you insist on dragging your world around in your suitcase you will be miserable and will be much happier spending a vacation in Europe or in a "5 star" luxury hotel in Kathmandu.

Similarly, do not attempt to treat Nepal as a weekend jaunt and carry your own backpack, petrol stove, freeze-dried food and tent. The trekker who packs his segment of our culture along with him is little different from that rich tourist ordering his martini. He will see the same scenery as the trekker who follows the suggestions in this book but will develop little understanding of Nepal, its people and its culture.

If you visit Nepal, be aware of the possibility of learning from people whose background and life-style are radically different from yours. Try to make every effort to ensure that your influence, both cultural and economic, on the people you encounter is as positive as possible. Trek with these thoughts in mind and you will enjoy the most rewarding experience of your life and develop new understanding of yourself and your world.

Geography of Nepal

Nepal is a small, landlocked country shaped like a rectangle 800 km long and 200 km wide. In the longitudinal 200 km, the terrain changes from the glaciers along the Tibetan border in the north to the flat jungles of the terai on the Indian border, barely 150 metres above sea level. The country does not ascend gradually from the plains; instead it rises in several chains of hills running in an east-west direction, finally terminating in the highest hills in the world — the Himalaya. Beyond the Himalaya is the 5000 metre high plateau of Tibet. The Himalaya is not a continental divide, so a number of rivers flow from Tibet through the mountains and hills of Nepal to join the Ganges in India. These are joined en route by many other rivers flowing southward from the glaciers of the Himalaya itself. The country, then, is scarred by great gorges in both north-south and east-west directions, resulting in a continual series of hills, some incredibly steep. Kathmandu lies in the largest valley of the kingdom — according to legend, once a huge lake. This valley is connected to the outside world by narrow mountain roads running north to China and south to India. The only other major road in the kingdom is the new East-West Highway that runs near the Indian border. Other than these roads and a few tracks that lead a short distance into the hills, all travel is on systems of trails that climb the steep hills of Nepal as no road possibly can.

The southernmost region includes the terai, the flat plain, until 1950 a malarial jungle inhabited primarily by rhinoceros, tiger, leopard, wild boar and deer. Now, with malaria eradicated, a large number of farming and industrial communities cover the terai. The southern region also includes the first major east-west chain of hills: the Siwalik hills and the Mahabharat range. In some parts of Nepal these hills are inhabited only by farmers, but in others they are the sites of large and well-developed villages.

The midlands, or middle hills, a band only 80 km wide, is the most populated region. This is the home of the ancient Nepalese people. The cities of Kathmandu, Patan, Bhadgaon, Pokhara, the ancient town of Gorkha (from which the term "Gurkha" — a name give to the Nepalese who enlisted in the British and Indian armies — was derived) and Jumla in the far west of Nepal are all within this region. Other than the Kathmandu and Pokhara valleys, the midlands region is hilly and steep. Extensive farming takes place on thousands of ancient terraces carved into the hills.

The Himalayan foothills and the Himalaya itself comprise only a small portion of the kingdom along the northern border. This inhospitable region is the least inhabited part of Nepal. Most of the villages sit between the 3000 metre and 4000 metre levels, although there are summer settlements as high as 5000 metres. Winter temperatures here are cold, but the warm sun makes days comfortable. Because of the short growing season, crops are few and usually small, consisting mostly of potatoes, barley and seasonal vegetables. The primary means of support in these regions is trading and herding sheep, cattle and yaks. Part of this region, Solu-Khumbu, is inhabited by Sherpas; much of the economy of this area is influenced by mountaineering and trekking expeditions.

From east to west the kingdom is divided into regions which are less clearly defined, although the political division is from east to west, not from north to south. The primary difference between eastern and western Nepal is the diminishing influence of the monsoon in the west. In the east, the climate is damp and ideal for tea growing; the conditions being similar to Darjeeling in India. In the far west the climate is quite dry even during the monsoon season. Another influence on the east-west division is the large rivers that flow southward in deep canyons, often limiting travel as they wash away bridges during monsoon.

How to Trek

There are hundreds of alternatives to bush walking or climbing in the west — from the "go-light" backpacker who carries but five kg for a weekend trip, through the surplus store backpacker who hauls an axe and a cast iron skillet, to the technical climber who carries 25 kg of climbing hardware, but neglects to bring a cooking pot. In Nepal, there are all these options, plus a considerable number of others as a result of the availability of inexpensive (by our standards) professional and non-professional labour and the large population that inhabits most trekking areas.

For simplicity I have condensed the infinite possibilities for trekking into four approaches: backpacking, living-off-the-land, do-it-yourself and arrangements made through a trekking agency. In order to discuss these approaches in detail, I have relied on a considerable amount of physical and cultural background about Nepal that has not been presented elsewhere. The discussion on how to trek will be preceded, therefore, by a discussion of some aspects of how people live in the hills of Nepal.

People of the Hills

It is important to understand the distribution of population throughout the kingdom. Nepal has a population of 13 million, but only 600,000 live in the Kathmandu valley. The rest of the people live in the terai or the hills in a primarily agricultural economy. In these regions, every possible piece of land is cultivated except where the hillsides are too steep or rocky to carve out even the smallest terrace. Extensive systems of trenches and canals provide the irrigation necessary to assure adequate food production. Houses are built near a family's fields, so a typical Nepalese 'village' extends over a large area and may have an elevation differential of several hundred metres or more between the highest and lowest homes.

Most Nepalese families are self-sufficient in their food supply, raising all of it themselves and selling the excess in the few places, such as Kathmandu, Pokhara, Biratnagar and Birganj, that do not have a strictly agricultural economy. In return, the villagers purchase the items that they are not able to raise or produce themselves; sugar, soap, cigarettes, tea, salt, cloth and jewellery. This exchange of goods creates a significant amount of traffic between remote villages and large population and manufacturing centres throughout Nepal. The goods are transported exclusively by porters carrying bamboo baskets with a tumpline across their foreheads. During the many days they travel in each direction, porters either camp alongside the trail and eat food that they have carried with them from home, or purchase food and shelter from homes along the trail. There are occasional tea shops called *bhattis*, on some trails, but porters rarely patronise them for more than an occasional cup of tea, because prices in a *bhatti* are much higher than sharing an already prepared meal with a family. Often porters travel in groups of five or more and take turns cooking, thus securing a substantial saving in the cost of food.

A typical meal for hill porters might consist of a thick paste called tsampa, made from coarse ground barley, corn or millet, often mixed with a few hot chilis. Another favourite food is dal bhat; rice (bhat) with a soup made of lentils (dal) poured over it. Rarely is meat or an egg included in local diet; protein is gained from dal. An unleavened bread (roti) is another frequent addition to a meal, often substituting for rice. Other items may be added to a meal, usually a curry made from seasonal vegetables.

Second to the transportation of goods is the flow of people between the warmer climates of the terai and the colder Himalayan regions. People also travel extensively in connection with weddings, funerals and special festivals. Several of the hundreds of festivals that occur annually in Nepal require that people visit the homes of their relatives. Of particular importance is the Dasain festival in October during which hundreds of people travel from urban centres to hill villages. Those who travel at these times are from a wide variety of economic backgrounds, so their mode of travel may range from hillside camps to those of the porters to service by an entire household staff. It is certainly rare, but not impossible, to see a woman being carried by a porter in a chair or a basket. Men who were born in hill villages and served in a Gurkha regiment of the British or Indian armies often return home on leave, or upon retirement, with a huge retinue of porters carrying items they have collected during their assignments in Singapore,

Rai woman making
millet chang

Hong Kong or England.

Therefore, a wide variety of modes of travel exists on the trails of Nepal, influenced almost exclusively by one's economic and social position. Whatever his means of travel and whatever his economic status, a traveller makes a direct contribution to the economy of every village through which he travels. In some cases, it is the purchase of food, in others it is the sale of necessary goods or services and in others it is the hire of locals to serve as porters for a few days. The inhabitants of villages situated on major trails have come to expect and depend on this economic contribution — in much the same way as our transport cafes, roadhouses, motels and petrol stations rely on travellers of all sorts to provide much of their income.

Another phenomenon that occurs in the hills is people coming into continual personal contact. There are no trail signs, no hotel signs and no maps. No matter how shy a person may be, he must continually ask for directions, help in finding food and other items, and information about places to stay, how far it is to the next village, and so on. This is a habit many of us have lost in the west; we rely on the isolation of our car to insulate us from strangers, we rarely need to ask directions because of the abundance of road signs and maps. We can easily shop in a supermarket without speaking a word to anyone.

Because of the people of Nepal are constantly exchanging important information, it often develops into long exchanges of pure conversation or useless information ("What time is it?" "What are you carrying in that basket?") or a traveller may waste an hour or two discussing trail conditions, where he has been, politics, the weather, crop conditions, the price of rice in a neighbouring village, who is married (and who isn't, but should be), who died recently, or hundreds of other topics with a complete stranger whom he may never meet again. This is an important part of life in the hills. There are no telephones, no newspapers, no televisions and few radios. Most of the news comes from travellers — it is certainly more interesting to hear first-hand experiences than the radio news broadcast. Once the crops are planted for the season there isn't much to do, beyond the day-to-day activities of housecleaning, cooking and taking care of the children, until harvest time. Besides their economic importance, travellers are valued as a diversion, a source of information and a glimpse into a new and different world.

A Nepalese View of Foreigners

Although Nepal has been accessible to foreigners only since 1950, there are few places in the kingdom that have not been visited by either trekkers, photographers, expeditions or foreign aid representatives. Foreigners, particularly light-skinned westerners, stand out readily in Nepal, and must realise that they are viewed by the Nepalese according to the stereotype created by those who have preceded them. They too will contribute to the image of the next westerners who happen to come along.

Unfortunately, the image which has predominated is one of great wealth and of a superior culture which westerners wish to share with the Nepalese. Such traditions as passing out balloons, candy and pencils to kids contribute to this view, but it is on a far grander level that the real image has been developed. Mountaineering expeditions have spent seemingly limitless sums of money for porters, sherpas and equipment, including much fine gear for the high altitude sherpas. At the conclusion of the expedition, the excess food and gear is usually given away — this being cheaper than repacking and shipping it home. This type of extravagance, even though it is often supported by foundations and other large organisations, not by the expedition members themselves, leads many Nepalese to believe, justifiably, that westerners have a huge amount of money and will simply pass it out to whomever makes the most noise. An interesting by product of this phenomenon is that all sorts of used mountaineering gear in Kathmandu was once sold at ridiculously low prices — because nobody in Nepal has ever had to pay for it. A Nepalese received it as a gift, or bought it for a very cheap price and then sold it for whatever he could get. Now, however, prices are the same or higher — than in the west because shopkeepers have seen equipment catalogues and charge according to the retail prices for new items.

The sherpas who deal with trekkers and expeditions quickly discovered that the airfare to Nepal from Europe or Australia is as much as $1000, which seems an astronomical amount of money. No matter how small a trekker's budget may be, he still was able to get to Nepal. The sherpas know this and are generally unable to accept a plea of poverty from someone who, according to their standards, has already spent the equivalent of about two years wages, or enough money to build three large houses. It is impossible to explain the difference in our relative economic positions to a Nepalese in the hills. We ourselves find it difficult to comprehend that a dollar buys the equivalent of ten dollars in Nepal.

Many trekkers and expedition members in the past have given huge tips to sherpas. Reports of $100 tips are not unheard of; one group recently tipped each of three sherpas $40 for a six day trek (for which their total salary was only $10). This type of extravagance not only forces up wages, resulting in higher demands on the next trekker or expedition, but also contributes to an unhealthy view of westerners as rich, lavish and foolish. It makes it impossible for an individual on a tight budget to convince Nepalese people that he can't afford outrageous salaries, tips or huge amounts of food during a trek.

A number of schools and hospitals have been built in Nepal, particularly in Sherpa villages. These facilities are largely supported by contributions from organisations of the western world, although a great effort has been made to require contributions of local labour and money. These unquestionably perform a great service and are sorely needed, but this method of financing does help to sustain the preconception of a westerner as a person with a huge amount of money with which he will readily part if he is approached with sufficient cleverness. Many trekkers, feeling a strong affinity for villagers or sherpas they have met, have supported the education of children or even provided free overseas trips for them. This practice is certainly worthwhile and kind, but it does encourage Nepalese people to actively seek such favours in their dealings with westerners.

Nor is the problem confined to the hills and the efforts of some thoughtless individuals. Many nations, eager to have a foothold in what they feel is a strategic part of the world, contribute vast sums of money to aid programmes in Nepal. Such programmes might not contribute further to an unhealthy view of westerners (and would undoubtedly do more good) if they did not also support the westerners who work for them in lavish style. Many foreigners live in Kathmandu and other places in Nepal in conditions similar to their western homes, eating food flown from home at their own government's expense and being served by more servants than they could conceive of at home.

Most foreigners carry with them an astonishing array of camera gear, tape recorders and other gadgetry. The exact cost of such items is unknown to the Nepalese, but it's obvious that they're expensive, even by western standards. Yet a surprisingly large number of people seem to have no care for this wealth and leave cameras behind on rocks or give their watches away at the conclusion of a trek. Not only can we afford to buy such expensive things, but we don't even take care of them. Compare this attitude to that of the porter carrying a duffle bag or the sherpa kitchen boy with patched and re-patched jeans, shoes and rucksack.

This is the westerner with whom the Nepalese is familiar. They may also recognise the qualities of sincerity, happiness, or fun, but the primary quality they see is wealth. Many Nepalese consider it their personal obligation to separate a share of a westerner's money from him by calling on his sense of fair play, through blackmail (a porter's strike in a remote location), through shrewdness and trickery or, fortunately still rarely, through thievery. Westerners are stuck with this image, no matter what they do personally to dispel it, and an appreciation of this situation is very helpful in developing an understanding of local attitudes during a trek in Nepal.

A Note about Sherpas

There are a great number of ethnic groups in Nepal. Although the Sherpas are the most famous of these groups, they form only a small part of the total population, and live in a relatively small and inhospitable region of the kingdom. Sherpas first came into prominence when a number of them were hired for the 1921 reconnaisance of Mt Everest from the Tibetan side. The expedition started from Darjeeling, India, where a number of Sherpas were living. Therefore it was not necessary to travel into forbidden Nepal to hire them. Later expeditions, impressed by the performance of Sherpas at high altitudes and their selfless devotion to their jobs, continued the tradition of hiring Sherpas as high altitude porters. Most of the hiring was done in Darjeeling or by messages sent into the Solu Khumbu region of Nepal (where most Sherpas live) through friends and relatives.

This practice continues to the present day with a number of trekking organisations hiring Sherpas on a seasonal basis, and others hiring them on a per trek basis. The emphasis has been shifted from Darjeeling to Kathmandu and to the Solu Khumbu region itself as these areas have become accessible to foreigners.

It is confusing to discuss the roles of Sherpas on an expedition or a trek. The word "Sherpa" can refer both to an ethnic group and to a function or job on an expedition. The job of "sherpa" implies someone who is reasonably experienced in dealing and communicating with westerners, and who often speaks some English. A sherpa has a good knowledge of his job, either cook, kitchen crew, sardar (head sherpa on a trek, who is responsible for all purchases and for hiring porters), orderly (who takes care of the needs of two or more trekkers), or high altitude porter. The term also implies a knowledge of the region a trek will visit. A sherpa acts as a guide in the lowlands, asking directions from the locals, if necessary, to find the best trail to a destination. The term sherpa does not, however, imply any technical mountaineering skill. Sherpas, although they live near the high Himalayan peaks, never set foot on them, except to cross high passes on trade routes, until the British began to introduce the sport of mountaineering. Many trekking sherpas have served as high-altitude porters on mountaineering expeditions, carrying loads along routes already established by technically proficient mountaineers; but it is only in the past few years that sophisticated mountaineering training has been made available to Nepalese at the Nepal Mountaineering Association school in Manang.

Chorpen Nima Tashi Sherpa from Khumjung

The term "Sherpa" with a capital "S" refers to members of that ethnic group. On a trek or expedition, the role of "sherpa" (without that capital "S") is generally fulfilled by a Sherpa, but there have been many recent exceptions from this tradition. Sambhu Tamang, who reached the summit of Everest with the Italian expedition in 1973, was the first non-Sherpa Nepalese to reach the summit of a major Himalayan peak.

A porter is a person who carries loads and whose job is completed once camp is reached. The job of a sherpa, on the contrary, is just beginning once the group is in camp. A porter may be a member of any of the ethnic groups. Many Rais, Tamangs and Magars spend almost their entire lives on the trail serving as porters, not only for trekkers, but also bringing supplies to remote hill villages. On an expedition, the term "high-altitude porter" is often used interchangeably with "sherpa" to denote those who are carrying loads to high camps on the mountain.

On the subject of nomenclature: a western (or Japanese) man is a *sahib* (pronounced "sob"), a western woman is *memsahib*, and a porter is a *coolie*. These terms no longer hold the derogatory implications that they did during the British Raj.

Four Approaches to Trekking

It is into this environment that a trekker must fit. The only similarity between the hill regions of Nepal below 4000 metres and the places you may have bushwalked or climbed in the west is that both are accessible only by trail. Even this similarity is misleading, because National Park and Forest trails tend to switchback and follow established standards for maximum gradient. But Nepalese trails take the most direct route up a ridge or through a valley, diverting only to visit a village or to avoid trampling a field of rice or millet.

With this background in mind, let us consider the major ways in which a trekker can outfit himself for a trek, and how various approaches to trekking may result in a wide variety of experiences for a trekker. It should become obvious that the way a trekker interacts with the people he meets will be a primary influence on his enjoyment of a trek.

Let me admit at the outset to being prejudiced in favour of the complete arrangement approach, where everything is arranged before you leave home and the trek is accompanied by the traditional sherpas and porters. My prejudice has been derived from several concerns:

An effort to encourage trekkers to make a positive, not a negative, impact on the hill country.

A desire to be reasonably comfortable when I travel; a decent meal and a good night's sleep are important after a full day of walking.

A desire to follow the established traditions in places I visit.

Conservatism that makes me uncomfortable stepping into a totally unknown situation without some help, particularly when my time and money are somewhat limited.

This does not mean, however, that I feel that only the rich should trek in Nepal. If you follow my advice, and arrange your trek through a trekking agency, you will almost be assured of an enjoyable and rewarding experience at a reasonable price. If you do not share my conservatism and are willing to buy a plane ticket to Nepal without making prior arrangements, you can, by following some of the advice in this book, probably have a similar experience — probably a little less costly, but possibly more so, depending on your luck and how much extra time you must spend in Kathmandu getting things organised before you begin your trek. I should point out that the majority who go trekking without prior arrangements are young people on overland trips or those who have a round-the-world air ticket. For them, Nepal is only one stop on a trip taking from three months to two years. Unlike most readers of this book, their time is not limited, and the expense of travelling to Nepal is not a consideration — they are already there. This is an important factor to keep in mind as you read or hear accounts of trekking in Nepal on your own. For if Nepal is your only destination, and the trek will be your only long vacation for two or three years, you'll probably be as conservative as I am, and want to have as great a chance as possible of making the trek an overwhelming success.

THE BACKPACKING APPROACH

Hundreds of people each year load a pack with a stove, freeze-dried food, a light tent, and set off for the trail. Many of these people are under the mistaken impression that they will be in wilderness once they leave the Kathmandu valley. They have envisaged a campsite with a stream, some trees to sleep under, and a quiet night. Instead they soon discover that running water means a village, or at least a house, nearby; that many trees have had most of their lower limbs cut off for firewood; and that barking dogs keep them awake all night long. With all their fancy equipment, most of which is unavailable in Nepal, they become the centre of attraction wherever they stop — a situation they had not envisaged and are often not prepared to deal with after a full day on the trail. It is enough trouble to light a stove, follow the instructions on the food packet, try to get some clean water to cook in, and set up a tent without continually having to chase kids, dogs and goats away from camp.

The backpacker breaks two cardinal rules for travellers in Nepal: he does not contribute to the economy, and because of the multitude of camp chores he has to perform, doesn't have the time or the inclination to entertain villagers. I know a few trekkers who have had meaningful and successful treks with this approach, but I have met many more who were either frustrated and completely alienated by the villagers they confronted, or who had given up their backpacking approach and hired a porter, taking up the "live-off-the-land" approach described in the next section. If there is one message this book conveys, I hope it is that the western approach to backpacking, as we practice it, is not a viable approach to trekking in Nepal.

At higher altitudes the backpacking approach may be useful. Depending on the terrain and local weather conditions, villages extend up to 4000 metres and there are summer settlements as high as 5000 metres. Many of these high villages are deserted from autumn to early spring, and it is in these regions that you may wish to alter your trekking style and utilise a backpacking or mountaineering approach to reach high passes or the foot of some remote glaciers in uninhabited regions. In many areas it is difficult to arrange for porters who have the proper clothing and footgear for travelling in cold and snow. It is often the best solution to leave much of your gear and food behind at a temporary "base camp" in care of a trustworthy sherpa, and spend a few days carrying your own food and equipment. This will provide the best of both worlds: an enriching cultural experience in the lowlands, which conforms to the standards and traditions of the country, and an interesting wilderness or mountaineering experience in which you deal directly with high mountains.

LIVE OFF THE LAND
Another type of trekker visits Nepal armed with a pack containing only clothing and bedding, and spends several weeks trekking throughout Nepal. Many of these trekkers, either at the beginning, or as their packs become too burdensome, hire a porter to carry their extra gear. A large number of people operate with a bare minimum of equipment and carry it themselves. For food and shelter they rely on *bhattis*, homes, and small "hotels" along the major trekking routes. In this manner, a trekker can operate for about $3 a day, often less though sometimes more, depending on his personality and on local economic conditions. I've trekked in this manner, and talked to many others who have done so, and am convinced that it takes a special type of person to make it work. There are probably more people who have had unhappy experiences than have had an enjoyable trek. But perhaps the rewards for the minority are far greater than for others.

On the Jomsom trek (from Pokhara to Muktinath) and in Khumbu (from Lukla to Pheriche) the conditions for "live off the land" trekkers are much different than in other parts of Nepal. There are Thakali inns on the Jomsom trek, and in both regions there are several hotels financed by NIDC, the Nepal Industrial Development Corporation. There are reasonable imitations of these facilities along the Sundarijel-Mahenkal-Tarke Gyang route to Helambu and along the Lamosangu-Jiri-Lukla route to Khumbu, but there still are many places on these routes where the only food and accommodation available is in private homes. The Jomsom trek and the Khumbu region are the only places where the facilities are consistently good.

If you are considering this style of trekking, first make a trek near Pokhara, perhaps as far as Jomsom or Muktinath. You can travel from inn to inn throughout the entire trek. It is possible, though slightly more expensive and difficult, to do the same from Lukla as far as Pheriche, and sometimes even to Lobouje. Most of the inns in these regions have dormitories or private rooms separate from the family living quarters, and most rooms have beds. Most Thakali inns have bedding — usually a cotton-filled quilt — available; sometimes the bedding has the added attraction of lice and other interesting bed companions. There are usually tables and chairs for eating. Several inns on the Jomsom trek even have sidewalk cafes where you can enjoy a meal in the sun. Beer, coke and other soft drinks are available everywhere, and the menus are often attractive and extensive. Too often, however, the menu represents the inkeepers fantasy of what he would like to serve, not what's available, so the choice almost always comes back to rice, dal, potatoes and pancakes. Thirty years ago, Tilman observed that one can live off the country in a sombre fashion, but Nepal is no place in which to make a gastronomic tour. It hasn't changed.

In many places, even along these developed routes, you will have to wait two hours or more for a meal. This means that many breakfasts and lunches will be tea and biscuits unless you are willing to keep your itinerary flexible and wait until the innkeeper gets around to preparing food. The alternative is to carry some food and cooking pots with you, but this can easily get out of control with porters, cooks and all the complications of a more organised trek.

Nepal has much more to offer than Jomsom and Khumbu. In most other areas, however, the facilities for "live off the land" trekkers are spartan or nonexistent. There are a few good hotels here and there, but you may not be able to find reasonable accommodation during the many days it takes to walk to a hotel, so the situation often becomes self-defeating. You must be able to count on finding food and accommodation *every night* of your trek. If you carry food, cooking pots and a tent to use even one night, you have escalated beyond the "live-off-the-land" approach into a more complex form of trekking with different problems and benefits.

There are many things to consider about a trek that relies entirely on locally available food and accommodation if you stray from the more developed routes.

Inflation

Trekkers can have a devastating effect on the economy of villages as they pass through them, especially if they trek in large numbers. The $3 a day that a trekker might spend is higher than the average daily wage in Nepal and twice the daily wage of a porter! By competing with local people in remote areas for the limited food supply one cannot help but drive the price of food higher, since a westerner always pays a higher price than the locals. An example: on the Lamosangu to Solu Khumbu route a chicken costs $3, in Jomsom a chicken may fetch as much as $7; yet on a route visited by very few trekkers a chicken sells for about 80c. Even though you continually bargain the price down to what, to you, is low, you're always outbidding the natives and contributing to an inflationary situation. Remember, the shopkeepers have seen a lot of trekkers and know how much you can afford. An important exception to this problem occurs in areas with well-established inns where food has been specially grown or purchased independently of the local supply. Fruit, especially oranges and apples, is a cash crop, so this can be purchased in quantity when it is available.

Food

A feature of the "live-off-the-land" approach that makes it unappealing to some people, including me, is the almost total lack of variety in the diet. "Dal bhat" twice a day for a month presents a pretty boring prospect to the western palate. Although it's sometimes possible to obtain variety, it is along the lines of the basic local diet already described. Trekkers often destroy their budget completely when they buy cans of beer or tins of food left by an expedition. It takes a considerable amount of imagination to provide the variety in diet that westerners are used to, even in Kathmandu, where a considerable amount of imported food is available. It is almost impossible to provide this variety in remote regions unless you've brought the food with you. Most people can adapt to a Nepalese diet, but try it for a few days at home — boiled rice with a thick split pea soup poured over it is the closest approximation — before you opt for this alternative.

Routes

You are dependent on facilities located, for the most part, in villages, so you must trek only in inhabited localities. Because you need to know where and if you can eat, you will usually have to stick to the better-known routes as well. Your schedule may often be altered in order to reach a certain place for lunch or dinner time. Many trekkers have gone without lunch, or even dinner, because they mistakenly assumed that a village or hotel existed at a convenient time for stopping. Most of the major routes are well documented but are also well-travelled. A hotel can be out of food if there are a number of other trekkers there, or if you are late. Your destination for the day can also get severely altered when you discover that the lunch you ordered at a tiny inn will take a very long time to prepare. You will usually discover this only after you have waited an hour or so already.

Bargaining

In Asia, a price, once agreed upon, is sacred. If no price has been fixed in advance, however, any outrageous demand is acceptable. Your first contact with most people will be the negotiation of a price for food, sleeping, tea or whatever. Asians regard bargaining as a game; once over it's all forgotten, and great friendships can ensue. Westerners are not used to this technique and often cannot forget their first impressions, thereby developing a negative view toward those with whom they argue — which in Nepal can be anyone who tries to sell you anything. Most shopkeepers have seen enough trekkers to know what you will be willing to pay if they hold out long enough, so you're at an initial disadvantage. English, though widely understood in the Kathmandu valley, is rarely spoken in the hills (although it's a safe bet that the average Nepalese speaks more English than you speak Nepali — a fact to keep in mind when you get angry because of communication problems), so there is a fair chance that once an agreement has been reached, you will later discover that there was a misunderstanding and everyone thought you had agreed to a higher price. Many trekkers I have met were convinced that everyone in Nepal was a crook, and were completely alienated because of the continual problems caused by bargaining and misunderstanding. Most *bhattis* and shops in the hills have fixed prices for food, sleeping, and staple items. Bargaining is confined mostly to fruit vendors, trinket salesmen and anyone selling livestock — goats and chickens, for example.

Your Reputation

Because of misunderstanding, or simply just because they felt they wre being "ripped off" by locals, a surprisingly large number of trekkers have retaliated by walking off without paying for the food and accommodation they used. This phenomenon provides some insight into how strongly people feel they have been cheated — it's usually for, say, 30c (a few minutes work in the west, but 1/5 of a day's pay for a porter). There's not much an innkeeper can do when a trekkers walks out on a bill, so he usually accepts his loss and tries to recoup it from the next trekker who happens along. If that's you, your bill may suddenly be doubled, or the total fee demanded in advance, a custom that is becoming quite prevalent. The whole situation is most unfortunate and has been caused by a number of thoughtless and unpleasant trekkers. Since you are following in their footsteps, your reputation is built by the actions of those who have preceded you. This helps explain the attitudes of some villagers and provides the "live-off-the-land" trekker with yet another obstacle to overcome.

Safety

Despite the caution advised by the US Embassy that is reprinted in the section on "Dangers of a trek", most people in the hills of Nepal are friendly, helpful and honest. It is, however, a good idea to travel with a well-chosen companion — either another westerner or a guide — for reasons of personal safety. The chance of theft is still remote, but a sprained ankle, debilitating illness or other misfortune can occur at any time. It is only common sense, applicable to a hiking trip anywhere, that you should not travel alone in the mountains.

Sleep

When you visit the house of a relative or a friend, you normally have to make some concessions to his way of living, particularly as it relates to bedtime and waking up. The same is true throughout the world, including the hills of Nepal. If you stay in someone's house, whether it has a sign that says "hotel" or not, you may expect to have a difficult time sleeping until the entire household has retired. Since you are a guest in the house (and your command of Nepali isn't good enough to ask everyone to be quiet) it is pretty near impossible to inflict your schedule on the entire household.

Most people who walk and exert themselves all day require more sleep than they normally do at home. Trekkers often will sleep ten or eleven hours each night. But the village people, who are not exerting themselves during the day, can get by with six to eight hours. This presents an immediate conflict in life styles and sleep requirements, particularly when the inevitable booze and card party erupts in the next room, or worse yet in your bedroom itself. Another universal deterrent to sleep is the ubiquitous Radio Nepal, which must always be listened to at high volume, and which does not stop broadcasting until 11 pm. The simple solution to this problem is to take your tent and pitch it a few hundred metres from the nearest house, but the tent is extra weight and may require a porter to carry it. Most "live-off-the-land" trekkers are unwilling to bear this additional expense. It seems a small price to pay, however, for the assurance of a good night's sleep.

Accommodation

Except for the places already mentioned, there are only a few real "hotels" in the hills of Nepal. The accommodation available in most places is in an often dirty, always smoky, home. Chimneys are rare, and a room on the second floor of a house can turn into an intolerable smokehouse as soon as the cooking fire is lit in the kitchen below. Often it is possible to sleep on porches of houses, but your gear is then less secure. The most common complaint among "live-off-the-land" trekkers is dirty and smoky accommodation. If you choose this type of travel, reconsider again the advantages of bringing your own tent.

Guides and Porters

From Lukla to Pheriche and from Pokhara to Muktinath you do not necessarily need a guide — although a good guide will always make things easier (and often cheaper) by negotiating on your behalf and will hopefully show you places of interest and trail junctions that you might have otherwise overlooked. In Khumbu, there is the additional benefit of being invited (almost always) to the house of your guide where you can become familiar with the Sherpa culture, and where your guide — and you — will (almost always) get drunk. On other routes, where there are fewer signs that say "hotel", accommodation and food is found by asking from house to house. A guide can be indispensible in such situations.

Tradition dictates that guides receive a salary (about $3 a day in 1981) plus accommodation and food. If you are staying at inns, you will be amazed at how much your tiny guide can eat and drink at your expense. It is usually cheaper to carry a small amount of food and cook it yourself. The guide can do this. This leads, however, to hiring a porter to carry the food and cooking pots; tradition also dictates that a guide does not carry a load. Suddenly your trek is transmogrified into a "do it yourself" trek with all its attendant bureaucratic hassles.

If you are considering hiring only a porter, think again. You can often find reliable porters, but the large majority are uneducated people who are subject to whims, fears, ill health and superstition. Your porter may vanish, or he may decide that he has gone far enough and wants to return home. If you have a (hopefully) reliable sherpa, and he has hired the porter, it is his responsibility to assure the porter's performance, and he will be intimidated into carrying the load himself (the only situation where a sherpa will willingly carry a porter load) until he can find a replacement for the porter — and you can be sure that he will do so in a hurry. If you have hired the porter yourself, you sit alongside the trail until a replacement comes along.

Porters are expected to buy their own food locally out of their wages ($2 a day in 1981), therefore you do not have to carry food for your porters. Unless you provide food and shelter for the porters, however, you will have to camp near a village where they can obtain food every night. If you are going into snow, you *must* provide goggles, shoes, shelter and clothing; porters are not expendable.

On the Brighter Side

As a "live-off-the-land" trekker, you can move at your own pace, set up your own schedule, move faster or slower than others, and make side trips not possible with a large group. You can spend a day photographing mountains, flowers, or people — or you can simply lie in bed for a day.

You will come into contact with other trekkers from throughout the world in a unique situation where both of you are out of place. Bonds can develop that would not be possible in either his home or yours. Often you will discover that you're travelling at much the same schedule as several others and you can share experiences, expenses and information during your trek.

You are free (within the limits imposed by your trekking permit) to alter your route as you learn about other interesting places in the vicinity or to join up with other trekkers and head off in their direction.

The "live-off-the-land" method offers the best opportunity to see how the people in the hills of Nepal live, work and eat and to develop at least a rudimentary knowledge of the Nepali language. The problem, of course, is that not only do you learn how the Nepalese live, but you must also live like them   and it may be too late when you find that you don't enjoy it.

DO-IT-YOURSELF APPROACH

A third alternative style of trekking is to gather sherpas, porters, food and equipment and take off on a trek with all the comforts and facilities of a trek arranged by an agent abroad. The size of the party for such a trek may range from one or two persons on to an almost impossible size — twenty or more. For many, this is a satisfactory solution and trekkers who opt for this approach, particularly with a small group of friends, are often rewarded with an enriching and enjoyable trip.

It is possible to wander through Kathmandu and pick up a sherpa or two, have him hire porters, visit shops and purchase food, then set off on your trek. There is a major drawback to this method. You have no way of knowing the honesty of the individuals you may hire, other than the letters they produce from the past (always satisfied) customers. Since those you hire obviously know the market prices and can bargain better than you, there is a significant opportunity to charge you much more for many goods and services — with the surplus making its way back to your employee. This is more a conformity to tradition (remember, you are wealthy!) than dishonesty; every tour guide in Asia, for example, receives a commission on whatever you buy from the shops to which he guides you.

October, November, March and April are very busy trekking seasons, and any sherpa who does not have a job during these months is probably of questionable reliability. During other months, it is often possible to find excellent staff with the help of a trekking agency in Kathmandu. You will find them more willing to help you if you offer them a fee for their assistance or hire some equipment from them. Trekking equipment shops are another place to ask for advice.

It is also possible to hire sherpas and porters on the spot in Lukla, except during October and early November, so you might be successful if you fly in and try to organise a "do-it-yourself" trek without a lot of advance preparations. There are no sherpas or porters available at Jomsom or Langtang, however. It is becoming imperative to be cautious when you hire either sherpas or porters. Hotels, trekking agencies or recommendations of other trekkers should be consulted before you employ anyone whom you do not know.

There are a host of recent regulations that govern trekking, although the degree of enforcement varies. Trekking agencies charge what they do because they are always subject to these rules, and compliance with them adds considerably to the cost of a trek. You should be aware that any of the following regulations could be strictly enforced at any time; your trek may be curtailed, and you could be fined, if you do not follow them.

Visa Extension

You receive a free visa extension in connection with your trekking permit, but you are obligated to prove that you actually went trekking for the full period. How to do this? You should get your trekking permit endorsed at any police checkposts that you come across. There is a whopping fine for overstaying your visa extension. You cannot leave the country until the fine is paid.

Trekking permit

At $5 a week, you may be tempted to understate the duration of your trek. You may be turned back or fined at a police checkpost in the hills if your trekking permit has expired. Be sure that the destination is shown correctly on your trekking permit; it cannot be altered except in Kathmandu.

Insurance

Trekkers are required to insure all their sherpas and porters for Rs 25,000 (about $2100) against accidental death. Trekking companies have a blanket policy that covers all their staff. There are insurance companies in Kathmandu that can provide coverage for a fee of about $8 per person.

Fuel

The current National Park regulations (see day 13 of the Everest trek) prohibit the use of firewood in Sagarmatha, Langtang and Rara National Parks. But there often is no alternative fuel — such as paraffin (kerosene) — available in these regions, and the Indian pressure stoves are troublesome and inefficient, especially at high altitudes. You could be stopped at the park entrance if you are not self-sufficient in fuel. Note that this means that your whole party, including the porters, must cook on stoves.

To obtain a little more reliability and to have things organised in advance, it is possible to contact a registered trekking company by mail and have them make arrangements for your trek. There are more than 30 trekking companies in Kathmandu that will organise treks for a fee and provide all sherpas, porters and, if necessary, equipment. Communication to Nepal is slow, however, and the volume of correspondence required to provide you with the information you require, to determine your specific needs, to define your precise route and itinerary, to fit you into an already overcrowded schedule and to negotiate a price that both parties understand, can consume months, and even as long as a year. One solution is to rough it out and travel to Nepal in the hopes of sorting out the details in an hour or two of face to face negotiations with a trekking company. You should be prepared to spend a week or so (less, if you are exceptionally lucky) in Kathmandu settling these details. The "rough-it-out" solution isn't possible with a group of more than three; here the best solution is to have a friend travel to Nepal early to make all arrangements, or better yet deal with an overseas agent of one of these companies. Dealing with an agent usually involves paying a fee to have them make all the arrangements and then this becomes the "complete arrangements" approach to be described in the next section.

Once you begin such a trek you are entirely in the hands of your sherpa sardar, and his resources are limited to the food, equipment, money and instructions provided by the trekking company. No matter how scrupulous the arrangements and how experienced your sherpa staff, there are bound to be complications and misunderstandings. These will be minimised by understanding and patience. The following advice can make a "do-it-yourself" trek much more pleasant:

A trek is organised according to a prearranged itinerary and the sherpas expect to arrive at certain points on schedule. If you are sick or slow, and do not communicate this to the sherpas, you may discover that camp and dinner are waiting for you far ahead. Many trekkers fail to communicate such problems and other desires to the staff and then blame the sherpas for the failure to provide the desired service. In most cases, the sherpas are true professionals and will make every possible effort to accommodate a trekker if they understand what he wants.

The sherpas have a daily routine similar to the one described a little later in this book. If you do not wish to follow this routine it is important to communicate this to the trekking company well in advance. A routine, once established with the sherpas, is difficult to change later.

You should be sure that you and the trekking company understand exactly who is expected to provide what equipment. It is most embarrassing to discover that there are no sleeping bags on the first night.

You will pay the complete cost of your trek in advance. Occasionally a sardar will ask you for additional money for special services or for baksheesh (a tip) in the form of clothing or money during the trek or at the end. As the demand for trekking increases, more and more men are placed in responsible roles as trekking sardars. While a trekking company does its best to assure you of the best and most qualified staff, its management cannot have possibly trekked with each sardar — they must rely on reports from trekkers themselves. It is rare that a man will make a totally unreasonable request, but occasionally it happens and a disagreeable situation can result. Remember, a sardar thinks you are rich (a preconception impossible to alter), so he may not feel that his demands are exorbitant. The best advice is to wait until you are both back in the office of the trekking company before yielding to such pressure — but such situations do demand delicate negotiations. Hence it is particularly useful to have a skilled and experienced leader on a trek.

Treks may be from two to five weeks in duration. How many people do you know with whom you could spend that period of time, twenty-four hours a day, often under difficult situations of bad weather, illness and confusion in a strange environment (plus a few drinks to loosen tongues) and not have some sort of disagreement? It is almost a certainty that there will be some, either among the trekkers, the sherpas or between the trekkers and the sherpas. It is possible that an irreconcilable conflict between two or more people may arise. This is not the fault of the trekkers, sherpas or the trekking company — just a simple part of living. You can only hope that your sardar is not involved, so that he can straighten out the problem, as he has the skill and authority to do so.

A westerner is viewed in the hills as possessing in his rucksack the sum total of modern medical science. You will be asked for medicines to cure an unbelievable range of diseases. I have often been asked for medicine without any clue to the symptoms, or even the personage, involved. The best solution is not to treat anyone unless you are a physician and are totally confident that you can effect a complete cure. Too many trekkers have casually passed out aspirin or other drugs that only cure the symptoms for a short while and have no effect on the disease. When the symptoms recur — often worse — faith in white man's medicine is undermined, making it more difficult for bonafide doctors to gain the confidence of the people of the hills. It's a great ego trip to make like a doctor, but please don't succumb to the temptation.

If you are travelling with porters, your progress will be limited by their ability to cover the required distance each day. Porters who carry 30 kg up and down hills cannot move as fast as a trekker who carries only a light rucksack. Other factors such as the weather, steepness of the trail, sickness and festivals (beware especially of the Dasain festival in October) can turn a schedule upside down. You will rarely experience a strike, but you may often find that the evening discussion of the next day's destination will turn into a delicate negotiating session. On major trails there are accepted stopping places, and it is difficult to alter them. I once congratulated myself on covering three days walking by lunchtime the third day, and anticipated covering a good distance after lunch. An embarrassed sardar then informed me that our lunch spot would also be our camp for the night because by definition it takes three full days to reach Ghandrung from Pokhara. Whether it had taken us that long or not was immaterial. Nothing I could say (or pay) would entice the porters to go further until the following day — when we were able to depart early in the morning, on schedule!

You may buy or bring some special food "goodies" that you are saving for high altitudes or an important occasion. If you hand these over to the cook at the outset of the trek, you are likely to find them (despite any instructions to the contrary) cooked during the first few days of the trek or, worse yet, served to the sherpas. You should keep any special food in your luggage to prevent such mistakes.

To the equipment list in this book add a huge dose of patience and understanding and you should be able to make a "do-it-yourself" trek with a minimum of problems and tribulations.

COMPLETE ARRANGEMENTS THROUGH A TREKKING AGENCY

The majority of trekkers in the hills of Nepal, especially those whose experiences are uniformly good, have organised their treks through a trekking agency with offices in their own country. Most of these trekkers have travelled as a group to Nepal, as this often results in lower airfares. The majority of trekkers come from the United States; many others come from Germany, Britain, Japan, Switzerland, France, Australia, New Zealand and Scandinavia. All the trekking agents that organise these groups work through one of the established trekking companies in Nepal. Some agents have agreements for the exclusive representation of a Nepalese company in their own country. Names and addresses of some of the major trekking agencies are to be found listed in the appendix.

I have already stated my prejudice in favour of this approach to trekking, whether it is a group you gather together yourself, a group organised by an outdoor club, or a group solicited by the trekking agency, there are significant advantages to an arranged trek. As should have been apparent from the preceding material, the application of ecology in the hills of Nepal is quite different from the concept as it applies to the west. The most important difference being that the people, their economy, food supply, wood supply and culture are severely affected by trekkers. A solution that least disturbs this environment, or better yet, makes a positive contribution to it, is clearly the best approach. Someone will always question "Why go there at all?", but taking all factors into consideration, this is not the soundest solution. Many people in Nepal have become economically dependent on tourism and trekking — it is also an important source of foreign exchange for the nation. Almost all tourists who stay in Nepal for more than four days are trekkers (about 20,000 trekkers in 1980). The Sherpas of Solu Khumbu and the porters in Pokhara and other regions have become highly dependent on this for their only real source of a cash income. Although these people are almost self sufficient at a subsistence level, a source of money has become increasingly important as they are exposed to luxury and convenience items, which abound in Kathmandu, being hauled in by the ton by trekkers and mountaineering expeditions — cameras, watches, down jackets, sleeping bags, plastic jugs, boots and so on. The Sherpas' earlier source of cash income, trade with Tibet, has greatly diminished. The relatively high risk of working for a climbing expedition (48 sherpas died between 1950 and 1974) turns many Sherpas off from this employment. Many Sherpas find trekking fun, financially rewarding and a wonderful excuse to leave the wife and screaming kids for months at a time. There are numerous other advantages to the arranged trek.

Minimising Inflation

A group trek is large enough to carry all its own food and, in areas of wood shortage, fuel for cooking. This practice ensures that trekkers are not competing with the locals for food. They can make a positive economic contribution if they hire local porters to carry their loads. The concern for minimising inflation should make any concerned environmentalist opt for the "complete arrangement" approach to trekking on this basis alone.

Trekking organisations in Nepal are working together to further decrease their impact on the land. Such problems as waste disposal, rescue insurance, wages and benefits to porters and sherpas are all of concern.

Food

Because the group carries its own food for the entire trek a greater variety is possible. This may include canned goods from Kathmandu and imported food purchased from expeditions or other exotic sources. If the group has been scheduled far in advance a skilled cook may be hired, providing an abundant variety of tasty western-style food. The meals a good sherpa cook can prepare in an hour over an open fire would put many western cafes to shame.

Bargaining

Money hassles are almost eliminated on an arranged trek. The sardar is responsible for whatever minor purchases are needed along the way. Unless you are particularly interested, or quite watchful, you may never be aware that these are taking place. Any bargaining or argument will be conducted in the Nepali language, so your personal involvement in disagreeable conflicts is minimal. On the trail you may stop in tea stalls or shops, but since you do not really need what you buy, you are in a better position when it comes to agreeing upon the price. A handy sherpa is always available if you feel a need for his services in negotiating.

Your Reputation

Because you have tents, sherpas, a kitchen crew and all the visible trappings of an arranged trek, villagers will know that a sardar will pay all bills and that the porters will probably purchase some food from the village. You are trekking according to Nepal's union standard and will be accepted and treated well along the way, particularly if your route takes you through the home villages of your sherpas or porters.

Sleeping

An arranged trek carries tents for the trekkers. This gives you a place to spread out your gear without fear that someone will pick it up, and usually you will have a quiet night. A tent also gives you the freedom to go to bed when you choose — to retire immediately after dinner to read or sleep, or to sit up and watch the moon rise as you discuss the day's outing.

Communication of Your Needs

A trekking agent ensures that each group is accompanied by an experienced and competent leader who is familiar with Nepal. A good leader provides an additional line of communication with sherpas. He can help you understand why things are done in a certain way and help the sherpas understand your special needs or desires. The leader should be able to solve any personality clashes or misunderstandings between the trekkers and sherpas and can provide information and advice to help you appreciate the culture, economy and traditions of Nepal.

Your Fellow Trekkers

Unless you are pretty good friends it is hard to spend a month or more together with only one or two people. A trekking agent usually arranges a trek with eight to 16 people, providing a small enough group to become intimate yet large enough to ensure several points of view on any issue, so that conversations never become too repetitive, even after a month. Since trekkers are generally recruited through outdoor-oriented stores, organisations and magazines, the group will usually have quite an interest in the great outdoors as a unifying factor, but may otherwise be quite diverse. It is not unusual to find a stockbroker becoming friends with a steelworker — an opportunity for an exchange of views with might never have been possible without the matchmaking of the trek. Read the brochures and other material prepared by the agent; see if it seems likely to attract the type of people you'd get along with.

Medical Problems

Trekking agents either partially subsidise a physician or provide a leader who has sufficient medical knowledge to take care of whatever problems may occur. You, therefore, have the assurance of good medical care and are spared the frustrations of being asked to play doctor for villagers along the route of your journey.

Timing

Most prearranged treks cater to people to whom time is more important (within limits) than money. For many, the most difficult part is getting time off from work. These people are willing to pay a little more to avoid wasting a week of their limited vacation sitting around in Kathmandu making arrangements or waiting along the way for available space on a plane. Your agent recognises this and tries to cram as many days in the hills as is possible in a given time span.

Expenses and Regulations

The expense of a prearranged trek is not much greater than organising a trek yourself, or travelling to Nepal and making those arrangements after you arrive. It is particularly true if you consider the value of your time and the additional money you may spend in a hotel in Kathmandu if you try to organise your trek yourself. An agent minimises the time spent in Kathmandu and other cities en route and keeps you informed of last minute considertions that might alter your itinerary — airline schedule changes, new restrictions on trekking in Nepal, new visa requirements and the like. It is a full time job to stay abreast of such developments and a good trekking agent maintains those contacts necessary to obtain up-to-date information.

Unless you make the mistake of signing up with a company offering a "deluxe trek" (a contradiction in terms) you will find that the per day cost of a trek is lower than many package tours. Be sure that when evaluating the cost of a trek or tour you subtract the airfare and divide the remaining cost by the number of days you are being accommodated. This per day figure is the true evaluation of the cost of a trip. I've heard it said a $1200 trek is cheaper than a $1600 trek, only to discover that the first was for only 30 days, while the "more expensive" trek was 44 days long. The comparison should have been between $40 and $36 per day. As a comparison, other tour packages average $60 a day and can easily run as high as $100, even up to $300 per day!

Beware of treks advertised at less than about $30 per day as these generally sacrifice some important elements of a good trek to cut the price. Be sure that there is more than one sherpa, tents are provided, enough porters are available to carry your luggage and that food is carried with the trek. One company used to offer treks with a single sherpa and one cook for a group of 15, slept in houses along the way and purchased food from villages and tea shops. Such a trek becomes a "live-off-the-land" expedition, but with more people to compete for limited food supplies — it therefore has all the disadvantages of such a trek, while you were being sold a prearranged one.

Tradition

By participating in a prearranged trek, you will conform to a tradition and routine that has been developed and refined for more than 50 years. You will have the opportunity to travel in much the same manner as the approach marches described in *Annapurna*, *The Ascent of Everest* and *Americans on Everest*, a feature not possible with other approaches. If your interest in the Himalaya was kindled through such books, take the opportunity to experience this delightful way to travel. There are a great number of reasons why these expeditions went to all the trouble and expense to travel as they did. It is an altogether refreshing experience to have all the camp and logistics problems removed from your responsibility so you are free to fully enjoy the land and the people which have attracted mountaineers for a century. A group of seven or more is desirable in order to fully appreciate this tradition.

Emergencies

If you have an established organisation with all of its contacts behind you,

You will have more help in case of emergency. Messages from home (heaven forbid) can be passed along to you through an agent in Kathmandu. If you become sick or unable to travel, a rescue helicopter or charter flight from a remote airstrip is easier to arrange if you have some definite proof that it can be paid for. It now costs $1500 for a helicopter evacuation from 4000 metres near Mt Everest and several whose lives were saved by such flights have left Nepal without paying their bill. Royal Nepal Airlines, who operate the service, are now quite reluctant to send a chopper unless they have absolute assurance of payment. All trek organisers have an agreement in Kathmandu that guarantees the payment, although you will be billed later for the service.

One Drawback

A condition of a prearranged trek through a trekking agent is that the group must usually stick to its prearranged route and, within limits, must meet a specific schedule. This means that an interesting side trip may have to be foregone, and if one trekker is sick he will probably have to keep moving with the rest of the group. Occasionally someone will not agree with a leader's decisions if a schedule must be adjusted because of weather, health, political or logistical considerations. For some people, this prospect alone rules out their participation in a prearranged trek, although it is unlikely that such an inflexible individual would be happy trekking under any of the other options. Such a person (and I have trekked with several) would be happier backpacking and climbing at home. On the positive side, by fixing the destination and schedule in advance, all members of the group may be prepared for the trip and have proper equipment and a clear understanding of the schedule and terrain.

Part 2

Preparing Yourself for a Trek

If you have finally decided to go on a trek and, hopefully, contacted one of the trekking agents listed in the appendix of this book, you are now in a position where you must prepare yourself physically and begin to gather the personal equipment necessary to make the trip comfortable.

The equipment supplied by various organisers of treks differs so you should read over the material provided by your trekking agent to assure yourself that he is not providing some of the equipment or services I suggest you provide for yourself. In addition, be sure that you are not expected to provide something, a sleeping bag in particular, that I do not include in my list. The recommendations here apply specifically to treks I organise through Himalayan Journeys in Kathmandu, but I have checked them against the literature of other agents and there are no significant deviations.

I have used the term "trekking agent" to define the company, travel agent or individual who has assumed the responsibility of organising the group abroad for a trek in Nepal. The trekking agent is generally a professional who takes care of all the myriad details of planning and arranging for equipment, plane and hotel reservations, leadership and information for trekkers.

The trekking agent is affiliated with a trekking company in Nepal which makes arrangements for trekking equipment, sherpas, porters and food for the trek. Because the Nepal affiliate deals directly with the trekking agent, most of these organisations discourage correspondence from individual trekkers. You should feel quite confident that the trekking agent with whom you are dealing is capable of handling any queries you may have and passing appropriate information along to their Nepal affiliate in case of special requests.

A Day on the Trail

A day begins about 6 am with a light breakfast of Darjeeling tea, coffee, porridge and eggs or pancakes. While the trekkers are eating, the sherpas take down the tents and pack up loads for the porters. The entire group is usually on the way by 7 am in order to take advantage of the cool morning to accomplish most of the day's hike. The trail is usually steep and often rough. In spite of the size of the group, many trekkers find an opportunity to hike alone for much of the day. The porters are slower and the sherpas, especially the cook crew, race on ahead to have lunch waiting when you arrive. There are numerous diversions on the trail and it is not unusual to find sherpas and fellow trekkers in shops or in some tea houses, or the entire group to be diverted by a festival or some other special event along the way. At a suitable spot, about 11 am, there is a stop of an hour or two for lunch: the inevitable tea (all water must be boiled for health reasons), a plate of rice, potatoes or noodles, some canned or fresh meat and whatever vegetables are in season.

The afternoon is shorter, ending about 3 pm, when you round a bend to discover your tents already set up in a (hopefully) flat field near a village. Tea and coffee are again prepared soon after arrival in camp and there is an hour or two to nurse blisters, read, unpack and sort gear, wash or explore the surrounding area before dinner.

A note on the menu: Asians eat meat perhaps once a month and rice is the basic staple. Trekking groups have a more western diet with chicken, goat, mutton or buffalo meat frequently, but not daily, and vary the rice diet by substituting potatoes, noodles and other items. (The cow is sacred in regions of Hindu influence, so beef is unavailable.) The food is tasty and plentiful, but may seem boring to a western palate after two weeks or so. Yet meals will tax the imagination of the cook as he provides a variety he has never experienced in his own meals. Most trekkers feel healthy and fit

lunch stop

on this diet; the food is fresh, organic, with no preservatives.

After dinner the sun sets early. There is time to read by candlelight in tents or to sit around talking in the dark. Since wood is scarce there will be few campfires. Occasionally, a visit to a nearby village provides an opportunity to sample chang and rakshi, the local brews. Most trekkers are asleep by 8 or 9 pm; face the next day refreshed; and continue the adventure that will have developed into a delightful and comfortable pattern of living, one that will be remembered fondly long after the views of the mountains and sore feet are forgotten.

Dangers of a Trek

The dangers of a trek include health problems caused by unsanitary conditions, the danger of acute mountain sickness, and the new problems presented by incidents of theft in the hills.

Health
If you take proper precautions, it is unlikely that you will have any severe illness during the trek. These precautions include the proper immunisations before you come to Nepal. Most stomach upsets are temporary, the major dangers are Hepatitis, Cholera and dysentary.

Hepatitis is totally debilitating, but proper sanitation practices and care go a long way towards preventing the disease. Gamma Globulin, injected just before the trek (it is available in Kathmandu at Kalimati Clinic) is a good preventative measure.

Cholera vaccine does not provide total protection, but is said to reduce the severity of the disease. Since there is almost none in the regions most treks visit, the dangers are minimal.

It is possible to contract amoebic·dysentery, a disease that can make a trek miserable and requires a long time to cure at home. If, however, you stick to hotel food in Kathmandu and the sherpa cooks' food on the trek, there is almost no possibility of being afflicted with dysentery. Trekkers who drink local brews, especially chang, who eat in out-of-the-way cafes or drink unboiled or untreated water, stand a better — but still remote — chance of contracting disease.

Altitude Sickness
Trekkers who have not previously experienced high altitude and who attempt to trek to places such as the Everest base camp may feel uncomfortable with headaches, nausea, and lethargy, although many make high altitude trips with few problems. Those in good physical shape, who slow down their pace as they trek above 4000 metres, seem to feel better. There is never any assurance, however, that everyone will be comfortable at extremely high altitudes. You should be emotionally prep-

ared to retreat to a lower camp if your condition is such that continuing might endanger your health. The leader will be watching for signs of altitude sickness (pulmonary oedema), but you should also watch yourself and other trekkers for visible signs of deterioration. Most fatal cases of altitude sickness have resulted from people pushing themselves beyond their capabilities when they were severely affected by altitude problems. Unless you completely disregard your health and ignore obvious indications, you'll have little to fear from hiking to high altitudes.

Theft

In 1974 I wrote "there is virtually nothing to fear in Nepal from thieves, hijackings or the other horrors of our urban civilisation". Unfortunately this has now changed, and it pays to be cautious about your companions — whether fellow trekkers or your porters — and with your belongings, especially when you camp. There are now frequent reports of items being stolen from the tents and hotel rooms of trekkers, even in the most remote villages. There have even been incidents of violent crime — something previously unheard of in Nepal. In March, 1981, the US Embassy in Kathmandu issued the following bulletin:

ATTENTION: ALL TREKKERS

The following has been prepared for your information concerning your personal safety while trekking in Nepal. Nepal has long enjoyed a reputation as one of the world's safest countries and many people have trekked alone into the most remote corners of the country without any danger. The vast majority of Nepalis are friendly and present no threat to tourists, but during the past year the number of violent incidents directed against visiting trekkers and tourists has increased. Most of these have occurred near Dhorpatan and along the Pokhara-Jomsom trail. Americans have been the victims of murder, knifings, stonings and verbal abuse. Two Japanese and a Briton have also been killed and another Japanese, an Italian, and two Germans are now reported missing. The general motive seems to have been robbery even though the possessions of some of the victims were insignificant by American standards. All of the victims were travelling alone or as a couple.

To help you enjoy your trek and to minimise the risk of unpleasant incidents, the Embassy recommends that you take the following precautions during your stay in Nepal:

1 Register with the Embassy Consular Section providing as much information as possible on your itinerary, your anticipated dates of departure and return, and emergency addresses in your home country.

2 Do not travel alone; select your companions carefully and make sure that someone knows with whom you are travelling.

3 Arrange for porters with a reputable trekking firm or hotel; register their names with the trekking agency or friends so that they can be traced if you have trouble during the trek.

4 Store all valuable items in Kathmandu (many hotels and small lodges will do this, just be sure to obtain a detailed receipt for the things you leave behind);

take only those things necessary for your trek and do not make ostentations of your cash or possessions.

5 Follow normal safety precautions, especially at night; try to remain near other trekkers or your porters; don't walk along the trails after dark.

6 Don't leave your passport as collateral for renting trekking equipment; you may need it as proof of your identity and as a means of notifying the Embassy that you need to be medically evacuated.

If you encounter problems during the trek, report them to the nearest police or immigration post. Provide as much information as possible to the officials. When you return to Kathmandu report any unresolved problems to the appropriate trekking agency or hotel, and to the police and Ministry of Tourism.

The most real and severe "danger" of a trek in Nepal is the strong likelihood that you will mortgage your entire future to return and trek again and again. This serious affliction has destroyed the careers of many people. Once you have visited the Nepalese hill country you may find bush-walking or backpacking at home far too tame and uninteresting. There are no shops, chickens, goats, laughing children or other such diversions along wilderness trails at home. Probably half the people who have made a "once in a lifetime" trek in Nepal have found themselves scheduling a trek as a biennial or even annual vacation.

Weather

Nepal is in the northern hemisphere, so the seasons are the same as in Europe. Because it is quite far south (the same as Miami or Cairo) the weather is, of course, warmer and the winters much milder. It rarely snows below 2000 metres.

The weather is governed by the monsoon in the Bay of Bengal. The monsoon creates a rainy season from about the middle of June through the middle of September. Because Nepal is in the northern hemisphere, it is hot during the monsoon and it rains almost every day, though not continuously. During this season, trekking is difficult and uncomfortable. The mountains are usually hidden by clouds and the trails are infested with leeches.

To avoid the monsoon, most treks are scheduled during the winter season from October through April. Temperatures are generally comfortable during this period: in the high 20°Cs during the daytime and falling to 5°C at night while trekking between 1000 metres and 3500 metres, and from about 20°C down to -10°C at higher altitudes. Mornings are usually clear with clouds building up during the afternoon, disappearing at night to reveal spectacular starry skies. It usually does not rain for more than one or two days during the entire fall season. During spring treks, there may be a week or so of rainy evenings.

Most of the precipitation occurs during the summer so there is less snow on the mountains during the winter. Everest itself is black rock during the trekking season, becoming snow covered only during the summer. Of course, there are exceptions to this weather pattern — you should be prepared for extremes. During December and January, occasional winter storms blanket the mountains with snow and produce rain in the lowlands. This snow may make an early spring pass-crossing difficult during years of winter precipitation.

Equipment Checklist

Footgear

boots or running shoes   *camp shoes*
socks — nylon thermal (3)   *socks — high for plus fours**
*socks — light cotton for under plus fours socks (2)**

Clothing

down or fiber-filled jacket   *down-filled pants**
wool shirt, sweater or acrylic pile jacket *nylon windbreaker*
nylon wind pants or ski warm-up pants   *hiking shorts for men*
*plus fours**   *long underwear*
poncho   *sun hat*
wool hat (or balaclava)*   *gloves*
down booties (optional)   *gaiters**
underwear (3 changes)   *bathing suit (optional)*
cotton or corduroy pants (optional)
T-shirts, cotton, for men (2 changes)
blouses, for women (2 changes)

Other Equipment

large duffle bag with lock   *stuff bags*
rucksack   *goggles or sunglasses (2)*
water bottles   *flashlight, batteries & bulbs*
sun cream   *sun cream for lips*
small duffle bag or suitcase for your city clothes

Additional Items for Comfort

insect repellant   *diary and pencils*
toilet articles   *soap*

toilet paper	toothpaste
shampoo	towel
laundry soap	medical and first aid kit
wash 'n' dris (pre-moistened towelettes)	sewing kit
small knife	bandana
length of parachute cord	umbrella
spare pair of prescription glasses	

Other Optional Equipment — bring only one or two

binoculars	altimeter
camera and lenses:	thermometer
lens cleansing equipment	compass
film — about 20 rolls	books and games
tape recorder and blank tapes	

* required only for treks exceeding 4000 metres.

Equipment

I wish to place considerable emphasis on the selection of equipment for a trek. The task of selecting proper gear can almost overpower some people, but it is not a complex or difficult undertaking. Preparing for a trek is not much more complicated than equipping yourself for a weekend backpacking trip; in some ways it is simpler. There is no food to worry about, no eating utensils or cooking pots, no tents or sleeping bags to stow, and even less overall concern with weight and bulk.

If you follow these instructions, you can have many happy hours — planning the trek, sorting gear, packing and repacking. It is a great way to spend boring evenings and will impress your friends when they find down jackets strewn over your living room floor in midsummer. On the other hand, if you don't have the time, you can probably get through most of the preparation in a week or less.

It is important to be certain you have the proper equipment — particularly down clothing, boots and sunglasses, before you leave home, as these items are difficult to obtain after departing. Some good used equipment may be available in Nepal (sometimes at lower prices than elsewhere), but you cannot depend on it. It is far better to have your entire kit organised in advance, rather than to spend the night before the trek begins scouring all over Kathmandu for an item of gear.

The equipment listed on the preceding page has been tested by many trekkers. Everything on the list is useful — most of it necessary — for any trek that exceeds three weeks in duration and ascends to above 4000 metres.

Items marked with an asterisk (*) may be omitted if you do not exceed this elevation. Note that all of this gear will pack into a duffle bag and weighs less than 15 kg.

Also remember that some of this equipment will not be necessary on a given trek. You might be lucky enough to trek during a warm spell and never need a down jacket, or it might be so cold and rainy that you never wear short pants. As you read the suggestions which follow, be sure to evaluate for yourself whether you feel that you need a particular item of equipment. Do not rush out to an equipment shop and purchase everything on this list; what follows is what works for me and has worked for many other trekkers. But you may decide that many items in this list are unnecessary for you.

Selection & Use

You will probably have most of the equipment needed for the trek if you do much hiking in cold weather. A trek is a good place to finally destroy clothing that is nearly worn out or outstyled. You may be uncomfortable, however, in completely disreputable clothing. Treks visit many villages where people dress in elegant local styles, even suits and ties. It is a distressing feeling to be clothed in torn and dirty garb while visiting the homes of people who are immaculately and colourfully attired (and who may display a fortune in jewellery). A long trek, five weeks or so, is just about the maximum useful life for some clothing items — so do be sure that used gear has enough life left to finish the trek. Repairs can easily be made at tailor shops at occasional points along the trail — they use hand-operated sewing machines.

Boots or Running Shoes

Proper footgear is the most important item you will bring. Your boots should be medium weight, 15 cm high, rugged enough to last, waterproof, well broken-in and must fit well. Be sure your boots provide enough room for your toes! There are many long and steep descents during which short boots can painfully jam your toes (causing the loss of toenails). The trails are often rocky and rough. If your soles are thin and soft, your feet will soon be bruised and walking will be painful. Soft rubber soles wear out very rapidly. Ensure that your boots have hard lug (Vibram) soles.

Many trekkers have found that tennis shoes or running shoes are a good substitute for boots whenever snow is not encountered. I myself have trekked many hundreds of kilometres in tennis shoes and find them quite comfortable. However, boots provide ankle protection and have stiffer soles. If you have done most of your hiking in boots, you may experience some discomfort in lighter and softer footgear. The shoes you wear on the trek should be tried out during several hikes (up and down hills) before you come to Nepal. Whenever there is snow (possible anywhere above 4000 metres), boots are an absolute necessity.

Camp Shoes

A pair of tennis shoes are comfortable to change into for the evening and can serve as trail shoes in an emergency. A pair of rubber "thongs" or shower shoes make a comfortable change at camp during warm weather. These may be purchased in Kathmandu. I always carry a pair of these in my rucksack and remove my boots or tennis shoes at lunch or on arrival in camp and put my shoes and socks in the sun to dry. I think this procedure has saved me a lot of foot troubles.

Socks

Thermal ski socks — a nylon/wool combination — are strongly recommended. You will wash your socks several times during a long trek and pure wool socks dry slowly. Nylon/wool socks dry in a few hours in the sun — often during a lunch stop. They are marketed as ski socks "designed for plastic boots" and come in a variety of colours, a useful feature since coloured socks hide stains. Most can wear these without a cotton liner. Try on a pair on your next local hike and see whether you need an inner sock. Three pairs should be enough unless you are a real procrastinator about washing clothes. If you bring plus-fours, you will need a pair of high wool socks and two pairs of cotton or nylon inner socks. Most treks do not spend enough time at high altitudes to require carrying more than one pair of high wool socks.

Down-filled or Fiber-filled Jacket

Down clothing has the advantage of being light and compressible. It will stuff into a small space in your bag, yet bulk up when you wear it. You must bring a good down jacket on a trek. Most ski jackets are not warm enough and most "expedition parkas" are too heavy and bulky. The secret is to choose one that will be warm enough even at the coldest expected temperatures, but also usable when it is warmer. Don't bring both a heavy and light down jacket. Choose one that will serve both purposes. If your jacket has a hood, you may dispense with a wool hat.

Your down jacket can serve many functions on the trek. It will become a pillow at night, protect fragile items in your duffle bag, and if you are extremely cold at high altitude, merely wear it to bed inside your sleeping bag. Probably you will not wear down gear to walk in; it rarely gets cold even at 5000 metres. Most leave their down clothing in their duffle bags and only use it during the evening below about 4000 metres. At higher elevations, carry your jacket and put it on at rest or lunch stops if it is that cold. Artificial fiber jackets, filled with Polargard, Thinsulate or Fiberfill are a good substitute for down — and much less expensive.

Down-filled Pants

Most stores do not carry these and consider them a luxury. I think that they are a necessity on a trek that goes above 4000 metres. You do not hike in down pants. Put them on when you stop for the night, over your hiking shorts or under a skirt. Bring a pair that has snaps or a zipper down the in-seam of each leg, a design that allows them to be used as a half-bag for bivouacs. This design also lets you put them on without taking off your boots. When made into a half-bag, they give additional insulation in your sleeping bag when the nights get particularly cold.

Often you will arrive in camp at about 3 pm and not dine until 6 pm. Unless you elect to do some exploring, there will be about three hours be-fore and an hour after dinner of physical inactivity. In cold weather, down pants are the only solution. Ski warm-up pants are an acceptable substitute, are much cheaper, and are available at all ski shops.

Wool Shirt or Sweater

With clothing, two light layers are better than a single heavy layer. One or two light sweaters or shirts are superior to a heavy wool jacket. Most of the time you will need only a single light garment in the morning and will shed it almost as soon as you start walking. A long-sleeved shirt or sweater will suffice. An advantage of a shirt is that you can open the front for ventil-ation without stopping to remove the entire garment. Wool is warm, even when wet, so make yours wool, not cotton.

I have recently used an acrylic-pile jacket on several treks and climbs and have been very pleased with its performance. Jackets and sweaters such as those made by Helly Hansen in Norway and Great Pacific Iron Works in California come in a variety of styles and thicknesses. I have found them to be light, warm (even when wet) and easy to clean. They are a little cheaper, they are much lighter, and dry much faster than wool garments.

Nylon Windbreaker

Strong winds are rare in the places visited by most treks, but a windbreaker is helpful even in light winds and light rain and drizzles, at a time when a poncho is really not necessary. Be sure that your windbreaker "breathes" — otherwise perspiration cannot evaporate and you will become soaked. A windbreaker is more in the line of emergency gear. If there is a strong wind, you must have it; otherwise it is seldom used.

Nylon Wind Pants

Many people use these frequently. The temperature will often be approach-ing 30°C and people prefer to hike in shorts. Early in the morning when it is cool, a pair of long pants is more comfortable. Wind pants provide the best of both worlds. Wear them over your shorts in the morning, then remove them to hike in shorts during the day. Most wind pants have special cuffs and can be removed over your boots. They can be indispensable.

Ski warm-up pants or even "warm-up" pants for running, can be substituted for both wind pants and down-filled pants at a substantially lower cost with not much sacrifice in versatility or comfort.

Hiking Shorts for Men, Skirts for Women

The weather will often be hot, frequently humid, the trails steep and the wind calm. Long pants tend to pull at the knees and are hot. For hiking at the lower elevations, the sherpas usually switch to shorts. I strongly recommend this procedure. Either "cutoffs" or fancy hiking shorts with ample pockets are fine.

Women may consider a skirt as an alternative. Many who have worn them on treks are enthusiastic about them; the most obvious reason being the ease in relieving oneself along the trail. There are long stretches where there is little chance to drop out of sight and a skirt solves the problem. Skirts are also useful when the only place to wash is in a stream crowded with trekkers, villagers and porters. A wrap-around skirt is easy to put on and take off in a tent. A large pocket in front is useful and a pair of bright tights under your skirt is a good addition to your wardrobe. Long "granny" skirts are not recommended; you will be walking through too much mud to make them practical.

Plus-fours ("Knickers" to Americans)

These are a classic example of the prime rule of selecting equipment for any hiking trip: make each piece of gear serve at least two purposes. The great advantage of plus-fours is that, combined with long wool socks, they provide both shorts and long pants — simply by rolling the socks up or down.

During the several days which some treks spend at high elevations, you will truly be "in the mountains" — where the weather can change quickly and sometimes dramatically. Although it will often be warm, it can cloud up and become cold and windy very quickly — a disaster if you happen to be wearing shorts. You can wear the socks up on cold mornings before the sun comes up (which, since you are surrounded by high peaks, is often about 10 am). As exercise and the heat of the sun warms you up, roll the socks down to your ankles. Because of this versatility, I recommend plus-fours rather than long pants.

Long Underwear

"Longjohns" are a useful addition to your equipment. A complete set makes a good warm pair of pyjamas for those late night emergency trips outside of your tent. Unless the weather is especially horrible, you will not need them to walk in during the day. I bring only the bottoms and use my wool shirt for a pyjama top. Cotton underwear is acceptable, though wool is much warmer. If wool is too scratchy, duo-fold underwear (wool lined with cotton) is an excellent compromise.

Poncho

There is really no way to keep dry while hiking in the rain, but a poncho, a large, often hooded, tarp with a hole in the centre for your head, is the best available solution. The weather is likely to be warm, even while raining, and a poncho has good air circulation. The condensation inside a waterproof jacket can make you even wetter than standing out in the rain. I have found that an inexpensive plastic poncho is better than the more expensive coated nylon gear. The plastic one is completely waterproof at a fraction of the cost. However, the most practical way of keeping dry is an umbrella. If you carry an umbrella, you can dispense with a poncho.

Sun Hat

A hat is an important item, but its design is not critical. Obviously, a hat with a wide brim affords greater protection. If the hat you choose does not have a strap to fit under your chin. put one on so that your hat does not blow away in a wind gust.

Wool Hat or Balaclava

A balaclava is ideal because it can serve as a warm hat or be rolled down to cover most of your face and — most important — your neck. You may even wish to wear it to bed on some nights. Much of your body heat is lost through your head, so a warm hat helps keep your entire body warmer.

Gloves

Warm ski gloves are suitable for a trek. I always take along a pair of woollen mittens in addition — just in case my others get wet. I do not recall ever having to use them though.

Down Booties

These are listed as optional since many people consider them excess baggage — I wouldn't be without them. They should have a heavy sole, preferably with ensolite insulation. They will serve as camp shoes. Down booties do make a cold night a little warmer since somehow your feet seem to feel the cold when everything else is warm — also for those midnight trips out of a tent.

Underwear

If you use nylon or cotton/nylon underwear, you'll save drying time. If it is coloured, you won't be so self-conscious about hanging it out to dry if it's dirty. Three changes should suffice, you could probably get by with less, but they weigh very little. Interest in the washing process diminishes at higher elevations because it is cold, particularly in the water. Once I measured the temperature of the Dudh Kosi. It was 1°C.

T-shirts and Blouses
Again you save drying time with a nylon/cotton combination and coloured clothing has that aesthetic value.

Gaiters
If your trek visits high elevations, there is a possibility of snow and some opportunity to do some scrambling off the trails. A pair of gaiters will help to keep your boots and socks cleaner and drier in such situations.

Bathing Suit
Almost nobody older than five goes without clothing in Nepal or India. You will probably offend sherpas, porters and an entire village if you "skinny-dip" in a river or stream, even to wash. There are numerous places to swim although most are just ridiculously cold — except along the Arun River in eastern Nepal where there are some great swimming holes. Either bring along a suit, or plan to swim in shorts and then wear them till they dry.

Duffle Bag
Several companies make good duffle bags that have a zipper along the side for ease of entry. Be sure your duffle bag is durable and has a strong zipper. Do not buy a cheap model. A bag 35 cm in diameter and about 75 cm long is large enough to carry your gear and will usually meet the weight limit — typically 15 kg. If you are trying to save money, an army surplus duffle bag will serve, but they are inconvenient because they only open from the end (but it will have no zipper to jam or break).

Most of your equipment will be carried in the bag by a porter. During the day, you will carry your camera, water bottle, extra clothing, and a small first aid kit in your rucksack. Do not overload the rucksack — especially on the first day of the trek.

It is impossible to describe how your duffle bag will look after a month on a trek. Load it with your equipment, take it to the second floor and toss it out. Pick it up and shake the contents to the far end then put it in the dirt and stomp on it a few times — get the idea?

Since your duffle bag will be carried by porters, you must realise that when it is raining, your duffle bag will be carried in the rain, as well as left outside tea shops in the rain, while the porters go inside to keep dry. Your duffle bag must be packed so that important items stay dry during rainstorms. A waterproof duffle bag and waterproof nylon or plastic bags inside your bag are both necessary.

Put a padlock on your bag. I suggest a small one that will fit through the zipper pull and fasten to a ring sewn to the bag. The lock will protect the contents from pilgerage during the flight to and from Nepal. It will also protect the contents on your trek. It is highly unlikely that a porter will disappear with your duffel bag, but a dishonest porter might be tempted to open a bag if it is not locked. People assume that you are very wealthy, and if something of yours is lying around, they may pick it up, figuring you won't even miss it. The porters make many stops during the day at tea houses and chhang shops and often leave their loads outside. The lock prevents kids, curious villagers and your porter from looking inside and picking up something they think is not valuable to you.

Rucksack
Select a rucksack that fits comfortably. Try to find one that has a light inside frame to stiffen the bag, and a waistband to keep it from bouncing around and also to take some weight off your shoulders. A rucksack has many advantages on a trek: its small size prevents you from carrying too much during the day; it is a good "carry-on" piece of luggage on flights; it will fit inside your tent at night without crowding you; and it is not overly cumbersome for you when going through low doorways into houses and temples. Some prefer a frame (kelty-type) pack, but it has few of these advantages.

Stuff Bags
It is unlikely that you will be able to find a completely waterproof duffle bag. Using coated nylon stuff bags helps you to separate your gear — thereby lending an element of organisation to the daily chaos in your tent — and also provides additional protection in case of rain. If you get stuff bags with drawstrings, the addition of spring-loaded clamps will save a lot of frustration trying to untie knots you tied in too much haste in the morning. Even plastic bags can be used, but they are much more fragile.

Sunglasses or Goggles
If you are travelling above 4000 metres, you may encounter snow. The sun reflects brilliantly off snow making good goggles or sunglasses with side protection essential. At this altitude, they are so essential that you must have a spare in case of breakage or loss. A pair of regular sunglasses can serve as a spare, if some sort of side shield can be rigged. The lenses should be as dark as possible. At 5000 metres, the sun is intense both visually and non-visually. At this elevation, ultraviolet rays can severely damage unprotected eyes. Be sure that you have a metal case to store them in because, even in your rucksack, they can be crushed. Sunglasses are at a premium in Nepal and it would be difficult to obtain a good replacement.

Water Bottle
Bring a one-litre plastic water bottle that does not leak. A water bottle is another important piece of gear that would be difficult to purchase in Nepal. Since all water must be boiled, or treated, your bottle provides the only completely safe source of cold water to drink. Each night, boiled water will be provided to fill your water bottles. If the bottle does not

leak, take it to bed with you as a hot water bottle on cold nights — very luxurious! By morning the water will be cool for your use during the day. I find that I rarely use my bottle and can get enough fluids by drinking numerous cups of tea at breakfast and lunch. On the other hand, many people require two litres of water during the day. If you are one of those, consider a second water bottle.

Sun Cream
Since most treks are in the winter season when the sun is low in the sky, except for the hazards of snow glare at high altitude, sunburn is not a problem for most people. I use a commercial suntan lotion. Those with more sensitive skin need a total sun screen such as zinc oxide cream. During spring treks, though, sunburn can be a problem.

Sun Screen for Lips
To protect your lips at high altitude you need a true sun screen which keeps out all of the sun. A heavy moustache works particularly well!

Torch (Flashlight for Americans)
Almost any torch will do, a headlight is not necessary. You can get spare batteries almost anywhere in the hills of Nepal if you have a torch that uses "D" cells. Larger batteries also perform better in the cold than small penlight "AA" cells.

Umbrella
This is an excellent substitute for a poncho (except on windy days). An umbrella can serve as a sunshade, a walking stick, and an emergency toilet shelter. Umbrellas with bamboo handles are available in Kathmandu for about US$2, but they are bulky and tend to leak black dye over you when they get wet. Collapsible umbrellas are an excellent compromise, although they cannot serve as walking sticks. An umbrella is necessary in October, April and May and optional for treks in other months.

Extra Duffle Bag or Suitcase
When you depart on the trek, you will leave your city clothes and other items you use and wear when travelling, in the locked storeroom of your hotel in Kathmandu. You should bring a small suitcase or extra duffle bag with a lock to use for this purpose.

Additional Items for Comfort
The check list that follows indicates most of the other equipment you will need for a trek. If there are two of you travelling together, double up on a lot of this material to save weight and bulk. There is not much to be said about soap, scissors and the like, but a few ideas may help:

laundry soap in bars is available in Kathmandu and along most trails.

"Wash-n-Dri's" are great for a last-minute hand wash before dinner — avoid many stomach problems by washing frequently.

A pair of scissors on your knife is useful.

Be sure your sewing kit has some safety pins — lots of uses!

Be sure all your medicines and toilet articles are in plastic bottles with screw-on lids — reread the section about how duffle bags may be treated.

One of the most visible indications of western culture are those streams of toilet paper littering every campsite. Burn your toilet paper after use.

Optional Equipment

The checklist suggests a number of items that might be interesting to bring along on the trek. Do not bring all of them; you will be overloaded and very busy if you do so.

Cameras

People have brought cameras ranging from tiny Instamatics to heavy Hasselblads. While most do bring a camera, it is equally enjoyable to trek without one.

Be sure your camera is winterised if it requires it (some do not). This involves removing heavy grease from the shutter and replacing it with graphite or some other lubricant that will be less affected by cold — a job for a professional cameraman.

The trek is long and dusty; be sure you have lens caps, some sort of lens tissue and a brush to clean the camera and lens as frequently as possible. Three lenses, a wide angle (28 or 35 mm), a standard lens (50 or 55 mm) and a telephoto lens (135 or 200 mm) are useful if you wish to take advantage of all the photographic opportunities during the trek. But three lenses can be heavy, since you will be carrying them in your rucksack day after day. If you must make a choice, I think that you will find a telephoto (or zoom) lens is more useful than a wide angle, as it will allow you close-up pictures of mountains and portraits of shy people. Don't overburden yourself with lots of heavy camera equipment.

Film is outrageously expensive in Kathmandu and not always available at duty free shops on the way to Nepal. Make certain you have enough. On a two or three week trek, 20 rolls of 36-exposure film is not too much. Most people want colour slides, but black-and-white photos are interesting too — you may want both. Shoot a roll or two on a new or borrowed camera if you haven't used it before. Be sure you are familiar with all your equipment before you invest in pictures for your trek.

Medical Considerations

FOOD & DRINK

You may have heard a lot of talk about sickness and intestinal problems in Asia. If you are reasonably careful, you should not have any problems — even in the more remote regions of Nepal — except perhaps a day or two of adjustment to a new environment somewhere during the trip. A sherpa cook crew boils all the water, thoroughly cooks all food and sterilises dishes in boiling water. There is a minimal danger of problems, if you stick to the regular food on your trek.

Problems may occur when you eat or drink in homes or local restaurants along the trail, where the people are not accustomed to the sensitive stomachs of westerners. Even if you ask if the water is boiled, for example, you will be assured that it is, despite the fact that the water has just been taken from the river. This illustrates several interesting facets of Nepalese culture and personality. The germ concept is not widely known or understood amongst the hill people. The peculiar insistence of westerners that water be boiled is accepted good naturedly, but is not understood — they often believe that we like only hot water. Besides, the locals always drink unboiled water, why don't we? Another consideration: Nepalese like to please and dislike answering any question negatively. So, you get a "yes" answer to almost every question, particularly "is this water boiled?" The best solution is to drink tea. Good tea must be made from boiling water. It is an easy way out.

Perhaps the best technique for preventing stomach and intestinal problems ("Delhi-belly" or "Kathmandu crud") is to keep your hands clean (a supply of pre-moistened towelettes and frequent wash stops at streams helps). Do not be continually concerned about the state of your bowels. There is virtually no history of severe problems among trekkers who ate only food prepared by sherpa cooks and kept themselves clean.

Before the trek, you will probably eat all meals in a hotel dining room where high standards of western hygiene prevail — these meals are often included in the price of the trek. There are numerous fine and inexpensive restaurants in Kathmandu. Restaurants such as the Rum Doodle or KC's in Thamel specially cater to trekkers and take extra care for health and sanitation.

PHYSICAL CONDITIONING

Obviously, the better the shape you are in, the more you will enjoy the trek. You do not have to be an Olympic athlete, but you should be in condition for the activity you are going to do — a lot of walking.

The best way to get into shape is to walk. If you take a strenuous back-

the dishwasher at work

pack every other weekend for a few months before the trek, you will be in good condition. Try to climb — and descend — as many hills as you possibly can. Walk up stiars rather than take a lift. Walk or bicycle to work. Be sure your boots fit and are well broken in. If possible, make your training jaunts in the same boots you will wear on the trek. This will also give you a chance to find out whether the nylon/wool socks are comfortable for you and weather tennis shoes or running shoes give enough support to your feet during long walks.

If you have the opportunity to climb a high mountain to get used to high altitude, this conditioning will certainly help, although it does not guarantee you will not have troubles at high elevations. If you don't have access to high peaks, find the tallest building around. When I was stranded in Washington DC one summer, I climbed the Washington Monument every day.

Although a trek is usually not particularly strenuous at any given time, and though you are waited upon almost to the point of embarrassment, a trek is long; probably longer than you have ever been in the outdoors. The continual day-to-day grind up and down hills can be a relaxing experience or just a nightmare. Be sure you do enjoy walking and are willing to put up with the regimentation of walking each and every day — whether you feel like it or not.

MEDICAL EXAMS

The worst place on your adventure to discover that you have a medical problem is on the trek itself. To assure yourself and your trek leader that you are in reasonably good health, contact your physician and have a rigorous medical exam. Most trekking agents will supply you with an examination form which must be completed and returned. This medical form is designed to outline to your doctor some of the potential problems of a trek and to ensure that he views the examination a little more seriously than a routine life insurance exam. Be sure that any abnormalities, chronic problems, or special medicines are listed on the form. This will help the leader to identify the problems in case you exhibit any symptoms along the trek.

Your doctor is the best source of information about immunisations and medicines. He both knows your medical history and is in touch with local public health officials. Ask and follow his advice on all medical matters regarding your proposed trek.

IMMUNISATIONS

The following vaccinations and preventive medicines are listed as required, strongly recommended, or recommended for all trekkers in Nepal. Begin your series of immunisations early. Some shots can be taken at the same time; others have to be spaced a week or two apart. Allow six weeks for the entire process.

Medical research is constantly finding new drugs and discovering new things about existing drugs. Therefore, the most recent medical advice may differ from recommendations here, and some immunisations are now said to be ineffective — cholera for example — or not necessary because the disease has been eradicated — in particular, smallpox. Follow your doctor's advice in any matters of question, as he is supposed to have the latest information. However, you should also be aware that many countries still require a smallpox certificate (and occasionally cholera) despite what your own public health office may tell you. It's far better to get a smallpox injection at home than at a remote border, or to sit in quarantine at a foreign airport.

Required
These shots must be recorded on your International Certificate of Vaccination, which is available at passport offices and many doctor's offices. Have your local health department certify the doctor's signature with a stamp on the vaccination certification — without the stamp the certificate is invalid.

Smallpox Vaccination Valid for three years. It is recommended that you have a revaccination if your last shot was over a year ago.

Cholera Immunisation A series of two injections spaced two weeks apart or a single booster after the initial series. Valid for six months only.

Strongly Recommended
The immunisations listed below are not required for entrance into Nepal or India, but most health authorities recommend them for travellers to parts of Asia visited by a trek. Have your doctor record these shots on your vaccination certificate for reference.

Gamma Globulin The best available protection against infectious hepatitis. The effectiveness of this injection diminishes rapidly. Get it just before departure.

Typhoid-paratyphoid A series of three injections, or a booster shot if you have already had the series.

Tetanus Booster You should have this if your last shot was more than a year ago.

Polio The Sabin trivalent booster.

Malaria Protection is gained by taking Chloroquine, Paludrine or Fansidar tablets starting before you leave for the trip, continuing once a week throughout your trek and for six weeks after you arrive home.

Recommended

The immunisations below are good additional protection. They are useful because you will be coming into contact with travellers from all over the world.

Yellow Fever Valid for ten years. Available only from certain designated vaccination centres.

Typhus Valid for six to twelve months. Two injections.

YOUR FIRST AID KIT

If you carry the items described below, you should be able to care for most of your medical needs on the trek. Bring along a sufficient quantity of these items for your own needs. A complete supply of first aid materials and emergency medicines is provided on most organised treks, but there may not be a sufficient supply of the most frequently used items listed here.

Your first aid kit should also contain any special items you normally take into the mountains with you. All medicines, particularly liquids and powders, should be in plastic containers with screw-on lids. Most doctors are willing to provide you with a supply of the prescription drugs recommended here. Follow your own doctor's advice regarding any substitutes or special needs you may have. The items you should carry are:

Chloroquine, Paludrine or Fansidar tablets for malaria
Sleeping pills for use at high altitude
Pain relief tablets with codeine for high altitude headaches
Lomotil tablets or other medicine for diarrhoea
Moleskin or Telfa pads for blisters
Tape and band-aids
Decongestant/antihistamines for high altitude congestion
Throat lozenges and cough drops
Aspirin for mild pain and discomfort
If you are allergic to any medicines (penicillin for example), bring your own substitutes
Any special medicines you require. Have your doctor describe them on the medical certificate

ACUTE MOUNTAIN SICKNESS

Acute Mountain Sickness (AMS), usually referred to as "altitude sickness", is the effect of ascending to high elevations, generally above 4000 metres, faster than the body can make the physiological changes necessary to adapt to the reduced oxygen and air pressure at such heights.

Most people are able to adjust to high altitude, but time must be allowed for this process. This adjustment is called "acclimatisation". Altitude affects everyone differently, so some individuals require more time to acclimatise, and some cannot acclimatise at high altitudes. There is no proof of a correlation between health, physical fitness or previous exposure to altitudes which indicate whether one person is more capable than another of acclimatising.

Symptoms of AMS are headache, loss of appetite, nausea and sleeplessness. These symptoms can develop further into pulmonary oedema (fluid in the lungs) or cerebral oedema (water in the brain). Either of these conditions can be fatal.

These problems are easily prevented by including specific "aclimatisation days" in the trek schedule and ascending no faster than the recommended itinerary developed by the Himalayan Rescue Association (HRA). If you go on an organised trek, the leader will have knowledge of the problems and symptoms of altitude sickness. This information is also available in Kathmandu in a pamphlet published and distributed by the HRA and in the medical books listed in the appendix. Most cases of altitude sickness can be cured by descent to a lower elevation. You should not delay such a descent even if it means splitting a group, travelling at night, or being carried by a porter.

You should be aware of the possiblity of not being able to reach high elevations in the event that you are one of those who do not acclimatise well, but you should have no fears if you follow the advice of the HRA and your trek leader. Almost without exception, fatal cases of altitude sickness have occurred only among those who ignored early symptoms and kept ascending when they should have retreated to a lower elevation.

IODINIZATION OF DRINKING WATER

A practical and safe alternative to boiling drinking water has recently been developed. The procedure requires a 30 ml clear glass bottle with a bakelite cap (do not use a plastic bottle) containing five to seven grams of crystal iodine. The iodine and bottle should be available for a very low cost from most pharmacies and this small amount will treat about 500 litres of water. Fill the bottle with water, shake it for a few minutes, then let the iodine crystals settle to the bottom. The resulting concentrated solution may be added to your water bottle to purify the water for drinking. The amount to be added depends on the temperature and degree of pollution of the water; the table below shows the amount of the solution that should be added to disinfect one litre of water in 20 minutes:

Near freezing (3°C)	add 20 ml per litre
Cold water (20°C)	add 15 ml per litre
Warm water (40°C)	add 10 ml per litre

If the water is heavily contaminated, either add more of the iodine solution or wait more than 20 minutes before drinking the water. After using some of the solution, refill the iodine bottle with water and shake it again to make more concentrated solution. This method kills all common forms of water carried diseases including amoebic cysts, salmonella and hepatitus virus. This method should not be used by people allergic to iodine.

The inclusion of an iodinization kit in your medical supply is highly recommended. It will allow you to fill your water bottle from any stream, treat it, and 20 minutes later have safe, cold drinking water. This saves having to wait for boiled water at night. If an entire trekking group used this method, it would also save scarce firewood by eliminating the necessity of preparing boiling water each evening. Note that halazone and iodine tablets are not a substitute for the method described above. For more details of this method, see *The Western Journal of Medicine*, May 1975, for the article "Water Disinfection in the Wilderness" by Frederick H Kahn, MD and Barbara R Visscher, MD.

Plane Tickets

Most trekking agents arrange air transportation to and from Nepal. Since their goal is to fill each trekking group they organise, it is to their advantage to find you the lowest possible airfare. Therefore it is to your advantage to make your travel arrangements through your trekking agent.

Airfares continually change, usually upwards, and the trekking agent will be aware of any alterations. You are thus spared the problems of discovering at the last minute that your fare has increased and having to pay the difference from money you had planned to use in Nepal. By travelling with the group, you are often eligible for a group or excursion airfare which can be, in some cases, even less than the one-way individual rate.

Your agent will assume that you will travel with the group. Be sure you inform him early, if you intend to make other plans. In some cases, there may even be an extra fee for doing so. Group airfares often depend on a minimum size group, ordinarily 10 to 15. If the group is not large enough (if one drops out at the last minute), everyone else has to pay additional airfare. It is only just to the others on the trek to let them know of your intentions as far in advance as possible, so that the minimum size can be maintained.

If you can conform to the group schedule and can arrange your travel through your trekking agent, I urge you to do so. Airline reservations are difficult to obtain in Asia. They must always be reconfirmed or they may be cancelled. This is no idle threat, it often happens. On some flights, a cancellation charge, sometimes as much as the entire cost of the ticket, will be forfeited if you do not cancel your reservation on time and have that fact recorded on your ticket for proof. All these details are taken care of for you, if you travel on the group itinerary. If you alter your individual itinerary, you'll either have to make new reservations yourself or pay a fee to an agency in Kathmandu to handle the changes.

Twin Otter in Lukla

Be sure that you understand any restrictions involved with your air ticket. A normal full-fare ticket can be switched to any other airline, can be refunded, can be used up to one year from its purchase date and can be changed or rerouted to allow stopovers. All group fares, excursion fares and other discounted tickets have specific restrictions that may complicate your travel schedule. In most cases you must travel on only one airline, you have a minimum and maximum stay overseas and you can make no stopovers, or only certain designated stopovers, en route. Be sure that you understand all these restrictions before you purchase your ticket so that you are not surprised and disappointed later. APEX tickets that involve heavy cancellation charges if you do not travel on a particular date are especially dangerous — it is very common for both domestic and international flights to be delayed — you must not count on leaving Nepal on a particular date to connect with a flight home.

Other Sightseeing

Most trekking groups have a few days in Kathmandu both before and after the trek for shopping and sightseeing. Some groups have additional stopovers and sightseeing arranged during their travel to and from Nepal. This limited duration is sufficient for most people, since they are already committed to an extended stay away from their home and job. If you wish to spend more time in conjunction with your trek, you should make firm reservations for any additional travel before you leave home — unless you are seriously committed to vagabonding it. Travel by bus and train in Asia is a fascinating experience, but it is quite different from anything you have experienced at home. I have met people who have hitchhiked through Europe, who could not cope with the bureaucracy, confusion, crowds and general uncertainty that are a part of everyday life in Asia. Be sure you are willing to accept all of this before you plan to travel on your own.

If, however, you do elect to have your trekking agent arrange additional travel for you, you will discover that you can travel in almost unbelievable luxury for a fraction of the cost you would pay at home for travel of any kind. For example, it is great fun to stay in a converted maharajah's palace, with a car and driver at your disposal — all at less than the price of a rental car at home.

Flights Within Nepal

All domestic flights in Nepal are operated by the national carrier, Royal Nepal Airlines Corporation (RNAC). RNAC operates a fleet of 19-passenger Twin Otter and 6-passenger Pilatus Porter aircraft to some of the most remote and spectacular airstrips in the world. Both these planes are STOL (Short Take Off and Landing) aircraft in order to accommodate the short, grass airstrips at Jomsom, Lukla, Shyangboche, Langtang and other places.

The approaches to these airstrips are difficult, they are all situated on mountainsides surrounded by high peaks. Therefore, if there are clouds or high winds, the pilot cannot possibly land the aircraft. The classic remark by one RNAC captain explains the picture perfectly: "We don't fly through clouds because in Nepal the clouds have rocks in them." Many flights to remote regions are delayed or cancelled because of bad weather.

If your trek involves a flight in or out of one of these remote airstrips, it is possible that you will experience a delay of several hours or (occasionally) several days. These delays are the price you pay for the time-saving and convenience of flights to remote airstrips in Nepal. It will be helpful to

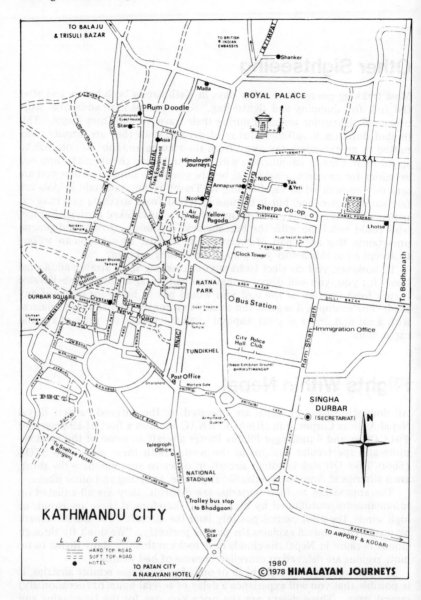

KATHMANDU CITY

L E G E N D
— — — HARD TOP ROAD
- - - SOFT TOP ROAD
● HOTEL

1980
© 1978 HIMALAYAN JOURNEYS

pack a good book into your hand luggage to make the inevitable waiting at airports in Nepal a little more tolerable.

Insurance

Many trekking agents can offer you a travellers' insurance policy, in force for periods up to 180 days. Coverage will vary from policy to policy, but will probably include loss of baggage, sickness and accidental injury or death. Most policies also cover the reimbursement of cancellation fees and other non-recoverable costs if you are forced to cancel your trip because of accident or illness of yourself, or illness or death of a family member. You should purchase this inexpensive protection. It will probably be suggested to you at the time you order your plane tickets.

Such a policy can often cover helicopter evacuation and other emergency services in Nepal. Be sure that the policy does not exclude "mountaineering" or "alpinism" or you may have a difficult time settling a claim. Although you will not be engaged in such activities, you may never be able to convince a flatlander insurance company of this fact. Note that neither your trekking agent nor its representative in Nepal can asskume any liability for lost luggage, lost money or plane tickets, or injury to any member of the party.

If you purchase insurance and have a loss, you must submit proof of this loss in order to make an insurance claim. If you have a medical problem, you must save all your bills and get a physician's certificate stating that you were sick. If you lose something covered by insurance, you must file a police report and get a copy to send to the insurance company, no matter how remote the location. No insurance claim will be considered without such documentation. Read your policy carefully and be sure you understand all its conditions.

Spending Money

On the trip you should have a supply of travellers' cheques for your expenses in Nepal (American Express is the most widely accepted). Since all of your expenses before and during the trek are covered, you will have a minimum of out-of-pocket expenditures.

Bring enough money to buy whatever souvenirs, incredible bargains, or art objects you may find along the way. In Kathmandu, there are Tibetan carpets ($90 to $150), fine oriental rugs ($100+), wool sweaters and jackets ($5 to $25), some genuine Tibetan art pieces ($20+) and semi precious stones ($5 to $25). On the trek you may have the opportunity to purchase some articles from Tibet (prayer wheels, thankas, butter lamps and bells) or Sherpa household articles (chang bottles, boots, aprons and cups) at prices anywhere from $1 to more than $100. How much money to take along is certainly your decision, but less than $100 should be sufficient.

If you plan to make a major purchase in Nepal, first visit a local importer and find out what is available and note prices. Especially note the quality so that you will have a basis for comparison in Nepal. Many pieces exported from India and Nepal may be available in your locale at prices lower than in retail shops in Kathmandu because of large volume discounts. I have noticed Tibetan carpets made in India for sale in San Francisco for less than it would cost to buy one in Nepal and ship it home.

You should also have enough money to buy such items as toilet paper and soap before you leave Kathmandu. A trick that is useful in international travel is to have a few dollars handy for tipping, bus rides and last minute purchases when you do not want to change a $10 or $20 travellers' cheque. All bus fares and baggage handling are usually prepaid, but you might want about ten $1 bills in your pocket. You will also need cash for a movie ($2.50) and drinks on the plane, if you opt for this form of entertainment.

If you will be trekking on your own, you must have enough money in rupees to cover all your expenses on the trek. It is usually not possible to change money or travellers' cheques outside of Kathmandu or Pokhara. It is most important to have enough money to purchase a plane ticket (or better yet, buy a ticket in advance) if you plan to fly back from Lukla, Shyangboche or Jomsom. In years past, flights to these airports were operated as charters and it used to be possible to bargain the airfare or leave a passport as a deposit and "fly now, pay later". Now all such flights are scheduled RNAC operations, so prices are fixed and all tickets must be paid for in cash and in advance.

Passports, Visas & Visa Extensions

You will need a passport and a visa for Nepal before you leave home. Do not put off these projects. They can sometimes take longer than you expect and a last-minute snafu could cause you to delay your trip.

When getting photographs for your passport, if you do not already have one, get about ten extra for your Nepal visa and trekking permit. It is also a good idea to carry a few photos along in case of some new regulation or restriction along the way.

If you already have a passport, be sure it is valid and will not expire during your trip. It can be a horrible project to get a passport renewed overseas. A new passport can be obtained well in advance of the expiration date of your old one.

A visa is simply a permit from a foreign government to enter their country. Obtain a visa for Nepal well in advance of your departure; during your stay the visa can easily be extended for the full period of your visit. If you enter Nepal without a visa, there can be problems. Although a visa can be obtained at Kathmandu airport, the procedure is lengthy and the initial validity is limited to seven days, although it can be extended. Visa extensions for a stay in Nepal for up to three months are available only in Kathmandu. Visa extension fees are expensive, Rs 400 ($32) for the second month and Rs 800 ($64) for the third month. Visas cannot be extended beyond three months for tourists. Visa extensions are free with trekking permits, but you are required to get your trekking permit stamped on your trek to prove that you actually did go trekking.

Your travel or trekking agent can obtain your visa for you at a small charge. If you decide to get your own visa, write, enclosing a stamped, self-addressed envelope, for the visa pplication form and information. When you receive it, fill it out and send the completed form, photos, your passport, the fee (currently $10) and a self-addressed envelope for its return. Send your passport both ways by registered post. The passport will be returned to you with the visa stamped in. The visa is valid only within three months of the date of issue, so do not apply too soon or the visa will not be valid when you arrive in Kathmandu.

Addresses of some of the Nepalese embassies and consulates abroad are:

Australia	— 3/87C Cowles Road, Mosman, NSW 2088 (tel 960 3565)
India	— Barakhamba Rd, New Delhi (tel 38 1484)
	-- 19 Woodlands, Sterndale Rd, Alipore, Calcutta (tel 45 2024)
Thailand	— 189 soi Puengsuk, Sukhumvit 71, Bangkok (tel 391 7240)
UK	— 12A Kensington Palace Gardens, London W8 (tel 01 229 6231)
USA	— 2131 Leroy Place, Washington DC 20008 (tel 667 4550)
	— 711 Third Ave, Room 1806, New York, NY 10017

Flying to Nepal from Europe you will most likely transit through New Delhi, from Australia or the US west coast through Bangkok. In either city it is quite simple to pick up a Nepal visa if you have a day or two stopover.

Trekking Permits

Your Nepal visa is only valid for the Kathmandu Valley, Pokhara and Chitwan (Tiger Tops). A trekking permit issued by the immigration office is required for all foreigners who travel outside these regions. The permit specifies the places you may visit, the route you are to follow and the maximum duration of your stay. If you have arranged your trek through an agent, he will see that your visa is extended and the proper trekking permit is issued once you arrive in Kathmandu.

If you travel on your own, you must go to the Central Immigration Office on Ram Shah Path (also called Putali Sadak) and fill in an application form stating the destination and duration you desire. This form, two photographs, a fee of Rs 1 plus Rs 60 for each week of trekking and your passport are necessary. Your trekking permit will be checked at several points along most trails and is always checked at Kathmandu airport (along with your passport) before you are allowed to board a flight to another part of Nepal.

It is no longer necessary (as it was in 1976) to have a trekking company arrange a trekking permit for you, although a trekking company can usually obtain a permit faster than you could do it yourself.

Follow the instructions of your trekking agent with regard to the formalities you should follow to help him secure your trekking permit. You must supply two identical passport photos for use on your trekking permit application.

Receiving Mail in Nepal

Your trekking agent will provide you with an address in Kathmandu at which you can receive mail. The only practical way to send letters to Nepal is airmail; surface mail (by sea) takes months.

Mail service to and from Nepal is not totally reliable. Important letters should be sent via registered mail. It is almost impossible to clear a parcel through customs — do not send packages to Nepal except in an extreme emergency.

Currency

The unit of currency is the Nepal rupee which has an official exchange rate of US$1 = Rs 13.1. The value of other currencies vary according to their rate against the US dollar. Approximate current values are:

US$1	=	Rs 13.1	Rs 10	=	US$0.76
A$1	=	Rs 14.9	Rs 10	=	A$0.67
£1	=	Rs 23.9	Rs 10	=	£0.42

You should change enough money in Kathmandu to cover all expenses on the trek, since it is impossible to change money outside the city. The money you receive should be in 5 and 10 rupee notes. There is a 100 rupee note but it would be difficult to change in the hills. Consider yourself lucky that paper money is now accepted throughout Nepal. On the 1953 Everest expedition, all their money had to be carried as coins — the money alone took 30 porter loads!

Some Cultural Considerations

I cannot emphasise too strongly the unique opportunities and responsibilities that a Nepal trek presents. You will have a chance to meet and become well acquainted with Sherpas and members of other Nepalese tribes — people whose background is completely different from what you are used to in the west. Treks are a fascinating cultural experience but require some concessions on your part to the customs and habits of other backgrounds.

Nepal is officially a Hindu country, although the Sherpas are Buddhists. In Kathmandu, you may be refused entry into a Hindu temple because you are wearing leather shoes or a leather belt; there are other temples that you will not be allowed to visit at all. Please respect these customs. Generally, Buddhist temples, or gompas, are less restrictive, but you should still ask permission to enter and remove your shoes when you do — and definitely ask permission before taking photographs in any temple.

During the trek you will have may opportunities to photograph picturesque local people. Some people, however, will not want to be photographed and you should respect this. There are always cases of shyness which can be overcome by a smile, a joke or using a telephoto lens — but don't pay people for taking their picture. They are not afraid of a camera "stealing their soul", as some African people are, but instead, according to information one friend supplied me, it is too much contact with photographers and cameras which cause the problem. Many photographs of hill people in Nepal, especially Sherpas, have been printed in books, magazines and brochures. The Sherpas, in particular the women, are afraid that a photo of them will be reproduced in quantity and eventually be burned, thrown away, or even used as toilet paper! This is a major reason for local people to refuse to allow photographs and it is probably a legitimate reason that you should respect.

You are travelling nearly halfway around the world to experience and, I hope, learn from a different culture. A traveller who embarks upon a trip with an open and enquiring mind gains far more than the condescending tourist who insists on seeing how "primitive" or "colourful" other cultures may be. You are not visiting a museum — you are visiting a country that is vibrantly alive, where the people live more comfortably and, in most cases, more happily than we do.

Nepal represents a culture far older and in many ways more sophisticated than our own. The more you listen and observe the more you will learn and

Sherpa woman

the more you will be accepted. Nobody likes to be told that his ways are "antiquated" or "wrong". If you must try to teach Nepalese hill people something, try teaching them English. This is one element of our culture that is universally desired. Spending your time conversing with a sherpa or porter in English as you stroll the trail together will be a good start towards a lasting friendship.

A few other suggestions and considerations that will make your trek more enriching:

— Don't pollute. Pick up papers, film wrappers and other junk.
— Burn all your toilet paper and bury your faeces.
— Don't pass out balloons, candy and money to village children. It encourages them to beg. Trekkers are responsible for the continual cries of children for "Mithai" (candy), "paisa" (money), and "boom boom" (balloon). Well-intentioned trekkers have thought they were doing a service by passing out pens for use in school, so clever kids now ask for pens.
— Don't tempt people into thievery by leaving cameras, watches and other valuable items around camp. Keep all your personal belongings in your tent. This also means that you should not leave laundry hanging outside at night.
— Don't make campfires; wood is scarce in Nepal.
— Don't touch food or eating utensils that will be used by local people. Most Hindus cannot eat food that has been touched by a foreigner; this problem does not apply to Sherpas, however.
— Do not throw things into the fire in any house — Buddhist or Hindu.

Part 3

Route Descriptions

> *The teacher can but point the Way,*
> *The means to reach the Goal*
> *Must vary with each Pilgrim* *

Scope & Purpose

This section provides descriptions of the best-known trekking routes in Nepal. The purpose of these descriptions is to provide some insight into the types of country and culture to be encountered on specific treks. In addition, these descriptions may help you to choose the area you wish to visit, because they provide some indication of the difficulty of each trek, as well as the number of days required to follow a particular route.

As you trek these routes, you can refer to the route descriptions for cultural background notes, but it is important that you understand that these are not self-guiding trail descriptions. There is no substitute for a Nepalese companion — a Sherpa or porter — who can ask questions on the spot and who can use his own knowledge of a trail to find the correct path. What to us may be a major trekking route may be, for the people of a village, only a path from Ram's house to Bir Bahadur's house to Dawa's house. In our minds we string all these sections of trail together to form a major route to some place that the village people may never go. There is nothing more frustrating than wandering around the hills of Nepal looking for the correct trail; and it is impossible, no matter how detailed the route description, to document every important trail junction. The descriptions that follow portray what you may expect if you follow the shortest available routes. But it will be all too easy to get lost if you try to walk through Nepal alone, using only this book as a guide.

Just as it is impossible to document every trail junction, it is also impossible to describe every trekking route. I have selected the major routes, included a few optional side trips, and pointed out some alternate routes to avoid backtracking. (You should seriously consider backtracking, however.

---

* This quotation is one of the Tibetan "elegant sayings" attributed either to Nagarjuna, the Indian mystic who lived in the second century AD, or to the Head Lama of the Sakya monastery in Tibet, 1270 AD.

Often the second time over a particular trail provides insights and views not seen or appreciated the first time through).

If you are making your first trek in Nepal, it is likely that you will choose one of these. Not only are they the best known, but they are generally the most interesting places to go. There is good reason for the fame of the Everest trek, the Jomsom trek and other well-known routes. Most of the routes described (with the exception of the Khumbu-Dharan trek) have some facilities for "live-off-the-land" trekkers and the trails are reasonably well defined. You may at first be tempted to go to some other region where there won't be so many tourists because of stories and articles you may have read about the "freeway" to Everest. When you listen to these discussions it is important to place them in their proper perspective. In 1979/80 the so-called overcrowded conditions in the Everest region consisted of less than 5000 trekkers over a period of eight months — this is fewer people than occupy a typical United States National Park campground on a single weekend night. Getting to remote and unexplored areas has little meaning in Nepal.

The following routes are described here:

The Mount Everest Region
Lamosangu to Everest Base Camp
The Lamidanda Escape Route
Gokyo
Thami

Eastern Nepal
Solu Khumbu to Dharan

North of Kathmandu
Langtang
Across Ganja La
Helambu Circuit
Gosainkund

Central Nepal
Manang and Jomsom to Pokhara via the Kali Ghandaki
Annapurna Sanctuary

Western Nepal
Jumla to Rara Lake

Other Destinations

In each of the sections there is a brief introduction outlining some of the many options possible in that region. There are many parts of Nepal, particularly thoses places near to the Chinese border, that are closed to foreigners. Many trips that a map may suggested are in restricted areas and you cannot obtain a trekking permit for those regions. Some areas specifically closed to foreigners are: Mustang (north of Kagbeni), Larke La (a circuit of Manaslu is not allowed), Dolpo (a circuit of Dhaulagiri is not allowed), Humla, Kanchenjunga Base Camp and the route to Nangpa La in Khumbu. It is advisable to respect these closed areas when you plan your trek and not count on a last-minute change in the rules. Police checkposts are frequent in the hills and you will get turned back if you try to proceed where foreigners are not allowed. In most cases there are very valid reasons for the restrictions; you do not want to be the centre of an international incident.

There are many routes that proceed over high passes. Two of these — Ganja La and Thorung La — are described here. These treks have the dangers of rockfall, avalanches and high altitude. It is important for all members of the party — including the sherpas and porters — to be well equipped before attempting these routes. The possibility of snow increases from December through April and a trek may be forced to turn back if the pass is snowbound.

DAY BY DAY

The route descriptions here have been separated into daily stages, a device useful to make them readable and to estimate the time required for a particular trek. The night stops I have suggested are the ones most trekking groups use; in all cases wood, water, food for porters (and usually *chhang* for sherpas!) and a place large enough to pitch four or five tents is available at

KEY TO TREKKING MAPS

1 · LAMOSANGU – NAMCHE BAZAR
2 · MOUNT EVEREST REGION
3 · DHARAN – MAKALU
4 · LANGTANG & HELAMBU
5 · MANANG & JOMSOM
6 · JUMLA & RARA LAKE

LEGEND
—·— International Boundary
—— Road
═══ Under Construction Road
〰 Rivers
▲ ○ Peaks & Towns

SCALE
0   16   32   48 miles
0 10 20 40 60 80 kilometers

each place mentioned. In most cases food and accommodation for "live-off-the-land" trekkers is also available, but as I don't often trek this way, I have never paid much attention to the availability and quality of these facilities.

You will find when you trek these routes yourself, either with an organised group or alone, that you may not be able to make your camp at the places I have suggested. Your actual stopping places will depend on the fitness of your group, whether someone is sick on a particular day, weather, trail conditions and arrangements with the porters. Porters are the primary influence on the speed with which you can travel, since their 30 kg loads make them much slower than a trekker with only a light rucksack. This variance from the schedule should cause no concern; you are not on a planned itinerary and your trek should allow the freedom and opportunity to move as fast or as slowly as you wish. A trek is supposed to be a vacation; don't carry schedules and timetables along where they are not necessary.

It is possible to alter the number of days suggested here. Perhaps you can cut a day or two off the time if you walk from first light to sunset each day, but since a trek is a continual experience, not simply progress to a particular destination, there is little point in rushing the trip just to get to some place that may not be as interesting as where you are now. At high altitues it is important to proceed no faster than the ascent times recommended here in order to avoid altitude sickness. The trek can be lengthened to almost any degree by side trips, rest days and further exploration of interesting villages.

TIME & DISTANCE

In the following route descriptions I have resisted the temptation to include approximate walking times. Instead, I have listed the routes in daily stages. I have hiked most of these routes myself and the stages I have detailed can all be accomplished in a single day by any moderately-fit trekker. The stages do, however, tend to get a little more difficult farther along in each trek, because you (and I) get fitter as the trek progresses. More importantly, however, each stage can be accomplished by porters in a single day.

I have had occasion to time my progress on several portions of a trail that I have hiked many times. (Much to the ridicule of my friends who do not believe it is in keeping with a lifestyle that emphasises outdoor living, I wear a wristwatch.) The elapsed times for any given portion of trail have varied considerably, depending on my own mood, physical condition, condition of the trail, the number of other people and cattle on the trail, and the weather. Because of my own wide variations in walking times, I have not even attempted to project approximate times for anyone else. Most days require from five to eight hours of walking.

Another statistic I have had trouble with is distance. Certainly we can judge distances from a map, but a printed map is two-dimensional. With the many gains and losses of altitude — and all the turns and twists of the trail — a map measurement of the routes becomes virtually meaningless. In researching a guidebook to Glacier National Park in the United States, a friend pushed a bicycle wheel-odometer contraption over every trail in the park to obtain accurate mileage measurements. I have neither the ambition nor the patience for such a project, and besides, it would take most of the fun out of a trek. One gains a different perspective of travelling by discussing how many *days* to a particular destination rather than how many *miles*.

For the route descriptions that follow I have only a very general idea of how far is covered per day. I know that my feet hurt if I walk much more than 25 km (15 miles) in a day so I conclude that most of the days listed here cover less than that — because my feet have not been overly uncomfortable. On the other hand (or foot), each day's trek must also be more than eight or ten km (five or six miles) because I am tired when I walk that far, and most of the days suggested here have tired me out enough to ensure a very sound night's sleep.

ON MEASURING ALTITUDE

I did make one concession to statisticians. I bought an altimeter, mostly because it impressed me to have such an expensive toy. I purchased one that reads up to 8000 metres (27,000 feet) — just in case! I also bought it to have a better altimeter than my friends. To put my toy to use, when I thought about it during a trek, I wrote down elevations at the tops of passes and at villages and other important places. Nevertheless, there are several gremlins that frustrated my attempts to report observations that are accurate. First, at many places I simply forgot or was too tired to write down the elevation. Second, according to the little book that came with the altimeter, it is necessary to reset the instrument frequently to compensate for barometric changes. Naturally I did not, as there are few known elevations in the hills of Nepal. Third, I later learned that the temperature must also be recorded to obtain accurate measurements. (I never bothered.) Fourth, I lost my notes for all the altitudes on the Everest trek. Therefore, the estimated elevations shown in these route descriptions are composites, based on my own measurements, the best available maps, and route descriptions others have prepared. Except for instances where everyone agreed on the same figure, I have rounded elevations to the nearest 10 metres. The elevations of peaks are those shown on the official mountaineering regulations of Nepal.

This uncertainty over precise elevations will cause no problems during a trek. The only purpose of knowing the elevation is to learn whether the trail ahead goes uphill or downhill and whether it is a long ascent (or descent) or a short one. The elevations shown here fulfill that purpose. The idea of precise elevations becomes even more complicated because villages are spread out over such large areas. What is the "correct" elevation of a village like Bung, which extends almost 500 vertical metres up a hillside?

CHANGES

The routes described here are undergoing constant change. Several roads are under construction that will make significant alterations in some of these routes, particularly when the roads (and bridges) from Dumre, Lamosangu and Dharan are completed. There is talk of a road from Pokhara to Jomsom and even talk of a road up the Dudh Kosi to Namche Bazar, but these haven't even reached the drawing board stage yet. Trails are constantly being widened, shifted or changed to avoid ridges, landslides or flood areas. Most descriptions here were accurate in the spring of 1981, but even by fall some portions will be out of date.

New hotels are being constructed at a fast pace in the hills. There seems to be an impression that "moderate" inns, charging US$3 to US$10 per person per night, can be successful. This may be true, but most local hotels charge much less, or even allow you to sleep for free if you buy a meal from them. Trekkers who have a completely arranged trek generally prefer their tents to even a reasonably priced hotel room. The fancy hotels at Poon Hill, Jomsom, Namche Bazar (under construction), Phakding and Lukla don't seem to offer much of an option until there is enough of a chain to allow sleeping in good hotels every night. But these establishments are exerting their own influence on the trekking routes and the trekking experience, so this will bring changes in the future.

There are many influences on the decision to open or close certain parts of Nepal to foreigners. Recent changes have liberalised both trekking and climbing and it is likely that more areas will be opened in the future. Rumours that the Kanchenjunga area will open are frequently heard; there are continual (and still seemingly unfounded) rumours that Mustang and Dolpo will be opened soon — but this rumour has been continuing for more than six years. A check with a trekking agent or the central immigration office should be made before planning any unusual trek, but it may be assumed that the treks listed here will not be affected.

The trek route may change because of the season. The routes described here work in the trekking season from October through May, though some high passes may be open only in October-November and again in May. If you trek in the monsoon, the trails may not bear any resemblance to what is described here. Bridges can get washed away and trails can get flooded during this season. In early October, and again in April and May, rice is growing in many of the terraces a trek passes by. Many campsites that are excellent in November and December are under water in the rice growing season.

NAMES

The route descriptions list many places that do not correlate with names in other descriptions of the same route or with names on maps. The diversity occurs because there is no universally accepted form of transliterating Nepali and Tibetan names into English, so the same place name may be spelled in many different ways. To make matters more complicated, a place may have several different names. Mount Everest, for example, is also known as *Sagarmatha* (Nepali) and *Chomolungma* (Sherpa). The same situation obtains for many village names.

Many maps made before 1950 had very little ground control and village names have little resemblance to reality. This is particularly true of the maps prepared by the US Army Map Service that have been subsequently copied and distributed as trekking maps in Kathmandu.

In the route reports that follow, names and descriptions have been translated in most cases, but to avoid a lot of repetition, several Nepalese and Tibetan words have been used throughout the text. These include:

khola — a river
kosi — one of the seven major rivers flowing into the Arun River
gompa — a Tibetan Buddhist temple
yak — the wonderful domestic beast that provides wool, milk, fuel and transportation in Solu Khumbu
nak — a female yak
Tamang, Chhetri, Brahmin, Rai, Sherpa, Gurung, Limbu, Newar and *Magar* — names of some of the many ethnic groups that populate Nepal's hills
chorten and *mani* walls — Tibetan Buddhist monuments
la — pass (Tibetan)
bhanjyang — pass (Nepali)
terai — the flat plains area along the southern border of Nepal
goth — an animal shed or small hut near an alpine pasture, usually inhabited only during the summer months
bhatti — a local inn
kani — an arch-shaped *chorten* that is built over a trail
kharka — an alpine pasture

MAPS

The maps included in this book are hand drawn by a cartographer in Kathmandu. As with everything else here, they are reasonably accurate, but not perfect by any means. In order to make them legible I eliminated most villages and landmarks not included in the route descriptions. In some cases, even major villages and mountains have vanished from the maps. Few elevations are shown; these may be obtained from the route descriptions. Instead of contour lines, only ridge lines have been depicted. This is the line of the highest point on a ridge; if the trail crosses one of these heavy black lines, you have to walk uphill; if the trail leads from a ridge line to a river, you must walk downhill. Peaks are shown in their true position, but villages may not always be located accurately — the problem occurs because of the size of villages. Where does the dot go for a village that is three km from end to end? The trails and roads follow the general direction indicated on the maps, but small switchbacks and twists and turns obviously cannot be shown in anything of this size.

For more detailed maps, there are several sources. The best series is the 1:50,000 series produced by Erwin Schneider for Research Scheme Nepal Himalaya and printed in Vienna. They are available outside of Nepal from many map shops and in Nepal from Thyssen House in Kathmandu. The fantastically coloured maps are also fantastically expensive — about US$8 a sheet, but if you are doing any serious trekking they are worth it. The available maps include: Khumbu Himal, Shorong/Hinku (Solu/Hongu), Dudh Kosi, Tamba Kosi/Likhu Khola, Rowaling Himal, Lepchi Kang, Langtang/Jugal Himal and Kathmandu Valley.

Other maps are available as blueprints of traced maps in Kathmandu. They aren't really very accurate, but they will give you some idea of where you are going. A few other printed maps, including an excellent series by Dr Harka Bahadur Gurung, formerly Nepal's Minister of Tourism, are available in Kathmandu.

A map titled *The Mount Everest Region* is published in England and covers about the same region as the map of the same name in this book in the section on the Everest trek. This map is available by mail from the Royal Geographical Society, 1 Kensington Gore, London SW7 at a cost of £5 per copy.

The Mount Everest Region

Interesting and justifiably famous, not only for its proximity to the world's highest mountain, but also for its Sherpa villages and monasteries, the Solu Khumbu area is the destination of most trekkers in Nepal. The primary destination for treks in this region is either the Everest base camp, about 5340 metres, or Kala Pattar, an unassuming 5545 metre bump on the southern flank of Pumori (7154 metres), which provides a fine view of Everest.

Trekkers should be prepared to forego these opportunities if they suffer any symptoms of acute altitude sickness at such a height. Less ambitious destinations include Namche Bazar, the administrative headquarters of the Khumbu region; Khumjung or Thami, more typical Sherpa villages; or

Thyangboche monastery, from which an excellent view may be had of Everest and its more spectacular neighbour Ama Dablam (6863 metres).

The Everest region may be reached by STOL (short take-off and landing) airstrips at Lukla (2800 metres) or Shyangboche (3700 metres), or by a two week trek from the roadhead at Lamosangu, 80 km from Kathmandu. Those who fly to Lukla miss the historic and culturally fascinating route followed by the Everest expeditions of the '50s and '60s. I recommend taking the time to walk from Lamosangu, then after acclimatisation and conditioning afforded by the trek, visiting the base camp area and either flying out or walking back by an alternative route to Kathmandu. Those who insist their time is limited can fly to or from Lukla or Shyangboche, and spend as little as six days to visit Namche Bazar and Thyangboche. It is ill-advised to attempt a visit to the base camp, because of the lack of acclimatisation, if flying up to these elevations. Clouds or bad weather can close either airstrip for several days at a time, so those with a tight schedule would do well to allow a few spare days — most trekking agencies do this as a matter of course.

LAMOSANGU to EVEREST BASE CAMP

This description details the route and suggested camping spots on a 25-day trek from Kathmandu to Everest Base Camp and flight back to Kathmandu from Lukla. If you are flying to Lukla, begin reading at day 12 and spend your first night at Phakding, but allow an extra day at Thyangboche for acclimatisation. An excellent 38 day trek — my favourite — may be made by walking to Dharan instead of flying from Lukla. This route is described in another section.

The Everest trek involves a tremendous amount of up and down walking. A glance at the map will show the reason why. All the rivers in this part of Nepal flow south (the Himalaya is not a continental divide) and the trek route proceeds east. Therefore the trail must climb to the ridge separating two rivers, descend to the river itself and climb to the top of the next ridge. Even though the trek begins at an elevation of 770 metres, on the tenth day it crosses the Dudh Kosi at an elevation of only 1500 metres — after considerable uphill walking. If you total all the uphill climbing, it will come to more than 13,000 metres (40,000 feet) of elevation gain from Lamosangu to Everest Base Camp.

The first part of the trek follows the new 110 km long road being built from Lamosangu to Jiri. The first 64 km of this road are now passable by vehicle, and there is even regular bus service (at irregular intervals) as far as Kirantichhap at a fare of Rs 30 for the full day trip. Breakdowns are common, so buses can get delayed for long periods. A special permit is necessary to travel the road; this is an amazing document issued in five copies that is valid only for a single trip. In 1980 it was not possible to get a permit for transportation with a trek, so most groups end up walking anyway. The development of roads has been a feature of this trek since the first Everest expedition. In 1953 the British Everest Expedition started from Bhadgaon. By 1963 the American Expedition could begin from the end of the road at Banepa, saving a day of walking over the British. The Chinese road to Kodari allowed the trek to begin from Dolalghat in 1967 and from Lamosangu in 1970. The road now stops at the Tamba Kosi, so unless you float a vehicle across the river, you must still be content with walking the rest of the way to Jiri for some time to come.

Maps and route descriptions for this trek become confusing because of conflicting names for the same place. Many of the villages along this route have both Sherpa names and Nepali names. This applies to both Sherpa and non-Sherpa villages. I have tried to standardise on the Nepali name, as these are the ones shown on all official maps and records. The Sherpa names for the villages along the route are given in parenthesised italics after the more common Nepali name.

Day 1

Kathmandu
↓
Lamosangu
↓

Pakhar

It requires about 2½ hours to cover the 80 km from Kathmandu to Lamosangu on the Arniko Rajmarg, the Chinese constructed Kodari highway, which links Nepal's capital with Tibet. If you are travelling by public bus, allow about five hours for the trip; buses leave frequently in the morning from a bus station near the Police Club in Kathmandu. After leaving the Kathmandu Valley and passing by the old Newar towns of Banepa and Dhulikhel — which offer excellent panoramic views of the eastern Himalaya (including Langtang Lirung, Dorje Lakpa and Manaslu) on a clear day — the road descends to the Sun Kosi at Dolalghat. It then follows the river north to Lamosangu, a bustling bazaar about 50 km south of the Tibetan border. Close to Lamosangu is a hydroelectric power plant built with Chinese aid.

Lamosangu (elevation 770 metres) means "long bridge" in Nepali. After leaving the road, the trail descends through the shops of the bazaar, then crosses the long suspension bridge that gives the town its name. The trail then begins to climb immediately towards the top of the 2500 metre ridge that forms the watershed between the Sun Kosi drainage to the west and the Tamba Kosi drainage to the east. The trek from Lamosangu to the eastern Himalaya, proceeding as it does from west to east, cuts "across the grain" of the country, crossing six major ridges enroute to Namche Bazar. The ascent is steep, particularly at the beginning, since the slope, as is usual in this region, is convex.

The road to Jiri begins a short distance south of Lamosangu and proceeds to switchback its way up the south side of the ridge, while the trail climbs initially up the north side. For the first day of the trek the road is not seen. The Jiri road is being built by the Swiss Association for Technical Assistance as part of a larger program of agricultural development in this region. The road is planned to serve the dairy and agricultural project at Jiri and the agricultural project at Kabre. It is being built by hand instead of machine in order to have a beneficial economic impact by employing hundreds of workers.

The trail climbs through terrace fields alternated with patches of scrub forest, past the tea shops of Kaping, to Perku, elevation 1660 metres, situated in a large ravine. The villages in this area are of mixed ethnic and caste composition. Most the population is either Chhetri or

Chorten at Bhandar

Brahmin, who speak Nepali as their mother tongue, or Tamangs, who speak a Tibeto-Burman language among themselves, but speak Nepali — the *lingua franca*, or "trade language" of the country — as a second language. Chhetris and Brahmins are Hindus, while the Tamangs practise a form of Tibetan Buddhism. Generally, Tamang people live at slightly higher elevations than their Hindu neighbours, but there is a great deal of overlap.

The afternoon is short, as the trail climbs gradually through the rest of the village of Perku, then on to the Tamang village of Pakhar, at 1980 metres. There is an excellent camping place here just before the village; the views of the mountains early the near morning are spectacular.

Day 2

Pakhar

Surkhe

The ascent continues up to the top of the ridge and joins the road, which has climbed up the other side. Most of the day's trek is on the road, straying off it only to avoid long switchbacks. Climbing through scrub forests and the village of Sildunga at about 2130 metres, the trail levels out near Muldi at 2540 metres. The train then continues to Nigale, located on the top of the pass at 2440 metres, where there are a few shops and teahouses. This and the nearby settlements are mostly Tamang. There are good views of the Himalaya to the north and of the trek route for the next several days (as far as Lamjura Pass) from the top of the first ridge.

The descent is steep, then becomes more gradual before crossing a stream and entering the village of Surkhe, 1750 metres, a mixed settlement of Tamangs and Chhetris-Brahmins. The motor road does not descend into the valley. Instead it turns north and contours around the ridge, passing by the large town of Charikot before joining up again with the trail near Kirantichhap.

Day 3

Surkhe

Kirantichhap

From Surkhe the trail descends to the Charnawati Khola, crossing it on a small makeshift bridge, then follows this stream through rice terraces to the Newar bazaar of Serobesi (*Shere*), at 1450 metres. After crossing the river on a large suspension bridge, the trail turns south and follows the river for about an hour, occasionally detouring to avoid places where the river washed the trail away during monsoon floods. There is a delightful spot for lunch in a grove of pine trees that afford some shade during what is usually a very hot day.

The trail begins climbing above the river through terraces, then descends slightly to Kirantichhap, located at about 1280 metres, on a bit of level ground at the end of the spur above the confluence where the Chandrawati Khola and Bhote Kosi join to form the Tamba Kosi. At Kirantichhap there are a few shops built in a semicircle around a pipal tree. Kirantichhap used to be a pleasant little market, but the road now cuts the village in half and has turned this delightful hill bazaar into a nondescript roadside village. The tea shops here serve a dreadful concoction of kerosene flavoured rice, and the dust from the road permeates everything. Just east of the village there is a reasonably good camping spot in the shade of another huge pipal tree.

Day 4

Kirantichhap
⬇
Yarsa

At Kirantichhap the trail rejoins the road and descends through pines and then through sal forests to the Tamba Kosi, which it crosses on a steel cable suspension bridge (imported from Aberdeen, Scotland!), at an elevation of about 850 metres. There is a major bridge for the road under construction over this large river at this point. This is a fertile valley, containing a good deal of terraced land for irrigated paddy cultivation. The population is mainly Brahmins and Chhetris, but there are also Tamangs and a few Newars. Just across the river is the village of Busti, which boasts a bakery that produces bread for Jiri, Those, and for the hungry trekkers who pass by. The trail climbs steeply through damp forests to the top of the ridge, then to Namdu at 1580 metres.

Namdu and its neighbouring village Kabre are large and spread out, with a school and a Swiss agricultural project. The trail through these villages is gradual, following the road in many places, but it climbs continuously past houses, shops, temples and fields. A short descent takes the trail to a log bridge that crosses the Yarsa Khola; then a steep walk of about an hour finally brings it to the village of Yarsa, elevation 1960 metres. The people of Yarsa are Jirels, a group whose language is related to that of the Sherpas. Although their culture and religion have been influenced by the Sherpas, in many ways they conform to regional practices in this part of the hills.

Day 5

From Yarsa the ascent continues steeply through oak and pine forests to the watershed between the Tamba Kosi and the Khimti Khola. This is the second major ridge to be crossed on the route; the pass is at an elevation fo 2510 metres. Like the first ridge, it provides an excellent view of the Himalayan peaks, especially Gauri Shankar (7150 metres) and Numbur (6954 metres). Just before reaching the pass, at a town called Chisopani (a very common Nepalese place name meaning "cold water"), there is a very welcome tea shop.

Yarsa

Those

From the pass, the motor road again remains high and contours around the head of the valley, while the trail makes a steep, slippery descent to Sikri, on the banks of the Sikri Khola at an elevation of 1860 metres. The road continues to Jiri, where it ends at the Swiss dairy and agricultural project. The Sikri Valley contains primarily Jirel settlements, although other ethnic groups are also represented. The trail follows the river southwards, then crosses a 2040 metre ridge to enter the Khimti Khola valley, which it then follows upstream to the village of Those, at 1750 metres. There is a good camp just beyond the iron suspension bridge that crosses the Khimti Khola, and there are several hotels a little bit further on in the village itself. Beware of second floor rooms above smoky kitchens here. Those (pronounced 'toe-say') (*Maksin*) is a large pleasant bazaar with a cobblestone street and whitewashed houses. It is the largest market between Lamosangu and Namche Bazar. Most of the shops are owned by Newir merchants. It is possible to buy soap, candles, candy, and items manufactured locally from the nearby sources of low-grade iron ore. Rooster lamps are a speciality. Occasionally it is possible to buy a bottle or two of beer that was carried from Kathmandu to tempt trekkers into parting with some of their money.

After lunch at Sikri, it is possible to make a side trip to Jiri (elevation 1860 metres) and see the Swiss project and then descend to Those by a different route. There is a weekly market in Jiri, at the top of the ridge, on Saturdays.

Day 6

Those

Bhandar

The trail, now completely free of the road, continues up the Khimti valley from Those to Shivalaya, 1800 metres. On this trail the first *mani* walls are encountered. These are stones covered with the Tibetan Buddhist inscription "Om Mani Padme Hum," which is most easily translated as "hail to the jewel in the lotus," though its true translation is much more complex and mysterious. You should walk to the left side of these walls as the Buddhists do.

From Shivalaya the route ascends steeply towards the

next pass. It is a climb of 480 metres to a school house at Sangbadanda, elevation 2080 metres. There is a small tea shop here, but there are three better ones between here and the pass, and another on the pass itself. On the top of the pass there is an impressive array of long *mani* walls, indicative that the trek is now entering an area dominated by Tibetan culture. At the top of the divide, at 2713 metres, there is an excellent view of the Likhu Khola valley and the village of Bhandar (*Chyangma*), the first Sherpa settlement on the trek, far below in a hanging valley. Just below the pass, take the left-hand trail to reach Bhandar. After an initially steep descent, the trail reaches the outskirts of the large village and descends gradually through fields and pastures to the village *gompa*, surrounded by two imposing *chortens*, at 2040 metres elevation.

A *chorten*, also called a stupa, is literally a receptacle for offerings, and often holds religious relics. Each of its elements has a symbolic meaning. The square or rectangular base symbolizes the solid earth. On the base is a half-spherical dome, symbolizing water. On top of the dome is a rectangular tower, the four sides of which are painted with a pair of eyes, the all-seeing eyes of Buddha, and what appears to be a nose, but is actually the sanskrit sign for the number one, symbolizing the absoluteness of Buddha. Above the rectangular tower there is a conical or pyramidal spire (symbolizing fire) with 13 step-like segments, symbolizing the 13 steps leading to Buddhahood. On top of the 13 steps is an ornament shaped like a crescent moon symbolizing air, and a vertical spike symbolizing ether or the sacred light of Buddha. The two *chortens* at Bhandar are usually freshly painted and are well preserved. A large *chorten* or *stupa*, may be seen at Bodhanath or at Swayambunath in Kathmandu.

An interesting side trip may be made to Thodung by detouring from the main trail just beyond Sangbadanda. Thodung, at 3090 metres, is the site of a government-operated cheese factory, originally built through the efforts of the Swiss in the 1950's. The long hard climb to the factory is rewarded by cheese, yoghurt and *yak* (specifically *nak*) milk for sale, though fresh dairy products are available only in the autumn season. The return route from Thodung rejoins the main trail at the top of the pass, then descends to Bhandar. Accommodation and food is usually available at Thodung if you have the courage to

chortens at
Bhandar

seek out the manager in the presence of several huge Tibetan Mastif dogs.

There are some hotels in the village of Bhandar, just below the *gompa*, and there is an excellent camping spot in a large meadow about 15 minutes walk beyond the village.

Day 7

Bhandar

↓

Sagar

From Bhandar the trail follows a small stream, crossing it on a wooden bridge, then descends into a steep canyon through heavy forests until it finally recrosses the same stream, now much larger, near a small water-driven mill. The trail turns north here, following the Likhu Khola, crossing the river on a new suspension bridge, at 1580 metres. This bridge replaces an ancient link bridge that collapsed under a load of 12 porters during the approach march for the American Mount Everest Expedition is 1963. As you follow the trail up the east bank of the river to Kenja it is often possible to see gray Langur monkeys in the nearby forests. Kenja at 1630 metres, is a small village inhabited by Newars and Magars. Several new shops and small hotels have been constructed here to cater to both trekkers and local people. When I first visited this village in 1969 there were no shops here, now there are more than 15 shops, restaurants and hotels, all operated by Sherpas who have migrated from the village of Kyama, several miles to the north. There is a weekly market here on Sundays; one specialty of Kenja's market is instant tailoring performed by on hand-operated sewing machines.

Leaving Kenja, the ascent towards the high Lamjura Ridge, a major watershed, begins. The first part of the ascent is very steep, then the ascent becomes less severe as elevation is gained. After about two hours of climbing, the trail takes a fork to the north and contours around the hillside to the Sherpa settlement of Sagar (*Chandra*), 2440 metres, a large village with two-storey stone houses and an ancient village *gompa*. It is possible to camp in the yard of the school, one of the projects of the Himalayan Trust, headed by Sir Edmund Hillary of New Zealand. The trek is now completely in Sherpa country. With only one exception, all the remaining villages up to Namche Bazar are inhabited by Sherpas.

If you are trekking on your own, you should continue on the main trail to Sete, elevation 2575 metres, a small monastic community, where accommodation may be found in a hotel.

Day 8

Sagar

Junbesi

From Sagar it is a long, but fairly gradual, climb — although in spots it gets steep — to the top of the 3530 metre pass over the Lamjura ridge. The way is scenic and interesting; it is one of the few parts of the trek that has no villages. Although the tops of some of the ridges crossed so far have been forested, the trek now for the first time gets into really fine, moist mountain forest, with huge, gnarled moss-covered rhododendrons, magnolia, maple and birch trees. In the autumn here there is often snow on the trail and the mornings are usually frosty. It is said that snow occasionally blocks the pass for a few days at a time, but I have not heard of this in the last eight or nine years. In the spring the entire ridge is alive with blooming rhododendrons: the white, pink, and red blossoms cover the entire hillside.

The ridge is the highest point reached during the trek between Lamosangu and Namche Bazar. It is a delight for the bird lover — Nepal has more than 800 species of birds, and many of the most colourful are found in this zone — sunbirds, minavets, flycatchers, tits, laughing thrushes, and many others.

After crossing the pass, the route descends through fragrant fir and hemlock forests to the small settlement of Tragdobuk, 2860 metres, then descends gradually to Junbesi (*Jun*), a splendid Sherpa village located amidst beautiful surroundings, at 2675 metres. Numbur, 6954 metres, known in Sherpa as *Shorong Yul Lha*, God of the Solu, towers over the large green valley above Junbesi. This village is at the north end of the Sherpa region known as Solu (*Shorong* in Sherpa Language). On the whole, the Sherpas of Solu are economically better off than their cousins in Khumbu, because the fertile valley here is at the lower elevation and a wide variety of crops can be grown. In recent years, however, employment with expeditions and trekking parties has done much to improve the lot of the Khumbu Sherpas.

Day 9

Junbesi

Nuntale

From Junbesi, the trail crosses the Junbesi Khola, then climbs over a spur separating the Junbesi Khola from the Ringmo Khola. There is an important trail junction here; the downhill trail leads to Phaphlu, the site of a hospital (operated by the Himalayan Trust) and an airstrip. South of Phaphlu is Salleri, the administrative centre for the entire Solu Khumbu region. After the uphill trail has climbed around the ridge, at about 3050 metres, there is an excellent view of Everest (this is the first point on the trek where Everest may be seen), Chamlang (7319 metres) and Makalu (8481 metres). The trail turns north, descending through Salung, 2980 metres, to the Ringmo Khola at 2650 metres. This river provides one of the last opportunities to wash clothes and bathe in a large river; the next river, the Dudh Kosi, is too cold for all but the most determined.

From the river the trail ascends to Ringmo where an enterprising (and very patient) Sherpa has succeeded in raising a large orchard of apples, peaches and apricots. The fruit has become so abundant that many fruit products — including delicious apple rakshi (spirits), apple cider and even apple pickles — are available at reasonable

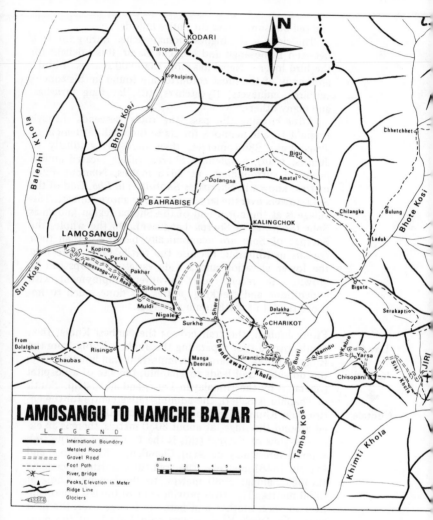

LAMOSANGU TO NAMCHE BAZAR

L E G E N D
- International Boundary
- Metaled Road
- Gravel Road
- Foot Path
- River, Bridge
- Peaks, Elevation in Meter
- Ridge Line
- Glaciers

miles
0 1 2 3 4 5 6

prices. At Ringmo the trail joins the 'road' that is being built from Salleri to Namche Bazar with the assistance of several aid programmes. From here to Namche the road is being widened and levelled by local labourers who are paid with food instead of cash. The result will probably never be a motorable road, but you can now walk side by side with your friends on the wide trail. It is a

short ascent from Ringmo to Trakshindo Pass, 3071 metres, marked by a large white *chorten*. About 15 minutes south of the pass on a clearly-defined trail is yet another cheese factory (closed in winter). A few minutes below the pass, on the east side, is a trail to the isolated monastery of Trakshindo, a superb example of Sherpa monastic architecture — certainly the most imposing building so far encountered on the trek. The trail then descends very steeply through a coniferous and rhododendron forest alive with birds to the Sherpa hamlet of Nuntale (*Manidingma*) at 2320 metres. You may also hear barking deer in these dense forests.

Day 10

Nuntale

Khari Khola

The descent continues to the Dudh Kosi ('milk river') — the largest river met since the Sun Kosi. The route passes through the scattered village of Phueli at 1980 metres, then descends steeply through forests to a suspension bridge, built by the Swiss, that crosses the Dudh Kosi at 1500 metres. The trail now concludes its trip eastward and turns north up the Dudh Kosi valley. After a short distance, the large spread-out village of Jubing (*Dorakbuk*), a maze of criss-crossing trails, is reached at 1680 metres. This village is inhabited by an ethnic group known as Rais. Like the Tamangs and Sherpas, the Rais speak a Tibeto-Burman language of their own and are basically of Mongoloid stock, but they have a very different culture and practice an indigenous religion of their own that is neither Buddhist nor Hindu, although it has been influenced by Hinduism in certain aspects. Rais have very characteristic facial features with make them easy to recognize. The Rais (along with Limbus, Magars and Gurungs) are one of the ethnic groups that supply a large proportion of the recruits for the well-known Gurkha regiments of the British and Indian armies.

Beyond Jubing there is a short but unbelievably steep climb up a rocky ridge and over a spu to Khari Khola (*Khatega*), at about 2070 metres. This village, while predominantly Sherpa, also has some Magars living in it. Khari Khola bazaar has become a bit dirty and crummy with a proliferation of tiny hotels clustered around the village drinking water supply. There is a better campsite beyond the village just across the bridge (and you avoid paying the fee for camping in the schoolyard); if you are on your own, consider one of the hotels that you reach when you first enter the village.

Day 11

Khari Khola

From Khari Khola it is a long climb to the top of the Bupsa Ridge, 3130 metres high, the sixth and last major ridge on the trail to Khumbu. The trail descends from Khari Khola village and crosses a stream beside some water-driven mills at 2010 metres, then makes a steep climb up to Kharte (*Dzomshawa*), at 2680 metres.

Puiyan

The trail then continues, climbing steadily, but gently, through forests to the pass at the top of Bupsa ridge. There is a large stone inn at the very top that has a good supply of local beverages for those who prefer something stronger than tea (also available for one rupee per cup). On the other side of the ridge there is a gradual descent to Puiyan (*Chitok*), a Sherpa settlement of only seven houses completely surrounded by forests, at 2830 metres. Much of the forest near this village is being cut down to make charcoal which is being burned for fuel by many users in the Khumbu region where wood is scarce.

There is a trail that goes from Khari Khola to Surkhe and avoids the long climb through Puiyan, but it is in disrepair and subject to rockfall. The new aid sponsored route to Namche will improve this trail eventually and it may soon be possible to avoid the Bupsa ridge entirely.

Day 12

Puiyan

Phakding

The trail climbs for about an hour after Puiyan to a ridge crest at 2945 metres. It is possible to see Lukla airstrip from this ridge by looking carefully through to the trees to the north-east. Lukla can easily be recognised by the large Sherpa Co-operative Hotel with its metal roof, and by the remains of two planes that crashed there. The trail descends to Surkhe, (*Buwa*), 2293 metres, located on a small tributary stream of the Dudh Kosi. From Surkhe the trail climbs again through the village of Mushe (*Nangbug*) to Chaunrikarka (*Dungde*), a large village at 2680 metres. The region from Khari Khola to Jorsale is called Pharak. The Sherpas in this area have slightly different traditions from their neighbours in Solu and Khumbu and have better agricultural opportunities due to the less severe climate in the Dudh Kosi Valley. Pharak villagers raise large crops of corn (maize) and potatoes in the summer; they grow wheat, turnips, cauliflower and cabbage in the winter season; and they raise herds of cows and yak cross-breeds, as well as sheep and goats. From Chaunrikarka the trail passes through Chablung (*Lomdza*), where the trail from Lukla joins the route, then continues north to Ghat (*Lhawa*), at 2550 metres, on the banks of the Dudh Kosi.

In September 1977, an avalanche from Ama Dablam fell into a large lake near the base of the peak. This created a wave of water 10 metres high that raced down the Dudh Kosi and washed away large parts of the trail, seven bridges, and part of the village of Jorsale, killing three villagers. At Phakding the first signs of this devastation becomes apparent; the river is crossed on a small temporary bridge just beyond the village at 2650 metres. There is a fancy new suspension bridge just south of Phakding, but nobody uses it because the trail from the bridge climbs steeply over a ridge; there is no climbing necessary if you use the old bridge. From Phakding to Jorsale the trail is continually undergoing repair and improvement; so portions of the description of the following day may be inaccurate because of recent modifications to the trail. At Phakding the 'Khumbu Alpine Camp' is under construction. Soon you may be able to stay here in a reasonably comfortable hotel room for about $10 a night.

Day 13

Phakding

Namche Bazar

From Phakding the trail continues north up the Dudh Kosi valley, climbing a hundred metres above the river on its west bank to avoid the flood damage, until the village of Benkar is reached at 2700 metres. Just past Benkar the trail crosses the river and passes through the village of Chomoa, the site of a Japanese agricultural project, and Monjo before recrossing the river at Jorsale (*Thumbug*), 2850 metres. All along this part of the trail, villagers are interspersed with magnificent forests — rhododendron and magnolia trees and giant firs. In both the early fall and late spring seasons, the flowers on this portion of the trek make it a beautiful walk. On the cliffs above the river it may be possible to see musk deer and Himalayan tahr.

At Jorsale the trail enters the Mount Sagarmatha (Everest) National Park. There is an entrance station here where a fee of Rs 60 (about $5) is collected from each trekker. The rules printed on the back of the entrance ticket are as follows:

Children below 12 years of age shall pay half the entry fee.
This permit is non-transferable and good for one entry only.
You enter the park on your own risk. His Majesty's Government shall bear no liability for damage, loss, injury or death.
Trekking is an acceptable challenge, but please do not:
— litter, dispose it properly.
— remove anything from the park.
— disturb wildlife.
— carry arms and explosives.
— scale any mountain without proper permission.
— scale any sacred peaks of any elevation.
Please keep all the time to the main trek routes.
Please be self sufficient in your fuel supply before entering the park. Buying fuel wood from local people or removing any

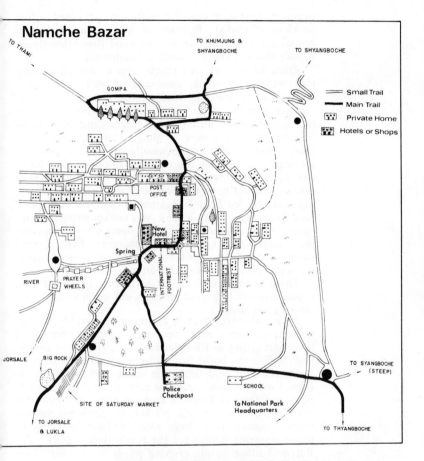

wood materials from the forest is illegal. This will apply to your guides, cooks and porters also.

Park personnel are entitled to arrest any person in charge of having violated park regulations or search his belongings.

For further information visit Park headquarter or ask any park personnel.

National Parks Family Wishes Your Trip Pleasant.

The degree of enforcement of these regulations varies, especially with respect to the use of firewood. It is difficult to obtain kerosene to use as a fuel, and almost impossible to obtain petrol or cooking gas. There is talk of a kerosene depot at Jorsale; if this materialises, it will ease the fuel problem somewhat. Trekkers on their own may eat in houses and hotels that cook over wood fires — but theoretically this will also be prohibited eventually.

From Jorsale the trail climbs over a spur up a soggy trail under a weeping, moss-covered wall, crosses the Bhote Kosi on the only bridge remaining out of the six "Hillary Bridges" in the valley, and begins the steep climb to Namche Bazar. From several places along the trail to Namche there is a view of Mount Everest, Nuptse and Lhotse, but because clouds usually obscure the peaks in the afternoon, Everest will probably not be visible. Namche Bazar (*Nauche*), 3440 metres, is the administrative centre for the Khumbu region and has a police checkpost, headquarters for Mount Sagarmatha National Park (with New Zealand advisers), a bank (you can sometimes change money here), several shops selling items of every description, and a few hotels and restaurants. Even a small bakery and a hotel with a hot shower are situated among the seventy-odd houses of this prosperous village.

There is equipment available for rent in Namche, so if you discover that your jacket is not warm enough, you can rent one here.

Each Saturday there is an important weekly *hot*, or market, in which corn, rice, eggs, vegetables and other items not grown in Khumbu are sold. The items are carried to Namche Bazar from villages several days away by Rai porters. It is an important social event, as well as the focus for the region's trade, as Sherpas from all the neighbouring villages in Khumbu come to purchase food. For the most part it is a cash market, in which Sherpas exchange money they have received from trekking or mountaineering parties for the goods they require. The Rais and other people carrying goods to the market are often told by fun-loving Sherpas that the money comes from Mount Everest, and it is not uncommon to find an unsuspecting lowland porter shivering with cold as he accompanies a trekking party to Everest Base Camp in search of the free money that tumbles from the highest peak on earth.

Day 14
Namche Bazar

Acclimatisation is important before proceeding higher. This is the first of two specific 'acclimatisation days' that must be built into the schedule. The day may be spent by taking a day hike to Thami, by visiting Khunde or Khumjung, or by relaxing and exploring Namche Bazar. There is a police checkpost in Namche where trekking permits must be presented and endorsed and the details entered into a register. Usually trekkers are required to sign the register, so you must appear personally at the police checkpost. Be sure to bring both your trekking permit and National Park entrance ticket for the police to examine.

Day 15

Namche Bazar

Thyangboche

There is a direct route from Namche Bazar to Thyangboche, but it is more interesting to take a slightly longer route that allows a visit to Khumjung, the largest village in Khumbu, and to Khunde, its smaller neighbour. From Namche Bazar it is a steep climb of one hour to the airstrip at Shyangboche, 3720 metres, where it is often possible to watch the spectacular landing of Pilatus Porter aircraft serving the Hotel Everest View in the mornings. From the airstrip it is a 20 minute walk to the hotel, which provides excellent views of Everest and Ama Dablam, as you sip an expensive cup of coffee or tea. The route descends to Khumjung village, 3790 metres, the site of a *gompa* possessing what is said to be the skull of a *yeti* or abominable snowman. It was this relic that was taken by Sir Edmund Hillary, in the company of the village headman, Khunjo Chumbi, to the United States in 1960 to be examined by scientists. The scalp turned out to be made from the skin of a serow — a member of the antelope family — but the *yeti* legend still goes on. Also in Khumjung is a school, built by the Himalayan Trust, that has succeeded in providing an excellent primary education for many of the children of Khumbu. It is only a short detour on to Khunde, the site of the Khunde Hospital, also built and maintained by the Himalayan Trust. From Khumjung the trail goes down the valley, continuously passing picturesque *mani* walls and *chortens*, and after a short descent it meets the main Namche Bazar-Thyangboche trail. It descends gradually to Teshinga, then steeply to Phunki Thanghka, a small settlement with several water-driven prayer wheels on the banks of the Dudh Kosi, at 3250 metres.

From Phunki Thanghla the trail climbs steeply, then gradually forests and around *mani* stones as it follows the side of a hill up to the saddle on which Thyangboche Monastery is located at 3870 metres, in a clearing surrounded by dwarf firs and rhododendrons.

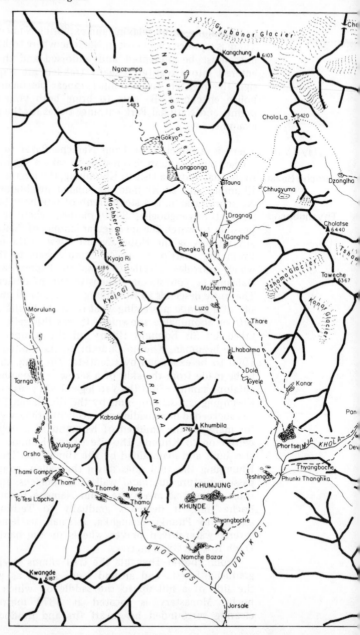

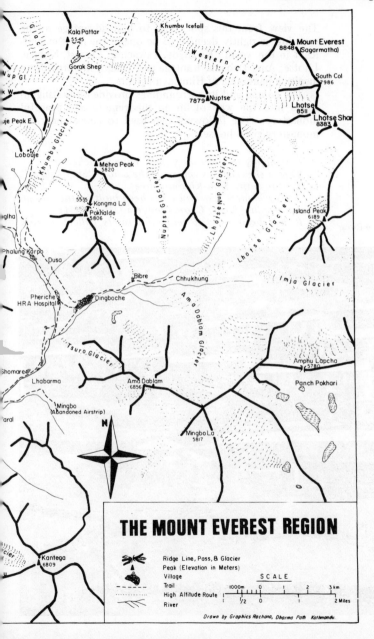

THE MOUNT EVEREST REGION

Ridge Line, Pass, & Glacier
Peak (Elevation in Meters)
Village
Trail
High Altitude Route
River

SCALE

Drawn by Graphics Rachana, Dharma Path, Kathmandu.

The view from this spot, seen to best advantage in the morning, is rightly deemed to be one of the most magnificent in the world. Kwangde, Tawachee, Everest, Nuptse, Lhotse, Ama Dablam, Kantega and Thamserku provide an inspiring panorama of Himalayan giants.

The *gompa* and its surroundings provide interesting insights into the way of life in this remote and peaceful monastery. The following sign used to appear near the monastery guest house:

I am happy to welcome you to Thyangboche.
This is the religious centre of the whole "Sherpa-land",
in fact the entire Solu-Khumbu area.
A very modest rest house has been built on the far end
of the meadow facing Chomo-longma (Mt Everest).
It has been erected with the funds collected from

Namche Bazar

friends and visitors who have come to this sacred and beautiful place. If you wish, you may contribute to our meagre funds to enable us to make it more comfortable when you come again, for we hope you will. Anything you wish to give will be gratefully accepted.

While you are a guest at Thyangboche, whether you stay in the rest house or in your own tents, I wish to request you to observe the few rules in observance of the Divine Dharma.

Please do not kill or cause to kill any living creature in the area of this holy place. This includes domestic fowls and animals, as also wild game.

Please remember that this holy place is devoted to the worship of the Perfect One, and that nothing should be done within these sacred precincts which will offend or cause to hurt those who live here in humility and serenity. May you journey in peace and walk in delight, and may the blessings of the Perfect One be always with you.

Nawang Tenzing Zang-Po
The Reincarnate of Thyangboche

Khumjung Village

The sign has long since disappeared, hauled off as a souvenir, no doubt, by a trekker. It has been replaced by a fancy carved sign directing visitors to the New Zealand-built Thyangboche Trekkers Lodge, a part of the Mount Sagarmatha National Park development. No longer is it necessary to endure the simple lodging offered by the Lamas — now you can sit around a stove burning charcoal (from Puiyan, outside the National Park) and write comments in the guest book either praising or damning the lodge concept.

Historical Note Thyangboche (the correct phonetic spelling is Tengboche, but most maps use Thyangboche) was founded about 50 years ago by Lama Gulu. The main temple was destroyed by an earthquake in 1933 and has since been rebuilt. Buddhism is believed to have been introduced into Khumbu towards the end of the 17th century by Lama Sange Dorje, the fifth of the reincarnate lamas of the Rong-phu (or Rongbok) monastery in Tibet, just to the north of Mount Everest. According to local legend, Lama Sange Dorje flew over the Himalaya and landed on rocks at Pangboche and Thyangboche, leaving his footprints. He is thought to have been responsible for the founding of the first *gompas* in Khumbu, at Pangboche and Thami. The *gompas* of Khumjung and Namche Bazar are of a later date. None of these were monasteries; their priests were married lamas and there was no monastic community with formal organisations and discipline. The first monasteries, at Thyangboche and, at about the same time, Thami, were established as offshoots of the Nyingmapa (Red Hat) sect monastery of Rong-phu in Tibet, and the young monks were sent there to study. Thyangbboche's charter bears the seal of the abbot of Rong-phu. A nunnery was later founded at Devuche, just north of Thyangboche. Trakshindo was established in 1946 by a lama from Thyangboche.

Each year, usually at the November-December full moon, the Mani Rimdu festival is celebrated at Thyangboche. On this occasion the lamas wear elaborate masks and costumes and through a series of ritualistic dances, dramatize the triumph of Buddhism over Bon, the ancient anamistic religion of Tibet.

Day 16 From Thyangboche there is a short descent to Devuche through a forest of birches, conifers and rhododendrons.

Thyangboche

Pheriche

Because of the ban on hunting at Thyangboche, almost-tame blood pheasants are to be seen here. Higher up, above the tree line, Nepal's national bird, the Danfay or Impeyan Pheasant, may be encountered. This colourful bird is only found at high altitudes. The tail is reddish, it has a shiny blue back, and has a metallic green tinge and pure white under its wings. It appears almost iridescent when seen in sunlight. Another common bird in this region is the Snow Pigeon, which swoops in great flocks above the villages of Khumjung, Namche and Pangboche. The crowlike birds that scavenge any food that you might drop (I have even seen them fly away with a full packet of biscuits that they have stolen) are Red Billed Choughs and occasionally ravens, called *goraks* by the Sherpas. Near Gorak Shep you are likely to encounter Tibetan Snow Cocks racing happily down the hillside. High above you may see Goshawks, Himalayan Griffons, Golden Eagles and Lammergeiers circling on the mountain winds.

After crossing the Imja Khola on a steel bridge swaying high above the river at a spot where the river rushes through a narrow cleft, the route climbs up past some magnificently carved *mani* stones to Pangboche at 3860 metres. Just before the village is a monument where the footprint of the patron saint Lama Sange Dorje may be seen preserved in stone. Pangboche is the highest year-round settlement in the valley. The *gompa*, which is the oldest in Khumbu, has relics said to be the skull and hand of a *yeti*, which may be seen by visitors for a slight fee. Pangboche is actually two villages, an upper and a lower village; on the way to the Everest Base Camp the lower route is used; on the return trip the upper trail may be used, allowing a visit to the *gompa*, 120 metres above the lower village.

From Pangboche the route enters alpine meadows above the tree line. Most of the vegetation is scrub juniper, tundra and wildflowers, including edelweiss. The trail passes several yak herders' huts, or *goths*, as it ascends on a shelf above the river, then climbs over a small ridge before crossing the Khumbu Khola on a wooden bridge and climbing to Pheriche, at 4240 metres. There is a trekkers' aid post at Pheriche supported by the Himalayan Rescue Association and Tokyo Medical College. A qualified physician is often in attendance during the trekking season. This establishment and the doctors who operate it specialise in the study and treatment of altitude

HRA Hospital in Pheriche — Lobouje peak in background

sickness and strive to educate trekkers in the dangers of too fast an ascent to high altitudes. There are a few hotels in Pheriche, mostly sod huts covered with a plastic sheet for a roof. There is also a national park lodge here. Several of these hotels also sell old expedition supplies and equipment. There is the usual jumble of climbing equipment for sale, but there is often an unlikely collection of expedition food available here, such as French snails or American soups.

Day 17

Pheriche

One of the most important aspects of acclimatisation to high altitudes is a slow ascent. Therefore, it is imperative that an additional night be spent at Pheriche to aid the acclimatisation process. This is the second of the mandatory acclimatisation days on this trek.

But the day may be spent in many ways. Some trekkers may wish to declare a rest day and relax in camp. Others may wish to do some strenuous exploring. A short trip may be made to the small Nangkartshang Gompa, a climb of about 400 metres above the village. From this vantage point there is a good view of Makalu, fifth highest mountain in the world, to the east.

A more strenuous trip may be made by climbing the hill to Dingboche, then up the Imja Khola valley past Bibre to Chhukung, a small summer settlement at 4700 metres. The views from Chhukung and further up the valley on the moraines towards Island Peak, 6189 metres, are tremendous. The great south face of Lhotse towers above to the north; Amphu Lapcha and the immense fluted ice walls that flank it dominate the horizon to the south; and the east face of Ama Dablam provides an unusual view of this picturesque peak to the south-west. This is a hike that should not be missed; it is one of the highlights of the trek. It is a fast trip back down the valley to Pheriche for the night.

Day 18

Pheriche

Lobouje

The trail ascends the broad, gently sloping valley from Pheriche to Phalang Karpo, at 4340 metres. The views of Tawachee and Cholatse are particularly good from this portion of the trail as it passes through country reported to be the habitat of the snow leopard and *yeti*. The trail climbs steeply onto the terminal moraine of the Khumbu Glacier at the village of Duglha, 4620 metres, just across a small bridge over the Khumbu Khola. There are two tiny tea houses here.

From Duglha the trail climbs higher on the moraine to a row of stone monuments that were built in memory of six Sherpas who died in an avalanche during the 1970 Japanese skiing expedition on Mount Everest, and another three monuments to climbers who have perished since then. The trail then drops a bit and follows the west side of the valley to Lobouje, two herders' huts and a small hotel at 4930 metres. The New Zealand National Park advisors have built a new lodge at Lobouje — a facility similar to the Thyangboche Lodge. If the project is successful, you may be able to find food and accommodation here. You should inquire at Thyangboche whether the lodge is operating or not before you rely on it. The sunset on Nuptse, seen from Lobouje, is a memorable sight.

Day 19

Lobouje

Gorak Shep

The first section of the trail from Lobouje follows the west side of the broad Khumbu Valley and ascends gently through meadows beside the glacial moraine. The ascent soon becomes steeper and rougher as it crosses several side moraines, although the trail is well-defined and marked by cairns at frequent intervals. After rounding a bend in the trail, the conical peak Pumori (7145 metres) comes into view; on the lower slopes of this mountain there is a ridge extending to the south, terminating in a small peak. This peak, called Kala Pattar, is 5545 metres high and provides the best vantage point for viewing Mount Everest (8848 metres). The ascent of Kala Pattar may be made easily from Gorak Shep in the afternoon or following morning.

The trail makes a short descent onto the sandy flat expanse of Gorak Shep, 5160 metres elevation. This was the base camp for the 1952 Swiss Everest Expedition and was called "lake camp" by the British in 1953. At Gorak Shep there is a small lake that is usually frozen, and several monuments to climbers who have died in various Everest expeditions. The carved stone in memory of Jake Breitenbach of the 1963 American expedition and the monument for Indian Ambassador H Dayal who died during a visit to base camp after the 1965 Indian expedition are just to the east of the hut at Gorak Shep.

Usually Gorak Shep is reached by lunch time; most people spend the rest of the day resting, but those who are not tired by the altitude can climb Kala Pattar or go to Base Camp in the afternoon. There used to be two buildings at Gorak Shep, but there is now only one, and the owner takes the roof off his hut when he goes to lower elevations. It may be possible to find some shelter and possibly a cup of tea here, but you should not plan on it. It is important to carry food, fuel and a tent if you plan to spend the night here, as you can never be sure when the hotel owner might plan a vacation. It is best to go from Lobouje to Kala Pattar via Gorak Shep and return to Lobouje for the night, avoiding the necessity of staying at Gorak Shep.

Day 20

It is impossible to explain the discomfort of high altitudes to someone who has not experienced it. Most people have an uncomfortable, often sleepless, night at Gorak Shep despite the extra time taken for acclimatisation. By de-

Kala Pattar &
Pumori above
Gorak Shep

Gorak Shep

Lobouje

scending 300 metres to Lobouje most people experience an immediate and noticeable improvement, so it is really not worth spending an addition night at 5160 metres.

Mornings are usually sparkling clear and the climb of Kala Pattar is one of the most rewarding parts of the trip. It is a steep ascent up the grassy slopes west of Gorak Shep to a shelf at the foot of Pumori. Even from this vantage point the entire Everest South Face is visible as well as the Lho La (the pass between Nepal and Tibet, from which George Mallory looked into Nepal in 1921 and named the Western Cwm), Changtse (the north peak of Everest) and most of the west ridge route climbed by Unsoeld and Hornbein in 1963. Those familiar with the accounts of early expeditions to Everest will be able to spot clearly the north ridge and the first and second steps, prominent obstacles during the attempts on the mountain in the 1920s and '30s. Continuing on to the top of Kala Pattar, more of the peak of Everest itself comes into view, and a short walk north from the summit of Kala Pattar, on the ridge towards Pumori will allow an unobstructed view all the way to the South Col.

The walk to base camp requires about six hours round trip, possibly more unless an expedition in progress has kept the ever-changing trail in good condition. The route follows the Khumbu Glacier, sometimes on the moraine and sometimes on the glacier itself. The walk is especially interesting for the views of the 15-metre high seracs of ice, a feature peculiar to Himalayan glaciers. "Everest Base Camp" is not actually a specific site; various expeditions have selected different locations for a semi-permanent camp during their assault on the mountain. Some of the base camp sites may be identified by debris on the glacier at 5360 metres or more. The trip to base camp, while interesting, is not as spectacular as the ascent of Kala Pattar because there is no view of Everest itself from base camp.

It is difficult to go to both base camp and Kala Pattar in single day; those who wish to do both should use the afternoon of the day at Gorak Shep for one trip and the next morning for the other. But the exhaustion and lethargy caused by the altitude limits many people to only one of the possible options. The descent to Lobouje is easy, but seems endless because of the many uphill climbs, from Gorak Shep. The night, however, will be much more comfortable than the previous one.

Day 21

Lobouje

Dingboche

The return is via the same route to Duglha, but then takes a different trail, staying high above the valley floor, past the yak pastures at Dusa, and descends steeply to Dingboche, at 4360 metres. The high pastures in this region are sometimes referred to as "summer villages". Sherpas with homes lower in the valley own small stone huts in the higher regions and occupy them in the summer months while they graze their herds of yaks in the surrounding pastures. A few crops, especially barley, are also grown in these high fields. While Dingboche does not have all the hotels and tourist facilities of Pheriche, it is a more typical summer village and the mountain scenery is outstanding.

Day 22

Dingboche

The route descends the Imja Khola valley, then crosses the Khumbu Khola on a wooden bridge and climbs up to rejoin the upward trail. Following the trail downhill, it is easy to make a detour and visit the upper part of Pang-

Thyangboche

boche and the village *gompa*, then continue to Thyangboche for the night. While ascents at high altitudes must be made slowly, descents can be made safely as fast as you wish.

Day 23

Thyangboche

Jorsale

The trail returns to Phunki Thanghka, then ascends the ridge towards Namche Bazar. The direct route to Namche follows the side of the ridge and avoids a lot of climbing; the alternative route through Khumjung allows a visit to Hotel Everest View or another visit to Sherpa villages before the steep descent to Namche, but involves climbing an extra 200 metres. In Namche Bazar you will have a last opportunity to buy (mostly) phoney Tibetan jewellery from a dozen Tibetan merchants who spread their wares beside every campsite and alongside the trail at the oddest places. The steep descent back to the Dudh Kosi at Jorsale makes it a rough day on the knees, but the warmer climate offers a good opportunity to finally shed down jackets and woollen sweaters.

Day 24

Jorsale

Lukla

It is necessary to be at the airport at Lukla the night before the flight in order to reconfirm reservations. The trail from Jorsale follows the upward route as far as Chablung, then turns off above the village of Chaunrikarka towards Lukla, situated high above the river on a shelf at 2800 metres elevation. Lukla is another classic paradox in determining altitudes as the runway is on a slope and there is a difference of almost 60 metres between the lower end and the upper parking place for airplanes.

Day 25

Lukla

Kathmandu

RNAC operates scheduled flights to Lukla in 19-seat Twin Otter aircraft that can carry only 14 or 15 passengers from Lukla because of the high elevation. The airstrip was built by Sir Edmund Hillary as part of the Khunde Hospital project in 1965 and expanded by RNAC in 1977. The landing is a visual one; there are no instruments or sophisticated navigational aids at Lukla. If there are clouds, therefore, the plain will not come — occasionally for days at a time during rare periods of extended bad weather.

When this happens, those who have planned to fly to Kathmandu must wait and a backlog of people builds up, each person convinced that he or she must fly on the next available aircraft. The situation often becomes ludicrous, but provides a great opportunity to develop patience and to become acquainted with trekkers from all over the

world as you wait together at Lukla. The stories of over-
crowding in the Everest area now become real. In the past
350 or more people have waited here — especially in late
October and early November each year. The problem
usually solves itself in a few days but it's important to be
prepared for a long delay for any flight to or from Lukla.
It's even possible to depart from Lukla exactly on schedule; it happened to me — once. The trek to Dharan
becomes attractive because it avoids the pile-up at Lukla
and explores some interesting country unlike any that has
been seen on the first portion of the trek.

The flight from Lukla to Kathmandu takes 30 minutes
and is a jarring return to the noise, confusion and rush of
a large city.

THE LAMIDANDA ESCAPE ROUTE

Ocasionally the pile up of people at Lukla becomes unmanageable. Imagine
350 people vying for seats on planes that carry 15 passengers. Many people,
having completed a great trek, make themselves miserable by fighting for
seats out of Lukla. It's a helpless feeling of course, to be in a place where
no amount of influence or money can make the planes come, but you did
come to an undeveloped country. If you expect things to operate on time
(or sometimes to operate at all), you should head for the mountains of
Switzerland.

Unbelievable things happen when people flip out at Lukla. I've seen the
station manager chased around the airport by a tourist brandishing an ice
axe; I've seen a chanting mob outside the airline office; I've seen rock fights
on the airstrip; twice I've seen planeloads of police arrive in Lukla to get
things under control; and I've heard endless tales of woe from people who
HAD to be at work the following day (they weren't). If it gets like this —
usually in late October and early November, and occasionally at other un-
predictable times — the only way to preserve your own composure is to be
sure your name is somewhere on the reservation list. Assign one of your
sherpas (or better yet, the Lukla representative of your trekking company)
to watch that other names are not slipped in ahead of yours, and retire to a
kettle or two of local *chhang* to consider your alternatives.

You can wait. It might be a day (I've seen a dramatic airlift of 14 flights
to Lukla in a single day), or as long as two weeks. You can walk to Lamosangu. If you go at a normal pace, it's nine days to Kirantichhap where you
may be able to get space on a bus back to Lamosangu. If you walk 10 to 12
hours a day (you save days in Nepal by walking a longer time each day, not
by walking faster) you could reach Kirantichhap in six days — perhaps even
five. Some people suggest trying the airstrip at Phaphlu, two long days (or
three comfortable days) from Lukla. It is an interesting walk, but it's

unlikely that it will hasten your return to Kathmandu because Phaphlu is served only by six-passenger Pilatus Porter aircraft and seats are in heavy demand for government officials stationed in nearby Salleri. You can walk from Phaphlu south towards Janakpur in six or seven days. The 12-day trek to Dharan described in this book is also a way to escape from Lukla. Another alternative is described here. You can walk to Lamidanda, an airstrip five days to the south. The important thing is to not make yourself, and everyone else, miserable by fighting and bemoaning your fate. Instead, do something positive. You can always go back to Namche Bazar for a few days and wait for things to clear up, or you can climb the ridge behind Lukla, where there are some wonderful high meadows and a good view of Karyolung.

The Lamidanda escape route works in either direction; groups have walked to Khumbu after a flight to Lamidanda. Although I've shown it as a five-day trek, it can be done (if the porters agree) in four days. The opposite direction, however, will certainly require five days because of the long initial climb up to Aiselukharka.

Day 1 **Lukla** **Kharte**	A trail leads off the end of the Lukla airstrip and descends to join the main trail from Kathmandu. The descent continues on the main trail to Surkhe, then the trail climbs to Puiyan, crosses the pass and descends again to Kharte. See day 11 and 12 of the Everest trek description.
Day 2 **Kharte** ⬇ **Wobsa Khani**	The trail descends steeply to Khari Khola (2070 metres). If you did not walk from Kathmandu, this will be your first view of extensive terracing and of the middle hills region of Nepal. There is a bazaar in Khari Khola on Wednesday if you need to stock up on provisions. There is only rice and dal available between here and the next bazaar at Aiselukharka. The trail climbs out of Khari Khola on the main route to Kathmandu, then turns south on a different trail just past 'Mother Hotel', about 20 minutes beyond the village. The path climbs over a ridge, then contours south, high above the village of Jubing. The route passes through scrub forests and a few cultivated fields until Jube (2100 metres), then through forests of rhododendron and oak. The trail descends, crosses the Thana Khola, then climbs steeply out of a side valley. There are a few houses and herders' huts, but for the most part the trail is through forests and is reasonably level (for Nepal). The Rai village of Wobsa Khani (1700 metres) is reached about two hours after the Thana Khola. Below Wobsa is Tamba Khani ('copper mine') where you can see the smelter and buildings for the mine that gave

the town its name.

Day 3

Wobsa Khani

Lokhim

Some oranges and rice from here are carried by porters to the market at Namche Bazar. Except for those porters, this trail is not often used by either locals or trekkers, so there are no hotels and few *bhattis* along this route. From Wobsa Khani the trail continues fairly level as the valley becomes wider, then it descends a bit to Waku, a Chhetri village at 1500 metres elevation. The trail descends further through forests to Suntale at 1100 metres and drops steeply to the Hinku Khola, crossing it on an old suspension bridge at 1000 metres. This is the same river (also called the Inukhu) that is crossed on Day 3 of the trek to Dharan. After a steep climb up a series of steps cut in the rock, the trail reaches a ridge at 1290 metres and descends a bit to the Rai and Chhetri village of Khorde. The trail descends further through trees to the Hongu Khola, crossing it on a temporary log bridge at 900 metres elevation. There are the remains of an impressive cantilever bridge here, but it looks as if this bridge collapsed years ago. There is some trade up the Hongu from here, and people who live in villages as far away as Bung travel down the valley to Aiselukharka on bazaar days. Climbing steeply past the herders' huts of Utha, the trail reaches a ridge at 1586 metres. It may be necessary to camp in Utha, because it's another 1½ hours to Lokhim from here. Lokhim is a huge Rai village with beautiful stands of bamboo situated in a large side valley at about 1800 metres elevation. This being Rai country, it is usual to encounter *dhamis* (shamans) walking the remote trails, or at least to hear the echoes of their drums in the distance.

Day 4

Lokhim

Ilim

Lokhim is a large village, almost 45 minutes walk from beginning to end. From the east end of the village the trail climbs through Chuwa towards the pass at Deorali (2400 metres). The Schneider "Dudh Kosi" map covers this part of the trek, but this section of trail is not shown on the map. The trail contours around the Dudu Khola valley before it ascends steeply towards Deorali. There is a tea shop, the first since Khari Khola, at the pass. Descending from the pass, the route travels through Harise, a Sherpa village at 2300 metres, then descends a steep stone staircase to Aiselukharka, a large town strung out along a ridge at 2100 metres elevation. There are a few shops and government offices here and a very large bazaar on Saturdays. The trail descends the ridge to the south on a wide trail to Ilim at 1450 metres.

Day 5

Ilim

Lamidanda

It is a steep descent through tropical country to the Ra Khola. There is a bridge upstream at 800 metres elevation or you can wade the river. This is a rice-growing region, and the trail follows a complex and intricate route amongst a network of dikes and irrigation canals. The trail makes a steep ascent up the Pippal Danda, then contours around the valley between 1200 and 1400 metres. The route is through terraced fields and there is little shade — it will probably be hot. Finally the trail (this trail also is not shown on the Schneider map, nor is Lamidanda) passes a school and follows a ridge out towards the airport. There is a hotel just across from the terminal building at 1200 metres elevation. From Lamidanda there are flights several times a week to Kathmandu and more frequent flights to Biratnagar. Take anything. From Biratnagar you can take a bus or plane to Kathmandu. The fare from Lamidanda to Kathmandu is less than from Lukla — only $30 each way. If you travel to Biratnagar from Lamidanda it will cost $55 by air from Biratnagar to Kathmandu and about $5 by bus.

Local people say that it is a two-day walk to Bhojpur and a one-day walk to Okaldhunga from here. Those timings are probably accurate. Once, however, the Lamidanda people terrified a trekking group that had landed there by all agreeing that it required at least 12 days to walk to Lukla (where none of them had ever been). There is nothing to see or do in the Brahmin village of Lamidanda, except wait for an airplane. There is a Buddhist shrine about a day's walk away, however, that might provide some diversion if you get stuck here for a long time. Lamidanda is the air traffic control point for this part of Nepal, so the radio is in constant use here (unlike Lukla) and it is easy to find out about flight movements.

TO GOKYO

The trek to Gokyo offers an alternative to the traditional trek to Everest Base Camp. From Gokyo more of Everest itself is visible, though from a slightly greater distance, then from Kala Pattar above Gorak Shep. The mountains are generally more spectacular, the Ngozumpa Glacier is the largest in the Nepal Himalaya and from a ridge above Gokyo, four 8000 metre peaks (Cho Oyu, Everest, Lhotse and Makalu) are visible at once. The view of the tremendous ice ridge between Cho Oyu (8153 metres) and Gyachung Kang (7922 metres) is one of the more spectacular panoramas in Khumbu. There are numerous options for additional exploration and high altitude walking, including a 5400 metre high pass into the Khumbu region.

Day 1

Namche Bazar

⬇

Phortse Bridge

Acclimatisation is essential for this trek, as it is easy to get too high too fast and run a danger of altitude sickness. Only after a MINIMUM OF TWO DAYS in the Namche-Khumjung region is it possible to begin this trek. From Khumjung, the trek begins by descending to the west of the village down the broad valley leading to the Dudh Kosi, but soon turns north, climbing above the more fre-

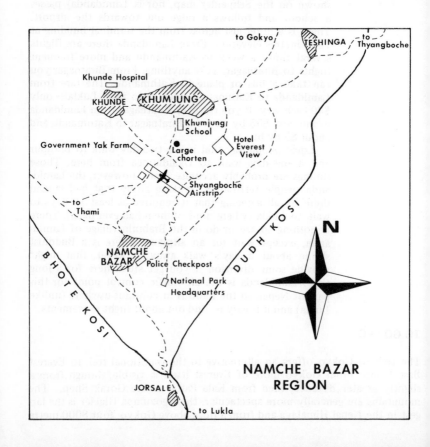

quented route to Thyangboche and Everest Base Camp.

There is a choice of routes in the beginning: the yak trail which climbs gently, but traverses a long distance around the ridge, or the steep staircase-like trail that is built of rocks embedded in a narrow cleft in a large boulder. The Sherpas claim that the steeper trail is better — for exercise. The two trails soon join and continue towards a large *chorten* on the top of a ridge at 3973 metres. This ridge descends from Khumbila, 5761 metres, the abode of the patron God of the Khumbu region. Khumbila (or more correctly *Khumbu Yul Lha*, translated as "Khumbu area God") is often pictured on *Thankas* and other monastery paintings as a white-faced figure riding on a white horse. Note that Numbur, which towers over Junbesi and the Solu region, is the protector God of that area and is called by the Sherpas *Shorong Yul Lha*, "Solu area God".

From the ridge the trail descends in a series of steep switchbacks down a sandy slope to the Dudh Kosi. There is an excellent camping spot near the river at 3500 metres, just before the bridge that provides access to Phortse, an isolated village of about 50 houses. It is possible to go much further in a single day from Khumjung — as far as Tongba or Gyele — but it doesn't serve much purpose.

Day 2

Phortse Bridge

Luza

This should also be an easy day in order to aid acclimatisation. The trail climbs steeply out of the valley through rhododendron forests which give way to fragrant stands of juniper and large conifers as the elevation increases. This portion of the trek is especially beautiful in the spring when the rhododendrons are blooming — generally late April and early May at this elevation. The trail passes through many summer settlements or *kharkas*, used when herds of *yaks* are brought during the summer months to graze in these high pastures. Some of the villages in this valley are occupied as late as December by people grazing their herds.

We tend to oversimplify the numerous manifestations of the *yak* into this single word, yet is is only the full blooded long-haired bull that truly has the name *yak*. The female is called a *nak*. A female crossbreed between a cow and a *yak* is called a *dzum*, and is prized for its milk, rich in butterfat, that is used in making cheese and butter. The male crossbreed, the infertile *dzopchuk*, is (relatively) docile and is used to transport loads and as a plow animal.

Most of the "yaks" seen along the trails of Khumbu are in fact *dzopchuks*. There are numerous other names for crosses between cattle and *naks* and for second generation crossbreeds, but the *yak*, *nak*, *dzum* and *dzopchuk* are sufficiently confusing for this lesson in *yak* husbandry.

Passing through the settlements of Tongba (3950 metres), Gyele (3960 metres) and Lhabarma (4220 metres), the trail finally reaches Luza at 4360 metres. The trail is steep in most places as it climbs through scrub junipers. *Kharkas* occur wherever there is a flat spot and the slightest hint of water available. In the winter months some of these villages may have no nearby water source, though Luza is on the banks of a large stream and has a year-round supply. The *kharkas* on this side of the valley are all owned by people from Khumjung; often a family will have houses in several settlements and move their herds from place to place as the grass becomes overgrazed and the snows melt.

The view of Khumbila and Tawachee is tremendous throughout the day, and it is possible to climb a ridge behind Luza for an even broader view up and down the valley.

Day 3

Luza

↓

Gokyo

The trail continues to climb along the side of the valley, high above the river, crossing sandy spurs to Machhermo at 4410 metres. It was in Machhermo, in 1974, that a *yeti* killed three yaks and attacked a Sherpa woman. This is the most credible *yeti* incident ever reported; be watchful as you visit this region. Beyond Machhermo the trail climbs a ridge and obtains an excellent view both down the valley to Kantega and up towards Cho Oyu (8153 metres). Beyond the ridge the valley widens as the trail passes through Pangka at 4390 metres, then descends to the riverbank before beginning the climb onto the terminal moraine of the Ngozumpa Glacier.

It is a steep climb up the moraine, switchbacking alongside the stream to the first small lake at 4650 metres, where a family of braminy ducks usually resides. The trail now becomes almost level as it follows the valley past a second lake at 4690 metres and finally up a boulder strewn path to Gokyo itself at 4750 metres. Gokyo is a *yarsa* of seven houses and walled pastures on the shores of a large lake; the setting is reminiscent of an abandoned summer resort.

Day 4

Gokyo

The views in the Gokyo region are tremendous. The best is obtained by climbing the small peak above the lake. Like its counterpart above Gorak Shep, this peak of 5318 metres is also often called Kala Pattar, meaning "black rock". It is only a two hour climb to the top of the peak, providing a panoramic view of Cho Oyu, Gyachung Kang, Everest, Lhotse, Makalu, Cholatse and Tawachee.

For those with more time and energy, a further trip may be made up the valley to another lake, marked with the name Ngozumpa on the maps, or even beyond to a fifth lake. There are several small peaks in this region that offer additional vantage points for the surrounding peaks and even of the Nangpa La, the old trade route into Tibet.

Everest from Gokyo's Kala Pattar

Day 5

Gokyo

⬇

Phortse

The descent back to Phortse may be made in a single long day, though it is possible to spend the night at Thare or Konar on the way in order to make the day less strenuous. Rather than retrace the upward route, the downward route follows the east side of the valley, offering different views of Khumbila and generally somewhat warmer weather because the sun stays on these slopes longer in the late afternoon.

Descending from Gokyo, the route passes the second lake. About half way between the first and second lakes a trail leads off across the moraine to the east. This is the route to the 5420 metre Chola La (or Chhugyuma) pass into the Everest region. The pass is not difficult, although it is steep and involves a glacier crossing on the east side. Allow three days from Gokyo to Pheriche on this high altitude route. An ice axe, crampons and a rope are necessary for negotiating the small icefall at the foot of

Mani Stone in the Solu Khumu

the glacier on the other side of the pass. The western approach to the pass varies in difficulty depending on the amount of snow. It can vary from a rough scramble up a scree (gravel) slope to an impossible technical ice climb. The best conditions are when there is snow soft enough for kicking steps up the slope. The pass is not passable for yaks and usually not suitable for porters.

The main trail follows its upward route through Pangka, then climbs to Na, 4400 metres, the only year-round settlement in the valley. The descent from Na along the east side of the Dudh Kosi valley is straightforward, with a few ups and downs where landslides and streams have carved side valleys. The trail enters Phortse at its upper part and a camp may be made in the potato fields of this large village.

Cho Oyu &
Gyachung Kang
from Gokyo's
Kala Pattar

Day 6

Phortse

⬇

Namche Bazar

The trail descends from Phortse to the bridge and rejoins the original route from Khumjung. It is easy to reach Namche Bazar, or even beyond to Jorsale, for the night.

An alternative route may be taken from Phortse up a steep trail towards Pangboche, joining the trail to the Everest Region at the bridge over the Imja Khola. A return may be made via Thyangboche, or the trek may be

> extended to Everest Base Camp by following the trail on
> to Pangboche.

TO THAMI

Thami lies at an elevation of 3800 metres near the foot of a large valley to the west of Namche Bazar. The village is the jumping-off place for the crossing of Tesi Lapcha, the 5755 metre high pass into the Rolwaling Valley. The crossing of Tesi Lapcha should only be attempted by experienced, well-equipped and well-informed parties, because frequent rockfall near the pass presents a very dangerous complication.

From Namche Bazar the trail turns west above the village past a large array of prayer flags and *mani* stones. The carved *mani* stones all the way to Thami are some of the most complex and picturesque in Nepal. Contouring around the hill on a wide, almost level trail, the route passes through Gonglha and Drama before reaching the large village of Thomde. Just before Thomde there is a trail leading uphill to the monastery at Mende. A few westerners are studying here under the partronage of the English-speaking head lama. At Thomde there is a new office building for the mini-hydroelectric project that may someday generate electricity from the Bhote Kosi to provide lights for the homes of Khumbu.

After a short climb followed by a descent to the river, which is crossed on a sturdy wooden bridge, the trail makes a steep ascent beside a stream to Thami, about three hours from Namche Bazar. The village is situated in a large valley with good views of the snow peaks of Teng Kangpoche (6500 metres) and Kwangde (6187 metres) to the south. Just to the north of Thami is a police checkpost. Trekkers are not permitted to travel further north than here; this is the trade route between Nepal and Tibet and it is a two day trip to the Nangpa La, 5716 metres high, that was once crossed frequently by trains of *yaks* carrying goods between the two countries.

About 150 metres above Thami is the Thami Monastery, a picturesque *gompa* situated amongst many homes occupied by both lamas and lay people, perched on the side of a hill overlooking the valley. This is the site for the spring celebration of the Mani Rimdu festival, held about the middle of May each year. The Mani Rimdu festival at Thami tends to be a little more spirited (literally) than the festival in the fall at Thyangboche, as the weather is warmer in the spring and the *rimpoche*, or reincarnate lama, at Thami is a little bit more liberal than the Thyangboche lama. The first day of Mani Rimdu involves prayers by the lamas in the monastery courtyard. The second day is the colourful lama dancing with elaborate gowns and wonderfully painted papier mache masks. Hundreds of local people attend the performance; it is an important social occasion as well as an entertaining spectacle. Along with the serious and intricate dance performances the lamas also stage two absurd comic sequences that make the entire performance a grand and amusing spectacle.

It is possible to make the trip to Thami and back to Namche Bazar in a single day, but more worthwhile to spend the night in order to see the peaks in the clear morning. This side trip provides a good acclimatisation day before proceeding to higher elevations.

Eastern Nepal

Treks in far-eastern Nepal generally begin from the village of Dharan, where the road abruptly ends as the flat terai terminates at the foot of the Siwalik Hills. Destinations include the Makalu base camp, an eastern approach to Everest and, if it is opened to foreigners, the area near Kanchenjunga — at 8598 metres it is the third highest mountain on earth. There is endless variety in this part of Nepal. Most ethnic groups are represented and many villages, such as Dhakuta, are large, prosperous and clean. The land includes hot, rice-growing country, the cooler tea-growing region of Ilam, the heavily populated middle-hills (gouged by the mighty Arun River at an elevation of less than 400 metres) and the major mountain massifs of Kanchenjunga and Makalu.

Treks here tend to be more expensive since the party and its gear must be transported to Dharan (two days by bus) and the treks are generally longer because two weeks are required to reach the high mountains. STOL airstrips at Tumlingar and Taplejung can shorten the time but greatly increase the expense. Inhabitants of this part of Nepal are not used to westerners and great care should be taken to avoid the mistakes trekkers made in the more popular regions, mistakes which have presented a distorted image of westerners and contributed to the problems now experienced in the Helambu and Dhorpatan regions.

SOLU KHUMBU to DHARAN
This section describes an interesting alternative to the Lamosangu to Everest Base Camp trek. Though shown here as a route from Khumbu to Dharan, it can equally well be used as an approach route to the Everest region — in fact, the first foreign visitor to Everest Base Camp, Tilman in 1950, used this route.

By walking from Lamosangu to Everest Base Camp and then walking via the route described here to Dharan, a rewarding 38-day trek may be made. Walking to Dharan avoids the flight complications at Lukla and lends a sense of continuity to the trek that is not felt when you fly back from Lukla.

Though some trekkers have made this walk as a "live-off-the-land" trek, it is not recommended. The first six days, from Lukla to Phedi, are through country that sees few tourists and not a lot of local travellers. It is most important to carry food for the nights at Gaikharka and Sanam, because facilities in these villages are poor.

Day 1 Lukla Puiyan	Instead of flying from Lukla you may take a leisurely stroll down the 550-metre long runway and drop to Surkhe, then climb back up to Puiyan at 2830 metres. If you are travelling from Namche Bazar, it is not necessary to go to Lukla; you can proceed from Jorsale to Chaunrikarka, then from Chaunrikarka to Puiyan.
Day 2 Puiyan ↓ Pangum	The trail follows the same route as the Lamosangu to Namche Bazar trail as far as Kharte, then heads into new country. Behind the large white house at the top of Kharte, the trail climbs over a fence and turns south-east up the broad valley between the Bupsa Ridge and Khari Khola. There are some ups and downs as the trail gradually gains elevation through forested slopes, passing isolated Sherpa houses and small streams, to the village of Pangum (also pronounced "Pankoma" locally), at about 2850 metres. Here is yet another Hillary school (there are 12 such schools in the region) and a paper factory that produces rice paper (actually made from the inner bark of a mulberry bush), which is carried to Kathmandu in huge loads by porters.
Day 3 Pangum ↓ Gaikharka	From Pangum it is a short climb to the 3173 metre Satu La, the pass between the watersheds of the Dudh Kosi and the Inukhu Khola. From the pass there is a great view, not only of the Khumbu Himalaya, but also of the peaks at the head of the Inukhu (also called Hinku) valley. The trail descends gradually to Chatuk, a small Sherpa settlement, then drops almost vertically in a series of short switchbacks to the river at 1855 metres, which it crosses on an exciting bridge suspended high above the river on two steel cables. The bridge was built by a Himalayan Trust team in 1971. One of the volunteers, when questioned about the fantastic engineering that must be required for the construction of a bridge in such a remote location commented, "We don't engineer them, we just build them".

The trail climbs a short distance alongside a picturesque waterfall that widens into a pool just above the river, a good place to take a bath after the cold of Khumbu. The trail then climbs up the side of the wild, sparsely-inhabited Inukhu Valley to the Sherpa hamlet of Gaikharka ("cow pasture"), at about 2300 metres. Although the only permanent settlements in this valley are those of Sherpas, the valley is also used by the neighbouring Rais for grazing their cattle and by the Gurungs to graze large herds of sheep, which they bring up from the south during the summer.

Day 4

Gaikharka

Bung

The route continues to climb past the abandoned houses of Najidingma, situated in a large meadow, then makes a steep ascent in forests towards Sipki pass at 3085 metres. Beyond the pass the trail descends a short distance through forests, then the valley suddenly opens up above the village of Khiraule, at about 2400 metes. There is a large *gompa* in this village that is particularly sacred. The *gompa* is surrounded by a large circle of trees and may be identified a long distance away.

The trek is now in the great Hongu Valley, one of the more fertile regions of Nepal. Much of the rice for the Namche Bazar market comes from this valley and is carried back across three ridges to Khumbu. Except for some Sherpas living at higher elevations and some Chhetris and Brahmins downstream near Sotang, the Hongu Valley population is exclusively Rai. Some of the Rai villages are extremely large and boast 200 or 300 households; typically the villages are spread out over the hillside with trails leading in every direction. Route finding in a Rai village is always an interesting challenge.

Rai people are very independent and individualistic. The two hundred thousand or so Rais in the eastern hills speak at least 15 different languages, which although closely related, are mutually unintelligible. When Rais of different areas meet it is necessary for them to converse in Nepali.

The trail descends down a ridge crest to the large village of Bung, spread out over the hillside from about 1980 down to 1500 metres elevation. The most direct route through the village follows a ravine downhill, but soon gets lost wandering among the houses and fields in the lower part of this typical Rai village.

A particularly interesting sight in regions of Rai influence is the *Dhami* shamans who are diviners, spirit mediums and medicine men. Occasionally they may be seen in villages, but more often they are encountered on remote trails dressed in elegant regalia and headdresses of pheasant feathers. The rythmic sound of the drums that a *dhami* continually beats while walking echoes throughout the hills, and you are almost certain to hear the drum of a *dhami* in the Hongu Valley.

Day 5

Bung

Sanam

From Bung there is a steep descent through bamboo forests to the Hongu Khola, crossed by a rickety wooden bridge at about 1280 metres, followed by an equally steep climb up to Gudel, another large Rai village, at about 2280 metres. It was this long useless descent and ascent that H Ẇ Tilman, travelling in the opposite direction, described poetically in his book *Nepal Himalaya:*

> *For dreadfullness, naught can excell*
> *The prospect of Bung from Gudel;*
> *And words die away on the tongue*
> *When we look back on Gudel from Bung.*

Beyond Gudel the ascent, up the side of the Lidung Khola, a tributary valley of the Hongu, continues more gradually. But it is a long and tiring climb through forests and the small Sherpa settlements of Sorung and Tigare, until Sanam (2620 metres) is reached. Rai villages in the valley have a maximum elevation of about 2400 metres; Sherpa villages exploit different resources; there is little economic competition between the two groups. Sanam is primarily dependent on herds of cattle and there is often milk, yoghurt and excellent cottage cheese available in the village, a compact settlement of houses arranged in a single row.

Day 6

Sanam

Phedi

The route continues to climb through a totally uninhabited area. The trail drops slightly to the floor of the canyon that it has been ascending, crosses a stream, and makes a final steep climb to the Salpa Bhanjyang, the 3475 metre pass between the Hongu and Arun watersheds. This area is deep mountain forest abounding in bird and animal life, including Himalayan bear and the lesser panda (a smaller, red-coloured relative of its more famous namesake). The pass is marked by a large *chorten,* the final influence of Sherpa culture on the route to Dharan. Note that the total climb up from the Hongu Khola is 2200 metres. The first available water is about an hour beyond the pass, making the lunch stop on this day quite late.

It is possible, by following the ridge to the south, to take an alternate route to the one described here. This route passes through Bhojpur, a large hill bazaar, famous for its excellent kukhris (the curved Nepali knife). There are weekly flights from Bhojpur to Kathmandu, or you can keep walking to the Arun, crossing it near Sati Ghat, and rejoin the trail described here on day 10.

The trail descends through forests and past small herders' huts as it follows a spur separating the Irkhuwa Khola and the Sanu Khola. On this portion of the trail there is ample evidence of forest fires that occur in the dry season each spring due to fires in villages, careless smokers and lightning storms. The trail continues through oak and rhododendron forests until it reaches a large stone overlooking the Irkhuwa Khola Valley, then drops almost vertically through bamboo forests into the Rai village of Phedi. The best camp is below the village, at about 1980 metres, on the banks of the Irkhuwa Khola. This is one of the longest days of the trek. The *rakshi* in Phedi is terrible, incidentally.

bamboo bridge
across the
Irkhua Khola

Day 7

Phedi

⬇

Dhubidanda

The trek has now emerged into the fertile rice-growing valley of the Arun River. The route follows the Irkhuwa Khola, a tributary of the Arun, crossing and recrossing the stream on a series of bamboo bridges, some quite substantial and some very flimsy, but all picturesque. After the continuous ups and downs of the last week, this is a particularly relaxing day. The trail loses elevation almost imperceptibly; yet by the end of the day, almost 1200 metres of elevation have been lost. There are numerous pools large enough for swimming, and the water temperature — especially in comparison with streams higher up — is comfortable. A few hours below Phedi, the first shops since Lukla are encountered. There is even a tailor shop that can outfit you with a new set of clothes while you wait.

Settlement in this part of the Arun basin is mixed; there are Rai villages, as well as those inhabited by Chhetris and Brahmins. Before the Gurkha conquest, which took place about 200 years ago, the entire middle hills region between the Dudh Kosi and Arun was populated almost entirely by Rais; but following in the wake of the conquest, when the Rais were defeated by the Gurkha army, considerable numbers of Hindus settled here, especially in the more fertile regions. The Rais and their neighbours on the other side of the Arun, the Limbus, are jointly known as the *Kiranti*. The *Kiranti* are the earliest-known population of Nepal's eastern hills and are believed to have settled here for at least 2000 years. Early Hindu epics such as the *Mahabharata* refer to the fierce *Kirantis* of the eastern Himalaya. This was the site of fierce fighting between Tibetan and Assamese warlords since the 7th century AD. The Kirantis joined the Gorkhali kingdom only in 1774.

There is a good camping place on the banks of the Irkhuwa Khola near the village of Dhubidanda at an elevation of about 760 metres.

Day 8

Dhubidanda

Chiyabesi

The trail makes a final crossing of the Irkhuwa Khola, this time, however, on an excellent new bridge built by the local government. It soon begins to climb over a spur separating the Arun River from the Irkhuwa Khola. The trail is difficult to follow as it crosses fields, doubles back on itself and traverses small irrigation canals that supply water to rice fields. The main trail in this region climbs much higher and goes to the large village of Dingla at the top of the ridge. To avoid this long, unnecessary climb, the trail follows a circuitous route through the fields and back yards of a larger village.

Finally the mighty Arun River is seen to the north. This river, which has its headwaters in Tibet, is one of the major rivers flowing into the Ganges in India. The trail now turns south and descends to a small tributary of the Arun, the Chirkhuwa Khola, where there is a small shop and a fine swimming hole overlooked by a huge and noisy band of Rhesus monkeys. This location makes an excellent, though usually hot, spot to stop for lunch.

A short distance on, the route crosses the Arun River, here at an elevation of only 300 metres, at what the maps call a "ferry". This consists of a lazy boatman who owns a single dugout canoe that his sons paddle back and forth across the fast-flowing river. The ferryman immediately doubles his price when a trekking group arrives, not only for the trekkers, but for the sherpas and porters as well. Fortunately such price fixing is rare in the hills, but since the only alternative is a long, cold and dangerous swim, there is little choice — and the ferryman knows it.

The ride is exciting, especially for the sherpas, who cannot swim and are usually terrified of the whole procedure. The river crossing can consume an hour or two; the boatmen drag the boat up the river, then paddle furiously across as the current carries them downstream. To return the canoe, the whole process is repeated from the other side of the river. From the ferry landing at Kartike

the Arun
River ferry

Ghat, the trail follows the east side of the river southward for about a half hour to a good camp at Chyawabesi, 280 metres elevation.

© 1978 Himalayan Journeys

Day 9   The trail follows the Arun as it flows south, sometimes climbing high above the river and sometimes on the sandy riverbed. The climate here is hot and tropical; the houses

Chyawabesi

Khare

are built on stilts for ventilation and the people are more dark-skinned than those encountered so far on the trek. Many of the settlements along the bottom of the Arun Valley are inhabited only during the planting and harvesting season by people who live higher in the hills above and own fertile farmlands in the valley.

It is a short uphill climb to a huge plateau that provides almost six km of completely level trail to Tumlingtar, a small village with an airport served by regular RNAC flights. Many of the inhabitants of Tumlingtar are of the *Kumal* (potter) caste and earn their livelihood from the manufacture of earthen pots from the red clay in this region. There is very little water on the plateau, so it is necessary to continue a long distance in the morning before lunch. A cup of tea, some oranges or bananas at the big shop under the banyan tree in Tumlingtar will provide the refreshment to keep moving under the hot sun. The reward comes immediately after the short descent from the plateau when the trail crosses the Sabbhaya Khola, a tributary of the Arun. There is an excellent lunch spot beside a fine swimming hole in one of the warmest and most delightful streams along the entire trek route. You can safely avoid the one rupee toll on the bridge by swimming or wading across the river. The afternoon is short, involving a climb of only a hundred metres over a ridge, then a descent to Khare, a tropical village on the banks of the Arun.

village in the Arun River Valley

Day 10

Khare

**Mangmaya
Khola**

The trail continues south along the east bank of the Arun. There are numerous porters on the trail from here to Dharan. These men carry goods from large warehouses in Dharan to the bazaars of Bhojpur, Dingla and Chainpur; they often walk at night with small kerosene lamps tied to their *dokos* (the bamboo baskets in which they carry their loads). In another of his classic anecdotes, H W Tilman imagines these porters nose-to-doko along the trail as they often seemingly appear. Each porter carries a T-shaped stick that he places under his *doko* whenever (and where-ever) he wishes to rest, usually as he stands in the middle of the trail. The entire trail then backs up, as each porter is forced to wait until the man ahead of him finishes his rest, thus halting a line of porters kms long. It presents a ludicrous picture, but a picture not totally removed from reality on this part of the trail. A short excursion into the villages here will often uncover such interesting items as papayas (called *mewa* in Nepali), peanuts (*badam*) and pineapples (*bhui katahar*).

The trail continues south, at no point climbing more than a hundred metres above the river, until it crosses under a cable that supports a river gauging station, just before a small village named Sati Ghat, the site of another dugout canoe ferry. Much of the vegetation along this part of the river has been devoured by herds of goats and sheep; these animals, more than humans, are responsible for the extensive deforestation of the entire country. After a short distance, the trail comes to a large pipal tree overlooking a huge side valley of the Arun. At the foot of this valley flows the Mangmaya Khola; the grassy banks of this stream, at 200 metres elevation, afford an excellent campsite.

Day 11

**Mangmaya
Khola**

Hile

The trail crosses the broad valley, then climbs through hot tropical forests to the delightful village of Piple, two tea shops facing a small village square, at about 700 metres elevation. The upper portion of this town has a number of large shops. The trail continues to climb through villages inhabited by Limbus, relatives of the Rais, to Gorlekharka, at 1250 metres elevation. The trail finally gains the ridge and allows a fine view of Makalu and Chamlang (7319 metres), almost 150 km away.

The route continues fairly level for some time to the British agricultural project at Pakhribas. This fantastic development presents a real contrast to the small gardens that surrounded every home throughout the trek. At Pakhribas there are huge rows of vegetables, all neatly labelled with signs; there are walls, roads and irrigation canals, all paved with stone and cement; and there are buildings of every description carefully labelled according to their function.

The trail then climbs a higher ridge crest to Hile, where there is the first real sign that the trek is approaching its end — Hile is served by electricity. This is a very pleasant town situated high on a hill at 1850 metres; the elevation and cool breezes provide a welcome relief from the heat of the Arun Valley. The village is inhabited primarily by people of Tibetan stock who resettled here from Tibet and other parts of eastern Nepal, particularly the village of Walungchung, when trade with Tibet was disrupted after the Chinese occupation in 1959. There is often some genuine Tibetan jewellery for sale here, and many Chinese goods are available at prices below those in Kathmandu. The village is also well known for its ample supply of *tongba*, an "instant beer" made from fermented millet, sipped through a bamboo straw from fancy

Rai porters
en route to
Dharan

wooden and brass containers. Eventually the road from Dharan will reach Hile; so it will someday be possible to end the trek here. There is a weekly market (*hat*) in Hile on Thursdays.

Day 12

Hile

Mulghat

The route descends gently on what will eventually become a motor road down a spur to Dhankuta at 1220 metres. This is a large, attractive, clean Limbu town, with white-washed houses and winding streets paved with stone. This is the largest town on the entire trek route; there is a police station flanked by polished brass cannon, a hospital, a cold storage facility, bank, bakery, telegraph office and hundreds of shops. Dhankuta provides an interesting opportunity to observe a quite-well-developed hill village that is still relying on porters and foot transport for all its manufactured goods. Some of the porters' loads en route to Dhankuta are unbelievable: huge corrugated metal sheets, machinery, tools and other items from Kathmandu and India. The motor road that is almost completed will soon change the entire economics of the town as it turns Dhankuta into a warehouse for goods to be carried further into the hills. The region is also famous for its wonderful oranges (*suntala* in Nepali).

From Dhankuta the trail continues to descend past a small bazaar that specialises in locally manufactured Nepalese caps or *topis*. This bazaar also has several cobblers who can perform instant repairs to shoes. The trail is quite crowded with porters between Dhankuta and Dharan, so there may be short waits along this portion of the route — the Nepalese hill version of a traffic jam. At the foot of the hill a large suspension bridge (toll — 10 *paisa* or one tenth of a rupee) crosses the Tamur Kosi. The Tamur Kosi flows west to join the Arun at the same point where the Arun is joined by the Sun Kosi, which has made its long trip eastward across Nepal, having collected all the rivers that have flowed south into it. Together these rivers form the Sapt Kosi ("seven rivers") that flows to the Ganges containing the waters of the Sun Kosi, Bhote Kosi, Tamba Kosi, Dudh Kosi, Arun Kosi, Likhu Kosi and Tamur Kosi.

Just across the bridge is Mulghat, the final campsite on the trek, at an elevation of about 300 metres.

It may be possible to hitch a ride to Dharan from Mulghat in a truck or jeep, and if I shared the optimism of the British engineers who are assisting with the road project, I would suggest that by the time you read this there will be regular bus service at least this far — it may or may not be operating.

Day 13

Mulghat

Dharan

The trail follows the Tamur Kosi west for a short distance, then turns south up a side valley alongside the new motor road, following this valley until it is halted by the Siwalik Range (in Nepal called the Churia Hills) - the last range of hills before the plains. The trail leaves the extensive tea shop complex at the foot of the hill and climbs steadily for about two hours to the small village of Dharapani. From Dharapani and other places on this ridge, there are excellent views of Kanchenjunga (8598 metres) and its prominent neighbour Jannu (7710 metres), on the eastern border of Nepal.

The trail makes the final climb to the pass, 1340 metres, on a broad trail in the company of hundreds of porters. At the crest is a most dramatic sight — to the south is nothing but plains. After weeks in the hills, it is unusual to see country that is absolutely flat as far as the eye can see. The trail descends quite steeply to Dharan, passing by rows of warehouses that supply the goods carried into the hills, until the paved road is reached, at about 370 metres.

Dharan is the major trading centre in the *terai* serving the eastern hills region and a good deal of resettlement of hill people has taken place in the surrounding area. Although located in the plains, most of Dharan's population consists of hill people. Dharan is also the site of a British Army recruiting centre for the Gurkha Brigade. In the old British Indian Army there were 10 Gurkha Rifle Regiments; when India gained her independence in 1947, she took six of the regiments and Britain retained four. By agreement with His Majesty's Government of Nepal, Britain was allowed to establish two recruiting centres within Nepal; one at Dharan which recruits Rais and Limbus (for the most part) for the 7th and 20th G.R., and one near Bhairawa, which recruits mostly Gurungs and Magars for the 2nd and 6th G.R. Recruits are accepted from other ethnic groups as well, but the bulk comes from these four groups in roughly equal numbers. The British camp development just to the west of Dharan is quite extensive, including an excellent hospital. There are hotels in Dharan, but those with tents will be more comfortable camped near the north side of town.

Day 14

Dharan

Kathmandu

An excellent all-weather road links Dharan and Biratnagar, Nepal's second largest city and the kingdom's industrial centre. The largest factories here process jute into carpets, bags and rope. There are also many smaller factories making matches, cigarettes and other items. The road passes through cultivated fields and villages for most of the distance between the two cities. Originally this was all jungle and fine sal forest, but over the years it has been cut back drastically. There is little to remind one now of the extensive malarial jungle that once blanketed this region — although there are still glimpses of this jungle to the west, in Royal Chitwan National Park.

The return to Kathmandu may be made by bus directly, travelling south from Dharan to Itahari, west on the east-west highway through Janakpur to Birganj, then up the Tribhuvan Rajpath to Kathmandu. An express bus service makes the long journey in a single day; the local buses, which are cheaper, take two days for the journey.

A more sensible route is by bus or Land-Rover to Biratnagar, then a flight back to Kathmandu. In contrast to Dharan, Biratnagar is a typical *terai* town, with noisy bazaars, inhabited mainly by plains people. There is very little of interest in Biratnagar and the noisy rickshaws and trucks make it pointless to spend much time there as a tourist. The drive from Dharan to Biratnagar requires about an hour and ends at Biratnagar airport, a fancy new facility built with South Korean assistance, to await the RNAC flight to Kathmandu. Unlike Lukla, the flights to Biratnagar are regular because there is rarely a weather problem, there are instrument landing facilities, the runway is paved, and the planes (44-passenger HS-748s) have enough capacity to meet the demands for flights. The return flight takes about 45 minutes and in clear weather provides an excellent overview of the entire trek, especially views of the Himalaya from Kanchenjunga to Langtang.

An alternative to the return to Kathmandu is to take a bus from Biratnagar to Kakarvita, cross into India and take a taxi to Siliguri. From Siliguri it is about a three hour drive by taxi (or a seven hour train ride) to Darjeeling, one of the most pleasant of India's hill stations. It requires a special permit to cross this border, and you will be certainly refused entry to India if you do not have it. The permit is easily obtained at an Indian Embassy, either in Kathmandu or overseas.

North of Kathmandu

Langtang is a narrow valley that lies just south of the Tibetan border, sandwhiched between the main Himalayan range to the north and a slightly lower range of snowy peaks to the south. The valley is dominated by 7246 metre Langtang Lirung at the north, Gang Chhenpo (6388 metres) to the south and Dorje Lakpa (6975 metres) to the east.

This high and isolated region is inhabited by people of Tibetan origin, who practice Buddhism. A visit to Langtang valley offers an opportunity to explore villages and monasteries as well as to visit glaciers at the head of the valley. According to legend, the valley was discovered by a Lama following a runaway yak, hence the name — "lang" is Tibetan for yak, and "tang" (more correctly "dhang") means to follow. Yaks still live in the valley, but are joined by numerous trekkers who make the 11 day round trip trek from the roadhead at Betrawati, a four hour drive from Kathmandu. Because the opportunities for moderate climbing excursions are good here, most trekking groups schedule a few extra days for exploration of the extensive glacier system.

A side trip to the holy lakes of Gosainkund at 4300 metres can be made from the Langtang region. These lakes are the destination of thousands of Hindu pilgrims during the month of August. The lake is also sacred to the Buddhists.

Helambu, about 75 km north of Kathmandu, may be reached directly from the capital, or from Langtang via Gosainkund or the 5106 metre Ganja La pass. In winter both of the high routes from Langtang are often snow covered and difficult, if not impossible. The seven or eight day trek to Helambu is one of the most popular in Nepal because it is short, stays below 3500 metres and is feasible all winter. It is also the easiest trek to organise because the transportation from Kathmandu to Sundarijel, the starting point for the trek, is readily available and inexpensive. The major inhabitants of the valley are Sherpas, but their culture and dress are different from those of the Solu Khumbu. The accessibility of Helambu has created an influx of tourists which contributes to begging, the sale of "genuine antiques" aged over the family fireplace, and a few reports of outright thievery. Many combine both Langtang and Helambu into a single trek of 14 or 15 days to avoid back-tracking.

LANGTANG TREK

This section describes the seven day approach to Langtang. From Langtang village or Kyanjin Gompa there are a number of alternatives for returning to Kathmandu. It is possible to make the trek back to Betrawati in only five days from Langtang because it is almost all downhill. An alternative route over the Ganja La is described in the following section. A third alternative is to trek back as far as Syabru from Langtang, then cross via Gosainkund into Helambu.

Day 1

Kathmandu

Trisuli

Manigaon

It is about a four hour drive on a paved highway twisting and climbing over ridges, to the Trisuli valley. Buses leave from the intersection where the Balaju road enters Kathmandu, close to the Malla Hotel, at about 7 am. Passing Balaju, the road climbs over Kakani pass (2145 metres), offering excellent views of Annapurna II, Manaslu and Ganesh Himal, climbs over another ridge, and descends into the broad Trisuli valley. Following the river upstream, the road passes a police checkpost, then crosses the river on an iron suspension bridge just before the town of Trisuli Bazar at 548 metres, 72 km from Kathmandu.

Trisuli Bazar is a large town with many shops, and is the site of a dam and hydroelectric project built by the Indian Technical Mission. There is a road, which is suitable only for jeeps, to Betrawati starting just before the bridge and following the east bank of the Trisuli River. The trail, for those who travel to Trisuli by bus, begins behind the village, and follows the canal supplying the hydroelectric project, on the west bank of the river. After about an hour's walking, the trail crosses the Trisuli River on a bridge carrying a huge pipe that feeds the hydro project and joins the road, climbing slightly to the village of Betrawati at 620 metres. Betrawati is a large town situated at the foot of the steep hill leading towards Langtang and Gosainkund.

Crossing the Phalangu Khola and passing the small hotels, shops, and police checkpost in Betrawati, the trail begins climbing immediately on a wide staircase-like track. It is a short climb to the first settlement of Bogota, 760 metres. There are frequent stops along the trail under the shade of huge Pipal and Banyan trees surrounded by rock walls standing near the trail. These trees, planted centuries ago, have broad leaves and branches that extend outwards for a long distance in mushroom fashion, offering welcome shade to travellers. It was under a Banyan tree that Buddha attained enlightenment in India, over 2000 years ago. The Banyan, a related species to the Pipal tree, can be differentiated from the latter by the long roots that droop down from the limbs, a peculiarity of the Banyan. Around

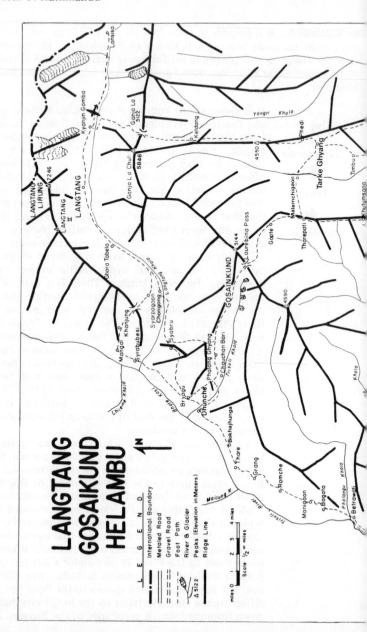

the huge shade trees have been built walls and *chautaras*, or stone benches, for porters to rest their loads upon as they pause during the hot, steep climbs. Many people build *chautaras* in the names of deceased relatives.

Continuing to ascend through an oak forest, the trail reaches Manigaon at 1190 metres. This village, like most during the first two days of the trek, is spread out over a large area on the side of the hill high above the Trisuli River. Most of the villages at the lower altitudes are inhabited by Brahmins and Chhetris; above 1500 metres the villages are generally Tamang settlements.

Day 2

Manigaon

Thare

The trail continues its steep ascent to Ramche at 1790 metres and Grang at 1860 metres. At Ramche there is a National Park station where the entrance fee of Rs 60 is collected from each foreigner. Be sure to keep the receipt because it will be checked at Ghora Tabela. The Trisuli valley is broad here and the trail follows many circuitous detours in and out of side canyons where small streams flow down. Some of these streams are particularly pleasant and offer outstanding lunch spots in the shade. The villages have become more spread out, and the intense cultivation of the lowland rice-growing country gives way to herding and small fields of corn, millet and vegetables as the elevation increases. Becoming more level, the trail contours, climbing only slightly through oak and rhododendron forests, to Thare at 1890 metres.

Day 3

Thare

Syabru

The valley is now even broader, and the climb continues gently through deep forests to Bokhajhunga at 1920 metres. This large Tamang village has a school and a hotel with an English signboard. From Bokhajhunga the trail climbs over a spur to Dhunche, the administrative headquarters of the region at 1950 metres. Dhunche is a compact and picturesque village with narrow streets lined by stone houses, shops, inns and government offices. There is a police checkpost, just before the village, where trekking permits are examined and endorsed.

From Dhunche the trail turns east down the village's main street, descends past a large government agricultural project, and drops to the Trisuli Khola, crossing it on a cantilever bridge at 1680 metres. The Trisuli Khola flows from Gosainkund where, according to legend, Lord Shiva released the waters of the holy lakes with his trident (*trisul*). The trail north, up the main valley, was once a major trade route with Tibet. The upper part of the river is called the Bhote Kosi ('river from Tibet'), as are most of the rivers that cross the Himalaya into Nepal. When it is joined by a Nepalese river, the Bhote Kosi assumes the name of its smaller tributary. Thus the Bhote Kosi becomes the Trisuli Khola below Dhunche.

From the bridge across the Trisuli, the trail climbs steeply up an almost vertical cleft in the rock beside a small stream for 250 metres. At the top of the steep climb is the intersection with the trail to Gosainkund, which follows the Trisuli Valley eastward. The trail to Langtang follows around the forested ridge past small herders' huts to the village of Bharku, 1860 metres.

From Bharku there is a choice of trails. The new trail descends to the Trisuli Khola and climbs over a ridge to Syabru, while the old trail continues north through Syabrubesi and Syarpagaon before turning eastward along the Langtang Khola. As the new trail offers a saving of a day, and passes both interesting villages and deep forests, it is the best choice.

Climbing steeply from Bharku, the trail reaches a ridge crest at 2300 metres where the trail finally enters the Langtang Valley. There are views northward of the snow peaks in Tibet, and to the east the top of Langtang Lirung becomes visible. The trail makes a short steep descent to Syabru at 2130 metres, a pleasant village strung out along a ridge. There are hotels at the upper end of the village just as the trail enters it.

Day 4

Syabru

Chongong

From Syabru, another trail leads to Gosainkund, climbing east out of the village. The main trail to Langtang descends along the ridge, through the village, then continues the descent to the Langtang Khola through forests. The trail meets the river at about 1890 metres elevation, then follows it on its southern bank as the river gains elevation very steeply. For the rest of this day and the following morning there is almost no human habitation, but the forest is alive with birdlife. The trail crosses to the north bank of the Langtang Khola at 2040 metres elevation on a wooden bridge, then continues up its northern bank. The forest is less dense and drier on this side of the river, consisting mainly of scrub oak as opposed to the damp forests of large pines found on the shady southern bank, which receives almost no sunshine all day. The tiny settlement of Chongong, a single house at 2380 metres elevation, offers either a camping spot or a primitive hotel for the night. There are also camping spots a short distance on in the forests.

Day 5

Chongong

⬇

Langtang Village

Trekkers' Camp

The trail climbs steeply above the river on the northern side of the Langtang Khola, in places so steep that the trail is on logs anchored to the valley wall. Tantalising glimpses of Langtang Lirung, 7246 metres, appear through the trees, until finally at Ghora Tabela the trail emerges into the open. Once a Tibetan resettlement project, Ghora Tabela, at 3000 metres, is now a Nepalese Army Post and has no permanent inhabitants. There is another police checkpost here. There is a check made to be sure that you pay the National Park entrance fee. If you somehow slipped past the station at Ramche, the fee of Rs 60 will be collected here. The trail ascends gradually, as the valley becomes wider and wider, through scattered Tamang villages until the large settlement of Langtang is reached

at 3500 metres. This village is the headquarters for Langtang National Park; park administration buildings, tourist facilities and yet another police checkpost are situated here. The houses of Langtang and neighbouring villages are of Tibetan style surrounded by stone walls enclosing fields of buckwheat, potatoes, wheat, turnips and barley. Herds of yaks and cattle are kept here and in the pastures above the village. There are plans afoot to build a series of deluxe facilities in Langtang. Bars, hot tubs and other amenities may sometime be available here.

Day 6

Langtang Village

Kyanjin Gompa

The trail now climbs gradually through small villages and yak pastures as the valley becomes broader and broader. After crossing several small streams and moraines, the trail reaches the settlement at Kyanjin Gompa. Here there is a small monastery and a government-operated cheese factory. The cheese factory was started in 1955 by the Swiss Association for Technical Assistance and produces many tons of cheese annually — all of it hauled by porters to the dairy in Kathmandu. It is easy to reach Kyanjin Gompa, at 3800 metres, by lunch time, allowing time to acclimatise and to explore the surroundings.

Day 7

In Langtang Valley

A day hike may be made up the moraine to the north of Kyanjin Gompa to an elevation of 4300 metres or more. From the moraine there is a spectacular view of Langtang Lirung and the foot of one of its major glaciers.

For the more adventurous, a walk up the valley to Yala will provide outstanding views and an opportunity to climb a ridge to the north of the village. It is also possible to continue further up the Langtang valley itself towards the peaks of Dorje Lakpa (6990 metres), Gang Chhenpo (6386 metres), and Lonpo Gang (7100 metres).

Return to Kathmandu
The return to Kathmandu may be made via the same route, or may be made by plane from the Pilatus Porter airstrip above Kyanjin Gompa at 3690 metres. This airstrip has no scheduled service. The charter flights are irregular, and in only 6-passenger aircraft, so it is best not to count on finding a seat back to Kathmandu unless you have made prior arrangements. The airstrip is also notorious for becoming snowbound in December, January and February for days at a time.

An alternative route to Kathmandu may be made either over Ganja La or via Gosainkund when there is no snow on these high altitude routes.

ACROSS GANJA LA

This description provides a picture of the route from Kyanjin Gompa in Langtang to Tarke Gyang in Helambu via the 5106 metre high Ganja La pass. This pass is difficult and dangerous when covered by snow, so local inquiries about its condition, good equipment and some mountaineering background are necessary for a safe crossing. The pass can generally be assumed to be open from April to November, though unusual weather can alter its condition at any time. A guide who knows the trail, a tent, food and fuel are imperative on a crossing of Ganja La.

Kathmandu to Kyanjin Gompa
As described in the preceding section. An acclimatisation day in Langtang valley is necessary before beginning the crossing of Ganja La.

Day 1	Kathmandu to Manigaon
Day 2	Manigaon to Thare
Day 3	Thare to Syabru
Day 4	Syabru to Chongong
Day 5	Chongon to Langtang village
Day 6	Langtang village to Kyanjin Gompa
Day 7	In the Langtang valley

Day 8

Kyanjin
Gompa

Ngegang

This is a short day from Kyanjin Gompa, but Ngegang is the last good place to camp before beginning the final ascent to the pass and it is necessary to minimise the elevation gain in order to aid acclimatisation. Crossing the Langtang Khola below Kyanjin Gompa, the trail makes a steep climb up the ridge on the south side of the valley through a forest of rhododendron and juniper. Finally becoming less steep, the trail raches the yak pasture of Ngegang at about 4000 metres elevation. There are *goths* here and on the other side of the pass but they have no roofs during the winter months, so a tent is a useful item to have along this trek. During the monsoon months, herders carry bamboo mats to provide roofs for the stone *goths* here and live the entire summer in high meadows with herds of yaks and goats.

Day 9

Ngegang

The trail continues south, following streams and moraines, climbing steeply towards the pass. As the trail climbs higher and comes under the shadow of the 5800 metre peaks to the south, more and more snow is usually encountered. Turning south-west the trail makes the final steep ascent towards the pass at 5106 metres; the last

Keldang

hundred metres of the ascent being a tricky balancing act on a snow slope above some steep rocks. The pass itself is flanked by gendarmes and topped by a large cairn of rocks and prayer flags. The views north from the pass of Langtang Lirung and snow peaks in Tibet are outstanding, and on a clear day there are views far to the south of many ranges of hills.

The descent from the pass is steep and dangerous as it follows a loose scree slope for about 100 metres before emerging onto a snow slope. Somehow the descent from Ganja La, like most mountain descents, seems more treacherous than the ascent — irrespective of which direction one crosses the pass. However, Ganja La is one of the steeper and more difficult of the major passes in Nepal. After the initial descent, the trail descends gradually in a huge basin surrounded by glaciated peaks. One peak, Ganja La Chuli, 5846 metres, is open to climbers upon prior application to the Nepal Mountaineering Association. A base camp in this region provides a good starting point for the reasonably easy climb.

The route descends in the large basin along an indistinct trail marked occasionally by rock cairns to a small stream. If you are proceeding from Helambu to Langtang, it will require a full day to reach this point, about 4400 metres elevation, from Keldang. Thus you should schedule two days from Keldang to the pass. From this campsite, the trail enters the steep Yangri Khola valley and drops quickly down a rough scree slope to the stream. Following the stream for some distance through grassy meadows, the trail reaches a few *goths* (again without roofs) at Keldang about 4270 metres.

Day 10

Keldang

Dukpu

This is a long and tiring day as the trail descends along a ridge, making many ups and downs. In winter there is no water from Keldang to the bottom of the ridge, near Phedi, so it is important to plan food accordingly for this stretch of the trail. In October and November there is usually no water problem, because the monsoon rains leave an ample groundwater supply in several small springs.

The route descends the valley, but stays high above the river, finally meeting the ridge itself and following the ridge line throughout the day. The small summer settlement of Dukpu is reached at 4080 metres.

Day 11

Dukpu

Tarke Gyang

From Dukpu the trail descends further along the ridge before making a 180 metre climb to a pass at 4020 metres, offering a commanding view of the Himalaya from Dorje Lakpa east almost to Everest, and a panoramic view of the first six or seven days of the trek from Lamosangu to Khumbu. Descending from the pass, the trail enters forests, descending through pines and rhododendrons, past tiny herders' settlements to a ridge high above Tarke Gyang. It is a steep descent to Gekye Gompa at 3020 metres, a small monastic community, and the first permanent habitation since Kyanjin Gompa. The trail continues its steep descent to Tarke Gyang, a large Sherpa village at 2560 metres.

Return to Kathmandu

For the route back to Kathmandu, see the Helambu route description below:

Day 12   Kiul
Day 13   Pati Bhanjyang
Day 14   Kathmandu via Sundarijel

HELAMBU CIRCUIT

This is the description of a 7-day trek that makes a circuit of the Helambu region. The best starting point for this trek is Sundarijel because of its proximity to Kathmandu. The trek may be made in either direction, as it closes a loop from Pati Bhanjyang, the first night stop of the trek. The best route is as described here, visiting the high ridge to the west of Helambu valley first, then going to Tarke Gyang and descending the Malemchi Khola before climbing back to Pati Bhanjyang. There are numerous other variations possible to this trek, including a direct route to Tarke Gyang from Pati Bhanjyang then down the ridge through Sermathang, ending at Panchkal on the Chinese Road.

The Helambu trek is the most popular short trek in Nepal, and is the destination of most people who decide to take a trek only after they have arrived in Kathmandu. The transportation to and from the starting point of the trek is fast and cheap, and the trek is at a low elevation so no fancy warm clothing is usually needed.

Day 1

Kathmandu

The trail to Helambu begins at Sundarijel, elevation 1265 metres, which is reached by an unpaved road from Bodhanath. It is possible to drive, or even take a taxi to Sundarijel, or the trek can begin from Bodhanath, taking a few hours to walk to Sundarijel along the level roadway.

At Sundarijel there is a large water project that supplies

**Pati
Bhanjyang**

much of Kathmandu's drinking water in a huge pipe. The trail begins on a set of concrete steps alongside the water pipe, then climbs continuously in forests beside the pipe and alongside a small stream to a dam. Crossing the dam, the trail leaves the water supply system and climbs steeply up to the top of the Seopuri Ridge. The first village, Mulkharka, is situated at an elevation of 1895 metres, and offers a chance to rest in a small tea shop while enjoying a spectacular panoramic view of Kathmandu Valley. If the trek is made early in the morning, you will meet hundreds of people walking uphill to gather wood to be used as fuel in Kathmandu. The forests of Seopuri Ridge are densely forested with pine, oak and rhododendron.

Beyond the Tamang village of Mulkharka the trail becomes a bit less steep, but continues to climb steadily through the scattered settlement of Chaurabas at 2220 metres, to the top of the ridge at 2440 metres. Just below the ridge on the north side is the village of Borlang Bhanjyang. A night stop in one of the hotels in this village will afford excellent mountain views the following morning. The sunrise on the Himalaya, from Annapurna to Everest, is particularly outstanding from this point.

The route continues down the ridge through a forest of oak and rhododendron, then across meadows and fields to Pati Bhanjyang, situated on a saddle at the bottom of the ridge at 1770 metres elevation. This is a large Tamang village with a few shops and hotels catering to trekkers, and a police check post.

Day 2

**Pati
Bhanjyang**

↓

Khutumsang

The trail climbs north out of Pati Bhanjyang and ascends the ridge through terraced fields, crosses a spur, descends and climbs again to Chipling at 2170 metres. Continuing on the ridge, through forests, the trail crosses a pass at 2470 metres, then descends and passes the Tamang village of Gul Bhanjyang, 2130 metres. The trail continues climbing up the ridge from Gul Bhanjyang to another pass at 2620 metres, then descends to Khutumsang, 2470 metres, situated in a saddle atop the ridge.

Day 3

Khutumsang

↓

The route continues due north up the Yurin Danda ridge and affords views of the peaks above Langtang and of the Gosainkund peaks. The trail now enters fir and rhododendron forests where there are no permanent settlements. The small huts in the region are used by herders during the summer months. Continuing to climb, steeply at first,

Tharepati then more gradually, though there are some ups and downs, the trail finally reaches Tharepati, the site of a few *goths*, at 3490 metres. The trail to Gosainkund turns north-west from this point, but the trail to complete the Helambu circuit turns east just before the hamlet of Tharepati. There is no hotel, but there are a few stone huts here. A tent is useful, though it is possible to continue on to Malemchigaon for the night if you have no shelter. The region is now truly alpine with meadows and shrubs typical of high elevations.

Day 4

Tharepati

↓

Tarke Gyang

Sherpani
porter

The trail turns east and descends steeply down a ravine. The vegetation changes rapidly to large firs, then to oaks and rhododendrons as all the altitude gained during the last two days is rapidly lost. Crossing a stream, the trail reaches the Sherpa village of Malemchigaon at 2530 metres. The Sherpas of Helambu are much different from their cousins in Solu Khumbu. Instead of the Tibetan-style black dress and colourful apron, the Sherpa women

of Helambu wear a dress of red printed cotton. The language is also quite distinct from the Sherpa language of Solu Khumbu. Helambu women have a reputation for being very beautiful, and many Helambu Sherpa girls were employed in aristocratic Rana households in Kathmandu during the Rana regime.

From Malemchigaon, the trail descends further to the Malemchi Khola, crossing it on a bridge at 1890 metres, and immediately begins the ascent up the other side of the valley towards Tarke Gyang. It is a long climb to this picturesque village at 2600 metres, situated on a shelf high above the river.

Tarke Gyang is the largest village in Helambu and the destination for most trekkers in this region. There is a large new hotel catering to trekkers at the southern end of the village. The *gompa*, with its impressive array of prayer flags, has recently been renovated. In 1949, Tilman described this *gompa* as in a state of sorry disrepair, but it is now well cared for, with new paintings and a huge brass prayer wheel. The stone houses of Tarke Gyang are closely spaced, with narrow alleyways. Inside, the homes are large, clean and often elaborately decorated and furnished, not only with traditional Tibetan carpets and brassware, but also with manufactured goods from Kathmandu and India. The people of Helambu do a lot of trading in India during the winter months. Many of the people are quite well-to-do, and own cultivated fields in the lower Malemchi Khola Valley. A special racket among the people of Helambu is the sale of antiques, usually purchased in Kathmandu and aged over smoky fires in the homes of Tarke Gyang — beware of such bargains here. It is illegal to export any item over 100 years old from Nepal, so it is best to purchase well made handicrafts in Kathmandu or Patan rather than attempt to beat the system by purchasing a phoney antique in the hills.

Day 5

Tarke Gyang

Kiul

From Tarke Gyang there is a choice of trails back to Kathmandu. The trail south along the ridge through Sermathang, down to the river at Malemchi, and down the road to Panchkal requires two days. The first part of this trail, along the ridge through Sherpa villages and forests, is quite delightful, but the later part of the route on the dusty road along the Indrawati River is less interesting, though it may be possible to get a ride in one of the infrequent jeeps plying this stretch of road. (But remember that you did come here to trek, and there's not much point in saving time by riding in a motorised vehicle.) This route ends on the Chinese Road at Panchkal (the name of the settlement where the trail meets the road is actually called Lamidanda), and it is a long ride back to Kathmandu by bus.

Most trekkers prefer to take an extra day in the hills and walk back to Sundarijel, where it is easy, cheap and fast to catch transport back to Kathmandu.

The route to Sundarijel passes the new hotel in Tarke Gyang, then begins the descent in a rhododendron forest, along a broad, well-travelled trail. Descending, the trail passes several Tibetan Buddhist monuments — *chortens* (small stone monuments in the same shape as Bodhanath Stupa), *mani* walls (walk to the left) and *kanis* (stone archways decorated on the inside with religious paintings). Passing through the Sherpa village of Kakani at 2070 metres and Thimbu at 1580 metres, the trail enters the hot rice-growing country of the Malemchi and Indrawati Valleys, and leaves the highland tribes for Brahmin; Chhetri and Newar people who inhabit the lower regions.

The steep descent continues to Kiul, 1280 metres, strung out along the terraces above the Malemchi Khola. The trail is now in semi-tropical banana and monkey country at an elevation below that of Kathmandu.

Day 6

Kiul

Pati Bhanjyang

From Kiul the trail follows the river, descending slightly, then crosses the river on a chain-link suspension bridge (do not take the first bridge the trail reaches, take the second a bit further downstream), at 1190 metres elevation. A short distance beyond the bridge the trail reaches Mahenkal (1130 metres) and widens into a roadway. This was once a motorable road, but a monsoon flood washed away the crossing of the Taramarang Khola years ago, and this portion of the road has fallen into disuse. It makes a good trail, however, though it is slightly incongruous to be walking on a disused road while frantic road-building is taking place throughout the hills in other parts of Nepal.

As the road descends the valley it passes through the village of Gheltum, the site of an imposing two-storey schoolhouse and a post office. Descending slightly, the trail cuts across some large switchbacks that the road follows, then descends into Taramarang, a pleasant village on the banks of the river at 940 metres. There are some small shops here, supplied by vehicles that come up the road and stop just across the Taramarang Khola.

Crossing the Taramarang Khola on a long, rather precarious, suspension bridge, the trail proceeds west up the south bank of the stream. From its good beginnings along rice terraces and fields, the trail deteriorates into a boulder-strewn route up the river valley. The same monsoon flood that destroyed the road at Taramarang also destroyed this portion of the trail and washed many fertile fields downstream in the process. After following the stream for a long distance, the trail begins a steep climb up towards the top of the ridge on a newly widened, well-constructed trail. From the uninhabited valley floor, the trail soon enters a densely populated region, passing through the village of Bhatache en route to the top of the ridge, which it reaches near the village of Thakani at 1890 metres. Following the ridge through meadows and terraced fields, the trail crosses over to its south side and descends to Pati Bhanjyang at 1770 metres, completing the circuit through Helambu.

| Day 7 | **Pati Bhanjyang to Kathmandu** |
| | Retrace the route back to Sundarijel, as described on the first day of the trek. |

GOSAINKUND

The trek through Gosainkund may be made in either direction combined with a trek to Helambu or Langtang. There is no dependable food or accommodation on the route, so everything, including fuel and shelter, should be carried. The description here is from Dhunche to Helambu, but the trail is also accessible from Syabru, or the trek may be easily made in the opposite direction.

| Day 1
 Dhunche

 Chenchen Bari | From Dhunche, at 1950 metres, the trail follows the route as described in Day 3 of the Langtang trek, crossing the Trisuli Khola and climbing up to the trail junction at 1920 metres. Leaving the main trail to Langtang, the Gosainkund trail follows the Trisuli Khola valley uphill through a forest of oaks, and higher up to a forest of firs and rhododendrons. The trail climbs to a Buddhist monastery, Sing Gompa, and a small cheese factory at Chenchen Bari, elevation about 3350 metres. |

| Day 2 | The trail continues to climb steeply up the ridge, leaving the forests below. The only signs of habitation are herd- |

Chenchen Bari

Gosainkund

ers' huts at the few points on the ridge where water is found. There are outstanding views across Langtang Valley to Langtang Lirung. To the west the view is even more dramatic with Himal Chuli (7893 metres), Ganesh Himal (7406 metres) and Manaslu (8156 metres) visible. On a clear day it is even possible to see all the way to the Annapurnas and Dhaulagiri.

Finally the trail descends from the ridge to the first of the lakes, Saraswati Kund, at 4100 metres. The second lake in the chain is named Bhairav Kund, and the third, Gosainkund, is located some distance beyond at an elevation of 4380 metres. There are three small stone shelters on the north side of the lake that are used by pilgrims who come here during the full moon festival each August.

Gosainkund Lake has a large white rock in the middle, said to be the remnants of an ancient shrine of Lord Shiva. According to legend, this high-altitude lake was created by Shiva himself when he pierced a glacier with his trident to obtain water to quench his thirst after consuming some poison. It is also said that the water from this lake disappears underground via a subterranean channel and surfaces in Kumbeshwar pond, adjacent to the five-storey temple to Shiva in Patan, more than 60 km away.

Day 3

Gosainkund

Gopte

The trail leaves Gosainkund lake and climbs further through rugged country past four more small lakes to Lauribina pass at 4610 metres, descends steeply alongside a stream, then ascends a ridge and enters forests. Gopte, at 3260 metres, has a cave that offers some shelter.

Day 4

Gopte

Tharepati

Descending along the ridge, the trail continues its steep descent through forests and past herders' huts to a stream at 3310 metres, then climbs to Tharepati at 3490 metres. Here the trail joins the Helambu route at Day 3 in the description, and you can travel on to Tarke Gyang or go directly down the ridge to Kathmandu via Pati Bhanjyang.

Central Nepal

Two major routes in this region are frequented by trekkers: Annapurna south face base camp, often called Annapurna Sanctuary (12 days round trip), and Jomsom (14 days round trip). Both trips begin in Pokhara, known for its large lake, Phewa Tal, and its spectacular panorama of Nepal's central Himalaya: the Annapurnas, Machhapuchhare and Manaslu dominate the skyline. The Annapurna base camp trek affords a fine opportunity to surround onself with Himalayan peaks in a short period of time without having to contend with the extreme altitudes of the Everest region. At an approximate elevation of 4000 metres you are well within the Annapurna Sanctuary and have a 360° view of Hiunchuli, the Annapurna south face (climbed by the British in 1970), Annapurna III (7555 metres), Gangapurna (7454 metres) and Machhapuchhare (6997 metres) — the 'fishtail' mountain. Campsites near the sanctuary are small and often crowded but the isolation of the high peaks quickly dispels any sense of constriction.

The trek to Jomsom is the best route for those who elect the 'live-off-the-land' approach to trekking. This is a major trade route in Nepal, and you will share the trail with trains of burros and ponies travelling to Mustang and other areas closed to foreigners. Many villages have *bhattis* or surprisingly well-equipped hotels operated by Thakalis, people of Tibetan origin who inhabit the Kali Gandaki Valley between Annapurna and Dhaulagiri. From the Kali Gandaki both the 1950 French Annapurna base camp and the base camp for Dhaulagiri may be reached by short side trips. The views of the mountains are spectacular and the route actually crosses to the other side of the main Himalayan range for some unusual views of the northern flanks. The entire route remains below 3000 metres, an important consideration for older persons who wish to avoid high altitudes, though the trek is still strenuous enough to be interesting.

Between Kathmandu and Pokhara there are three major groups of peaks: Ganesh Himal, Manaslu and Himalchuli, and the huge Annapurna Himal. A trek from Kathmandu to Pokhara starts from Trisuli Bazar, 65 km from Kathmandu, on the same road which leads to the start of the Langtang trip. Trekking west there are many alternatives: a northern route presents a trek close to the mountains — Manaslu (7945 metres), Himalchuli, Baudha (6674 metres) and a side trip to Bara Pokhari, a fine high-altitude lake. The more direct southern route to Pokhara allows a visit to the ancient town of Gorkha with its large bazaar and fort. This route has the attraction of lower altitudes and it avoids the extreme elevation gains and losses common to other treks in Nepal. Treks in this region can be of almost any length; nine days is sufficient from Trisuli Bazar to Pokhara. A round trip to Pokhara without backtracking is possible — or trekkers can fly to Pokhara and walk back to Kathmandu, gaining a preview of the route from the plane. The southern routes are often travelled by westerners, but many parts of the northern regions are both remote and untramelled by trekkers.

Jomsom is the district headquarters for the Mustang district of Nepal. To many people, however, Mustang implies the area of Nepal which extends like a thumb into Tibet. This is the region described in Michel Piessel's book *Mustang*, and includes the walled capital city of the one-time principality of Mustang, Lo Monthang. This part of Mustang, however, is closed to foreigners, and despite the reassuring and optimistic brochures printed by many trekking agents, there are no signs that it will be opened soon. Parts of the Mustang district are open, but the area that many people refer to as Mustang is certainly not open (in 1981) to foreigners.

The area most recently opened to tourists is Manang, the area north of Annapurna. The opening of this region has made possible a complete circuit of the Annapurna Himal, involving the crossing of a single high pass, Thorong La, at 5416 metres.

TREK AROUND ANNAPURNA

This is the description of a 19-day trek around the entire Annapurna massif, visiting the Tibet-like country on the north slopes of the Himalaya and the dramatic Kali Gandaki Gorge. The route to Manang was opened for the first time to trekkers in April 1977, although a few expeditions and scientific parties visited the region in the 1950's.

The last seven days of this trek are the popular 'Jomsom Trek' from Pokhara. By reading this description backwards from Day 19 to Day 13, a picture may be gained of this easy short trek. The Jomsom Trek can comfortably be done as a 'live-off-the-land' trek without sherpas or porters by staying in local inns (*bhattis*) run by Thakali innkeepers along the entire route. The trek from Dumre to Manang is much less developed and has (in 1981) only rudimentary food and lodging available; it is advisable to carry your own food supply for this part of the trek.

The Thorong La pass, 5416 metres, should be crossed only from *east to west*, as shown in the route description. Here's why: there are no camping spots or water sources on the west side of the pass from a meadow near Muktinath at 4100 metres, to a spot two to three hours beyond the pass on the Manang side at 4510 metres, if you travel in the *reverse* direction. This means that unacclimatised trekkers have to make a 1300 metre climb plus at least a 900 metre descent in a single day — a virtual impossibility for most people. If you are reading the description backwards, read from Day 19 only as far as Muktinath on Day 12 and turn around there. From Manang to Muktinath the pass is not difficult, but those making this trek must be aware of the possible necessity of returning to Dumre, should Thorong La prove impassable due to snow or altitude sickness.

Clothing and equipment for porters must be of prime consideration on any crossing of Thorong La. Many lowland porters from Dumre have died needlessly or been snowblinded on this pass because trekkers (and their Sherpas) have not provided the proper footgear, clothing and — most important — sunglasses for the pass. Porters from near-tropical villages like Dumre have no idea what to expect on a high snow-covered pass and often join a trekking party clad only in cotton clothing. If you employ porters for a crossing of Thorong La you incur both a moral and legal obligation for their safety and wellbeing. Most trekking agencies assume this responsibility on your behalf.

Day 1

Kathmandu

Turture

The trek begins with a 160-kilometre drive (that takes about five hours on the narrow road) from Kathmandu to Dumre. Leaving the Kathmandu valley, the road descends from the Chandragiri pass on a wild series of steep switchbacks along the narrow Indian-built Tribhuvan Rajpath. It then continues south through cultivated fields to Naubise, 26 km from Kathmandu. At Naubise the Ariniko Rajpath, completed in 1971 with Chinese assistance begins. The Tribhuvan Rajpath continues south from this point and winds its way to the Indian border at Birganj. The Chinese road heads east along the Mahesh Khola to its confluence with the Trisuli river. It then follows the Trisuli valley to Mugling, elevation 220 metres, at the confluence of the Trisuli and Marsyandi rivers. The large river thus formed flows south to become the Narayani river, one of the major sources of the Ganges. Many groups travel this stretch of river in inflatable rafts, finally emerging at one of the game parks in Royal Chitwan National Park. A new road follows the Narayani valley south from Mugling to join the East-West highway at Narayanghat in the terai. A short distance beyond Mugling, on the banks of the Marsyandi river, is Dumre, a new village that was settled by Newars from the nearby town of Bandipur after the completion of the Kathmandu-Pokhara road. At an elevation of 440 metres, Dumre exists because it is at the beginning of trails that lead both to Gorkha, a day's walk away, and to the Marsyandi valley, including Manang. Most of the village consists of warehouses, shops and small *bhattis* serving porters who carry loads from the roadhead to remote villages. A motor road is under construction from Dumre to Besi Shahar (sometimes called Lamjung), the headquarters of the Lamjung District. In 1981 the road was completed as far as Tarkughat, but jeep service on this stretch was sporadic. Before too long it may be possible to drive to Besi Shahar and eliminate two days of walking through country that is not particularly interesting.

After crossing the Nahala Khola, the trek begins in level country, passing through terraced rice fields and small villages inhabited by Newars, Brahmins and Chhetris. For the first 3½ days of the trek the trail intersects often with the motor road. While following the road, the trail is hot and dry (an umbrella is a real asset on this portion of the route), but it occasionally shifts back to the edge of a sparse forest of sal and mango trees, which

MANANG & JOMSOM TREK

LEGEND

━━━●━	International Boundary
═══	Paved Road
═ ═ ═	Gravel Road
‐ ‐ ‐	Trail
∿	River
▲	Peak
━━	Ridge Line

miles 0 1 2 3 4 5   10
kilometres 0 1 2 3 4 5   10

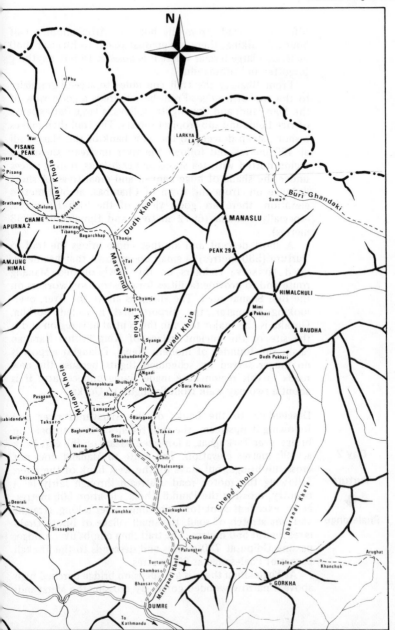

offer some shade from the hot sun. After about a half hour of walking, there is a gradual ascent to Bhansar (530 metres), a large bazaar where it is possible to buy anything forgotten in Kathmandu.

From Bhansar the trail continues to ascend gradually to the top of a ridge. From here there is a good view of the Marsyandi and Chyanglitar valleys, a large flat expanse of rice fields and sub-tropical forests. The trail then makes a short, steep descent to the west bank of the Marsyandi at 460 metres and follows the river upstream through a region dotted with tea shops and *chautaras*, resting places under the shade of huge banyan and pipal trees. A short distance on, from the town of Chambas, at 500 metres elevation, there are good views of the high Himalaya, especially Baudha (6672 metres) and Himalchuli (7893 metres).

A short descent and another climb brings the trail to Turture (530 metres), a small boom town that has developed to serve trekkers on the newly-opened Manang route and to provide facilities for construction workers on the Besi Shahar road. The village is above the river, overlooking Palangtar, the airport that is called Gorkha. Gorkha is the major town in the central hills region and is the site of the ancient palace of King Prithvi Narayan Shah, the founder of modern Nepal. Palangtar airport is no longer served by scheduled flights because the new roads to this region have made flying unnecessary. It is about a two day walk from Palangtar to Gorka.

Day 2

Turture

Phalesangu

Descending to the banks of the Marsyandi river and following it upstream, the trail reaches a large suspension bridge near Tarkughat, a fair-sized bazaar on the east bank at 490 metres elevation. The route to Manang does not cross the bridge, but stays on the west bank of the river, following the motor road upstream through fairly level country, crossing the Paundi Khola, elevation 505 metres, at an excellent spot for swimming. After a long, straight and hot stretch of road, the small village of Bhote Oralo is reached at 550 metres. The trail then climbs over a ridge, passing Udipu at 730 metres and descends to the Thakali bazaar of Phalesangu at 670 metres.

At Phalesangu there is a suspension bridge perched high above a narrow wooded gorge. By crossing the Marsyandi on this bridge a side trip to Bara Pokhari may be made. Bara Pokhari is a high-altitude lake (elevation 3100 metres) offering outstanding views of Manaslu, Himalchuli and Baudha. The trip requires a long steep climb, but it may be made in as few as three days, departing from the main trail at Phalesangu and rejoining the trail to Manang below Usta on Day four.

The bridge at Phalesangu also provides access to an alternate route to Manang that may be followed for the next day to avoid the motor road. From the bridge at Phalesangu the trail climbs to Chiti, then follows the river valley north through sal forests and rice terraces to Chaur, elevation 760 metres, where the trail enters a sugar-cane growing region. From Chaur (also called Simbachaur) the trail stays near the river, crosses the Bhachok Khola, and climbs through Baragaon, elevation 910 metres, and over a ridge before descending to Bhulbule where it joins the route described below. This route not only avoids the motor road, but also avoids the bazaars of Besi Shahar and Khudi — not such a big loss, however, because there are shops further on and the lowlands bazaars are not particularly interesting.

Annapurna Himal from Bara Pokhari

Day 3

Phalesangu

Khudi

From Phalesangu the trail climbs gradually along the motor road, which by now has become hot, dusty and rather boring, as it makes a few small ascents and descents before reaching Besi Shahar, 790 metres. The first of many police checkposts is situated here. Above Besi Shahar to the west is Gaonshahar (elevation 1370 metres); here there are the remains of an old fortress and palace. From the 15th to 18th centuries this region was a collection of independent kingdoms that continually waged war on each other. Lamjung, the principality ruled from this palace, was finally absorbed into the kingdom of Gorkkha in 1782.

From Besi Shahar the trail makes a steep descent of about 150 metres followed by the steepest climb so far. Finally leaving the motor road behind, it begins to feel like a trek in the mountains as the trail becomes a narrow footpath and the valley becomes a deep river gorge. Crossing the Khudi Khola on a long sagging suspension bridge, the trail enters Khudi, 790 metres elevation, a mixture of tin and thatch roofed houses clustered around the anchors of the bridge. There are a few rudimentary inns and shops here. The best camp is at the school, 10 minutes beyond the village.

Khudi is a Gurung village, the first to be encountered on the trek. Most of the wide river valley below Khudi is inhabited by Brahmins and Chhetris, although Gurung villages are found in the side valleys and slopes above the river. Gurungs are known largely for their service as soldiers in the Gurkha regiments of both the British and Indian Armies, as well as the Royal Nepal Army and police. It is not unusual to encounter ex-soldiers on the trail who have served in Malaysia, Singapore, Hong Kong and Britain; the stories of their exploits — in excellent English — provide fascinating trailside conversations. The most important source of income in most Gurung villages is the salaries and pensions of those in military service. The remaining income is from herding — particularly sheep — and from agriculture — rice, wheat, corn, millet and potatoes.

Gurungs are Mongoloid in their features, and the men are easily recognised by their traditional dress of a short blouse tied across the front and a short skirt of white cotton material wrapped around the waist and held by a wide belt. The Gurung funeral traditions and dance performances (the latter staged at the slightest excuse) are particularly interesting, and it is often possible to witness such aspects of Gurung life during a trek in this region — with a running commentary by an elderly English-speaking ex-Gurkha Captain who will explain the rituals and regale trekkers with long, involved stories of his World War I and II campaigns in France, Germany, Italy and North Africa.

Day 4

Khudi

Bahundanda

The trail continues northward up the Marsyandi valley, with views of Himalchuli dominating the horizon, then crosses the river on a suspension bridge at Bhulbule, elevation 825 metres, and travels up the east bank of the river, past a waterfall 60 metres high, and through small villages scattered amongst the extensive terraces. Beyond Bhulbule there are good views of Manaslu and Peak 29. After passing through the small stone settlement and shops of Ngadi the trail crosses the Ngadi Khola on a long new suspension bridge at 880 metres elevation. It is amazing to see the extensive public works programme in the hills of Nepal — the steel cables and towers for this bridge, for example, had to be carried for several days. There are thousands of bridges throughout the country in unbelievably remote locations that have required huge expenditures of time and money for their construction. It is all too easy to see only the undeveloped aspect of Nepal and ignore the progress that has been made in the last 30 years to develop an extensive network of trails and bridges.

Above the Ngadi Khola is the village of Usta; the trail from Bara Pokhari rejoins the route to Manang here. Climbing steadily through scrub forests, the trail finally enters a horseshoe-shaped village. This is the village of Lampata, elevation 1135 metres. Slightly higher is Bahundanda, a picturesque village situated at 1310 metres in a saddle on a long ridge. The school here is nestled in a grove of bamboo; there are also a few shops and an inn. Bahundanda ('the hill of the Brahmins') is the northern-most Brahmin settlement in the valley.

Day 5

Bahundanda

Chyamje

The trail descends steeply past amphitheatre-shaped rice terraces, across a stream and across a large slide area to Khane, 1180 metres, high above the river. Continuing in and out of side canyons, the trail drops to a long suspension bridge at 1070 metres. There are shops and *bhattis* in the village of Syange on the west bank of the river. Beyond Syange the trail climbs high above the river on a somewhat terrifying trail carved into the near-vertical cliffs forested with rhododendron and pine and festooned with healthy crops of stinging nettles and marijuana. Because of the steep terrain, the villages in this region are small and infrequent. In 1950, when Tilman visited Manang, this portion of the trail did not exist. Instead, the route followed a series of wooden galleries tied to the face of the rock cliffs alongside the river. At 1070 metres is the village of Jagat, which is inhabited, as are most villages in this region, by people of Tibetan stock. There are two reasonably well-stocked shops in Jagat now; when I first travelled this route in 1977 the last shops were in Bahundanda. From Jagat the trail climbs through forests to Chyamje, 1400 metres. There is a place to camp just across the suspension bridge on the west side of the river at Sattale, 1430 metres elevation.

Day 6

Chyamje

⬇

Bagarchhap

The path is rough and rocky in this portion and passes under a huge boulder that forms a tunnel over the trail. There are lots of lizards in this region as well as more stinging nettles. Following the east bank of the Marsyandi the trail climbs gradually except where it is necessary to cross steep ridges. The valley suddenly opens into a large plateau. In this picturesque setting, at the foot of a large waterfall, is the village of Tal, 1675 metres elevation. The trek has now entered the Manang District. The village is the southernmost in Manang and is in a region called *Gyasumdo*, one of three distinct divisions within Manang. Gyasumdo was once highly dependent on trade with Tibet. Since the disruption of this trade in 1959, herding and agriculture have assumed greater importance. Corn, barley, wheat, buckwheat and potatoes are grown in this region, which has enough warm weather and rainfall to produce two crops a year. The people of Gyasumdo used to hunt musk deer, and the sale of musk was once an important source of income and trade. Although they are Buddhists, the people throughout Manang slaughter animals and hunt in the nearby hills, unlike other Buddhists who have strict taboos against the taking of life.

The trail crosses the broad flat valley that was once a lake (Tal means "lake"), through fields of corn, barley and potatoes, then climbs steeply on a stone staircase high above the river, finally cresting on a spur at 1860 metres. The trail then makes some significant ups and downs before descending to a suspension bridge at 1850 metres. The forests in this steep valley are oak, rhododendron, spruce and hemlock. The trail climbs from the bridge to an unpainted stone archway, or *kani*, that marks the entrance to Dharapani, elevation 1890 metres. All the old villages from here to Kagbeni have these entrance *chortens* at both ends of the village; the *kanis* get more elaborate and picturesque as the Tibetan influence becomes stronger in each successive village. From Dharapani the trail passes a school and climbs over a spur before descending to Bagarchhap. The villagers in this region recently made extensive trail renovations, and the route to Manang was graded and widened to allow horse and mule caravans to transport supplies to these remote villages — though you may not believe this as you walk the rough trails. Across the Marsyandi, just beyond Dharapani, is a long covered bridge. This leads to Thonje, an important village at the junction of the Marsyandi and the Dudh Khola. It is not necessary to go to Thonje enroute to Manang.

Bagarchhap, at 2160 metres, is the first village on the trek with typical Tibetan architecture — closely-spaced stone houses with flat roofs piled high with firewood. The village is in a transition zone between the dry upper Marsyandi and the wet regions of the lower valley, so there are also a large number of sloping wooden shingle roofs here as well. Higher in the Marsyandi and Kali Gandaki valleys where there is little rainfall, the shingle roofs disappear, the houses are packed even closer together, and all have flat roofs. There is a well-maintained whitewashed *gompa* in Bagarchhap that contains many Tibetan Buddhist paintings and statues. From here the trail travels west up the Manang valley. The high Himalayan peaks are to the south; there are occasional glimpses of Lamjung and Annapurna II (7937 metres) through the trees. To the east, Manaslu (8156 metres) provides a dramatic backdrop to the tree-filled valley.

Day 7

Bagarchhap

Chame

Much of the Manang valley is virgin forest of pine and fir, but construction of new houses and the constant requirements of firewood are forcing people to cut down many of these fine trees. On the trail to Manang village there is much evidence of this cutting: huge piles of firewood are stacked alongside the path and great timbers are being hauled to homesites.

The trail climbs along the new mule track through

forests to Danejung (also called Syal Khola 'the river of jackals', and also sometimes called Tibang Phedi — 'lower Tibang'), a new settlement (elevation 2290 metres) inhabited by people from Bagarchhap. The 'Gurung Furniture Factory' is located here. From this village a trail leads to Tibang, 2600 metres, and climbs over Namun Bhanjyang (5784 metres) enroute to Ghanpokhara in the south. This was the old route to Manang; it is now rarely used except by herders. For trekkers, the Namun Bhanjyang is a difficult route — especially with porters because there is no food or shelter for four days.

Climbing further, the trail continues to be rough and rocky. Suddenly a broad level stretch of trail appears. There is a fine wooden bridge near a waterfall and the trail is supported by outstanding stonework for about 100 metres, then it degenerates again to a rock-strewn path. Construction projects, including trail construction, are allocated to local contractors; it is interesting to note the obvious difference in workmanship amongst contractors, even in such a remote locale. Climbing further, the route reaches Tyahgja, also called Lattemarang, elevation 2360 metres. The Gurung people call Chhetris *marang* and the Nepali word for a mentally retarded person is

Bagarchhap
Village

latta; thus this village was where a retarded Chhetri once lived. There is a tiny hot spring near the river below the village.

The track stays near the river in forests of oak, climbing and descending amongst river-worn boulders, then it crosses a large stream before reaching Kuparkodo (2590 metres), situated in a meadow surrounded by huge pine and spruce trees. This is a police checkpost controlling access to the Nar-Phu valley to the north. That remote valley, populated by only 850 persons, is one of the three regions of Manang. It has a heritage and traditions different from that of other parts of the district. The region is closed to foreigners.

The next village is Chame (2685 metres), the administrative headquarters for the Manang District. Here there is a wireless station, school, several shops, a health post, post office and bank amongst the closely-spaced stone dwellings. The incongruity of a shotgun-toting guard in front of the bank is almost worth a picture. Across the river there are two small hot springs; they are not big enough for swimming, however. Throughout the day there are views of Lamjung Himal (6986 metres), Annapurna II (7937 metres) and Annapurna IV (7525 metres).

Day 8

Chame

Pisang

From Chame the trail crosses a side stream, and then the Marsyandi itself on a cantilevered wooden bridge, passes by a few houses on the north side of the river, and proceeds through fields of barley to Talung (2775 metres). After passing a huge new apple orchard surrounded by a high wooden fence, the trail descends to a bridge at 2840 metres. The village just above this bridge, Brathang, used to be a *Khampa* settlement, although it is now largely abandoned. The *Khampas* had installed a gate on the bridge, thus controlling the traffic up and down the Manang valley; you can still see the remnants of the gate on the bridge. In Brathang, there is a small carved stone that is a memorial to a Japanese climber who died in an avalanche while trekking across the Thorong La — a grisly reminder to wait several days after any heavy snowstorm before attempting the pass.

The valley is steep and narrow here and the trail is in deep forests. The trail crosses the river on an extremely long cantilevered bridge at 2910 metres, then climbs steeply on the river's north bank to another bridge at 3040 metres. Here there is the first view of the dramatic

Paungda Danda rock face, a tremendous curved slab of rock rising more than 1500 metres from the river. Continuing, climbing over a ridge, the trail continues the steep ascent to the upper Marsyandi valley. The lower portion of Pisang, a cluster of houses near the bridge, is at an elevation of 3200 metres. Note the wooden canals for water to power the two mills in this village. The main village of Pisang (3300 metres) is across the bridge and uphill. There are excellent camping places in the forest on the south bank of the river. This is a better choice than camping inside Pisang, where the only suitable spots for pitching tents are the rooftops of houses.

Day 9

Pisang

↓

Manang

Manang Valley &
Tukche Peak

The trek is now in the region known as *Nyesyang*, the upper portion of the Manang district, comprising about 5000 inhabitants in six major villages. This region is much drier than the Gyasumdo region down the valley. There is only a small amount of rainfall here during monsoon because the Annapurna range to the south alters the climate significantly from that of the rest of Nepal, south of the Himalaya, so most of Nyesyang is quite arid. The people of Nyesyang raise wheat, barley, buckwheat, potatoes and beans, but the cold, dry climate limits them to a single crop annually. They keep herds of yaks, goats, cows and horses. Horses are an important means of trans-

portation in the relatively flat upper portion of Manang valley and are often used as pack animals and by riders as high as 5416 metres, over the Thorong La between Manang and Jomsom.

An interesting situation exists in Nyesyang as a result of special trading privileges the people enjoy through a decree of King Rana Bahadur Shah in the year 1784. These facilities continue today and include passports and import and export concessions not available to the general population of Nepal. Beginning long ago with the export of live dogs, goat and sheep skins, yak tails, herbs, and musk, the trade has now expanded into the large scale import of transistor radios, watches, silk, clothing, gems and other high-value items in exchange for gold, silver, turquoise and other resources available in Manang. The

Bryagu village & Gompa

trade-network of the Manang people extends throughout south-east Asia and as far away as Korea; it is not uncommon to see large groups of Manang people jetting to Bangkok, Singapore and Hong Kong. Many people in Nyesyang villages speak fluent English and dress in trendy western clothing purchased during overseas trading excursions, presenting an incongruous picture as they herd yaks and plow the fields of these remote villages. This exposure also makes them shrewd and eager businessmen, so the traders and shops of Manang are all expensive. There are few bargains to be had here.

A short distance beyond Pisang the trail climbs a steep ridge that extends across the valley. At the top of this spur is an excellent view of Manang valley with Tilicho Peak (7132 metres) at its head. After a short descent from the ridge, the broad forested valley floor is reached at an elevation of 3350 metres. Most of this valley is grazing land for sheep, goats, horses and yaks. Across the river, high on the opposite bank, is the village of Ghyaru. It is possible to take an alternate route from upper Pisang and stay on the north bank of the river, passing through Ghyaru and rejoining the main trail at Mungji. A side trip may be made to the new monastery of Ser Gompa that is located on a plateau high above the river on the north side.

The southern trail avoids all this climbing and follows the valley past the new airstrip of Hongde, elevation 3325 metres. There is a police checkpost here, the last in the valley; a few tea shops and hotels have grown up around the airport. The infrequent flights to Manang are usually charter flights arranged by rich Manangis enroute to and from trading excursions, so there is almost no chance of obtaining a seat either to or from Kathmandu. A half hour beyond the airport there is a huge valley with Annapurna III and IV at the head. Just south of the trail, in this spectacular setting, is the building that houses the mountaineering school funded by the Yugoslav Mountaineering Federation, and operated since 1980 by Nepal Mountaineering Association in cooperation with UIAA, the Union of International Alpine Associations. There is a 6-week course offered to climbers from Nepal and neighbouring countries during August each year.

The trail crosses the Marsyandi again near Mungji (3360 metres), then traverses to Bryagu, 3475 metres. The largest part of this picturesque village of about 200 houses is hidden behind a large rock outcropping. The houses are stacked one atop another, each with an open veranda formed by a neighbour's rooftop. The *gompa* perched on a high crag overlooking the village is the largest in the district and has an outstanding display of statues, *thankas* (ornate Tibetan paintings) and manuscripts estimated to be 400 to 500 years old. The *kanis* over the trail that mark the entrance and exit from Bryagu are particularly impressive. There is a good place to camp in the meadow below the village.

The country is now very arid, dominated by wierd cliffs of yellow rock eroded into dramatic pillars alongside the trail and by the towering heights of the Himalaya across the valley to the south. It is only a short walk past *mani* walls, across a stream where several mills are operating, to the plateau upon which Manang village is built at 3535 metres elevation.

Day 10

Manang

The day must be spent in Manang village and the vicinity to acclimatise for the higher elevations to be encountered towards Thorong La. There are many opportunities for interesting day excursions from Manang. It is possible to climb the ridge to the north of the village for excellent views of Annapurna IV, Annapurna II, and Glacier Dome (7193 metres), or to descend from the village to the glacial lake at the foot of the huge icefall descending from the northern slopes of Gangapurna (7454 metres). It is interesting to walk to the village of Khangsar, the last village in the valley enroute to Tilicho Lake. There are splendid

Manang Village & Annapurna II

views of the 'Great Barrier', the high ridge between Roc Noir and Nilgiri North, from Khangsar. Another

choice would be a walk to visit the Bhojo Gompa, the red edifice perced on the ridge between Bryagu and Manang. This is the most active monastery in the region.

Before Manang was opened to trekkers in 1977, the region saw few outsiders. The only traders in the region were the people of Manang themselves, and the population was generally intolerant of outsiders. Therefore,

Archery Contest in Manang village

there was little need of inns, shops and other facilities here. In 1950, Maurice Herzog came to Manang village in a futile search for food for his party, only to return nearly starving to his camp at Tilicho Lake. With the advent of tourism, however, there are grand plans for inns and even luxury hotels in Manang, and tourists — particularly those with lots of rupees — are warmly welcomed by the people of Manang. The resourceful Manangbhot people have been quick to adapt to this new source of income, selling semi-precious stones (from Tibet, they claim, but more likely from Bangkok), foodstuffs, Tibetan jewellery and other items of interest to tourists. An alternative to a day hike is a bargaining session with these skillful traders.

The village itself is a compact collection of 500 flat-roofed houses; the entrances are reached from narrow alleyways by ascending a steep log notched with steps. The setting of the village is most dramatic, with the summits of the Annapurnas and Gangapurna less than eight kilometres away, and a huge icefall rumbling and crashing on the flanks of the peaks.

Day 11

Manang

Phedi

The trek now begins the 1980 metre ascent to Thorong La. From Manang village the trail crosses a stream, climbs to Tengi, 120 metres above Manang, then continues to climb out of the Marsyandi valley, turning north-west up the valley of the Jarsang Khola. The trail follows this valley north, passing a few herders' huts as it steadily gains elevation. The large trees have been left below, and the vegetation consists of scrub juniper and alpine grasses.

The trail passes near the small village of Gunsang, a cluster of flat mud roofs just below the trail at 3960 metres, then through meadows where horses and yaks may usually be seen grazing. After crossing a large stream that flows from Chulu Peak and Gundang, the trail passes an ancient mani wall in a pleasant meadow at 4000 metres. Villagers from Manang collect firewood from the slopes above. An hour further on is a single two-storey house, now rapidly falling apart — the stone walls are falling down and the biscuit-tin roof is both rusting and blowing away — at 4250 metres. This is the next-to-last shelter before the pass and is a good spot for lunch. There is a description of the Manang trek that refers to the first, second and third 'base camps'. As far as I can determine this ramshackle building, called Leder, is the 'first base camp'. The second is apparently Phedi (where there is no shelter) and the 'third base camp' is the dilapitated *dharmasala* at 4510 metres.

From Leder the trail continues to climb along the east bank of the Jarsang Khola, then descends and crosses the river on a new covered bridge at 4310 metres. After a short ascent on the new trail built in connection with the bridge, the route follows a narrow trail along an unstable scree slope high above the river, then descends to Phedi, a meadow surrounded by near-vertical cliffs at 4420 metres. This is the best campsite on this side of the pass, although there is a small hut (with an erratic water supply) 100 metres above, and another small flat spot about an hour beyond that. Local traders ride horses from Manang to

Muktinath in a single day, but the great elevation gain, the need for acclimatisation, and the heavy loads carried by the porters all make it imperative to take at least two days for the trip on foot.

Day 12

Phedi

⬇

Muktinath

Phedi, which means 'bottom', is a common Nepali name for any settlement at the foot of a long climb. Phedi is a summer pasture used by the people of Manang, but there is no shelter here. In 1980 a *dharmasala* was built on a shelf about 100 metres above Phedi, but by 1981 the metal roof had blown off, the wooden door frames had been burned by firewood, and the toilets had become repulsive. Such, apparently, is the future of unattended public buildings in the hills of Nepal. I have heard stories of several hundred trekkers attempting to live in this building while waiting for the weather to clear. A camp at Phedi, using a tent, seems the only sensible way to approach the Thorong La.

The trail becomes steep immediately after leaving the camp, switchbacking up moraines and following rocky ridges as it ascends to the pass. This trail has been used for hundreds of years by local people travelling on horseback and bringing huge herds of sheep and yaks in and out of

Thorong La Pass
to Muktinah
from Manang

Manang. Thus the trail, while often steep, is well defined and easy to follow. The only complications to the crossing are the high elevation and the possibility of snow. When the pass is blocked by snow, usually in late December and January, the crossing becomes difficult — often impossible. It then becomes necessary to retreat back to Dumre or wait until the snow has consolidated and local people have forged a trail. The only shelter between here and Muktinath is a tiny hotel at 4100 metres, far down the other side of the pass. An overnight stop in the snow, unless well planned in advance, can be dangerous — especially for the porters.

The trail climbs and climbs, traversing in and out of many canyons formed by interminable moraines. It is a reasonably good trail unless there is snow, in which case the route may traverse scree slopes or ascend steep snow. It is only about four hours from Phedi to the pass, but the many false summits make the climb seem to go on forever. The pass, with its traditional *chorten*, prayer flags and stone cairn built by travellers, is reached at 5416 metres. The views from the trail and from the pass itself are outstanding high Himalayan scenes: the entire Great Divide with the Annapurnas and Gangapurna to the south, the barren Kali Gandaki valley far below to the west, the rock peak of Thorungtse (6482 metres) to the north and a heavily glaciated peak (6484 metres) to the south. Well-acclimatised, technically proficient and well-equipped trekkers have climbed high on this peak during a crossing of the pass.

The descent is steep and rough on the knees — a loss of more than 1600 metres in less than three hours. The descent usually begins in snow, which soon gives way to switchbacks down another series of moraines. During the descent there are excellent views of Dhaulagiri (8167 metres) standing alone in the distance across the valley. Eventually the moraines yield to grassy slopes and the final descent to Muktinath is a pleasant walk along the upper part of the Jhong Khola valley. In 1981 there was a tea shop at 4100 metres elevation where the grassy slopes begin, though I doubt that it will have enough business in this remote location to last very long. It is also possible to camp here if the tiny stream nearby is flowing. The trail crosses meadows, drops into a ravine that is the start of the Jhong Khola, and enters Muktinath near the temple at 3800 metres. There is a police checkpost here.

Muktinath, is an important pilgrimage place for both Hindus and Buddhists. Situated in a grove of trees, the holy shrines at Muktinath include a Buddhist *gompa* and the pagoda style temple of Jiwala Mayi, containing an image of Vishnu. This temple is surrounded by a wall from which 108 waterspouts cast in the shape of cows' heads pour forth sacred water. Even more sacred is the water that issues from a rock inside an ancient temple situated a short distance below the pagoda. Inside this *gompa* behind a tattered curtain are small natural gas jets that produce a perpetual holy flame alongside a spring that is the source of the sacred water — an auspicious combination of earth, fire and water that is responsible for the religious importance of Muktinath. It is often possible to see Tibetan women with elaborate headdresses embedded with priceless turquoise stones engaged in devotions at these shrines.

Perhaps the best description of Muktinath is that on the signboard erected by the Ministry of Tourism at Jomsom:

> *Muktinath is beautiful, calm and quiet, great and mysterious for pilgrims, decorated with god and godess. Although you are kindly requested not to snap them.*

There is no camping near the temple, but 90 metres below the shrine area is a large rest house for pilgrims and a host of hotels, *bhattis* and camping places. This area, called Ranipowa, is often crowded with both pilgrims and foreign tourists. The Tibetan traders here are unrelenting in their efforts to convince you to buy their wares. One item that is unique in this region is black stones that, when broken open, reveal the fossilised remains of prehistoric ammonites, called saligram. They are overpriced, and you may be able to find some yourself between here and Jomsom, but you can always purchase them from these traders — and then curse yourself all the way back to Pokhara for carrying a rucksack full of rocks. Hindu pilgrims also purchase these ammonites because they represent the god Vishnu.

The most colourful pilgrims to Muktinath are the ascetic sadhus who will certainly be encountered many times between here and Pokhara. They travel in various stages of undress, smear themselves with ash and often carry a three-pronged spear or *trisul*. A rupee or two donation to these holy men is not out of place. They are Shaivite mystics on a pilgrimage that, more often than not, began in the heat of Southern India.

Day 13

Muktinath

Jomsom

The trail descends, heading west, high above the Jhong Khola to Jharkot, an impressive Tibetan village at 3500 metres. There is a hotel here offering 'solar heated' rooms. The village itself, with its picturesque *kani* is well worth exploring. There are some peach trees nearby; the seeds are ground up to make oil. The walk from Jharkot to the next village, Khingar (3200 metres), is a delightful walk amongst meadows, streams and fruit trees. The trail descends beyond Khingar through country that is arid and desert-like, in the same geographical and climatic zone as Tibet. The striking yellows of the bare hillsides contrast dramatically with the blue sky, white peaks, and splashes of green where streams allow cultivation. The views of Dhaulagiri and Nilgiri are tremendous. When the trail reaches a point overlooking the Kali Gandaki valley and the village of Kagbeni, it begins a steep descent to the valley floor, finally dropping to the single house at Chancha Lhunba, elevation 2730 metres.

Here in its upper reaches the Kali Gandaki is known as the Thak Khola, thus the name *Thakali* for those who live in this region. The trail is now in the world's deepest gorge, and the flow of air between the peaks of Annapurna and Dhaulagiri creates strong winds that howl up the valley. The breezes blow gently from the north during the early hours of the day, then shift to powerful gusts from the south throughout the late morning and afternoon. The trek from here to Tukche is a constant push against these winds after 11 am each day. The trail follows the broad river valley, sometimes above the river, but mostly along the riverbed as it passes beneath vertical rock cliffs. Jomsom, the administrative headquarters for the region, straddles the Kali Gandaki at an elevation of 2713 metres.

Unless you are in a tremendous rush, you should take a side trip to Kagbeni. About a half-hour after Khingar, on the desert-like plateau above the Kali Gandaki, a trail leads to the right. Descending past hundreds of small piles of rocks made by pilgrims to honour their departed ancestors, the trail reaches Kagbeni (2810 metres), a green oasis at the junction of the Jhong Khola and the Kali Gandaki. Kagbeni looks like a town out of the mediaeval past, with close-packed mud houses, dark alleys, imposing chortens and a large ochre-coloured *gompa* perched above. The people dress in typical Tibetan clothing — though the children have, even in this remote village, learned to beg, rather insistently, for candy. Kagbeni is the northernmost village that foreigners are allowed to visit in this valley; the police checkpost here prevents tourists from proceeding towards Lo Monthang, the walled city of Mustang. From Kagbeni a trail follows the Kali Gandaki south to rejoin the main trail from Muktinath at Chancha Lhunba.

Jomsom is in three separate parts — the section on the east bank of the Kali Gandaki is the main part of the town, with dwellings, two lodges, a bank and the post office; on the west bank are shops, local *bhattis*, the telegraph office and a bakery; to the south, near the airport, are large hotels, restaurants and the RNAC office. Just north of the airport is an army post and the inevitable police checkpost. It is important to obtain the endorsement of this station on a trekking permit, because it will be required by all police posts to the south. Flights to Jomsom are notoriously unreliable because the wind makes flying impossible after 10 or 11 am. Kathmandu is often fogbound until 10 am during the winter season, so flight departures are delayed. When the combination of unfavourable weather conditions at both Kathmandu and Jomsom makes flights impossible for several days, the crush of local people and trekkers waiting for planes in Jomsom can become intolerable. It is a far better choice to walk back to Pokhara than to rely on good weather allowing flights to maintain their schedule. With light porter loads and long days it is possible — though not particularly pleasant — to reach Pokhara in four days or less, if necessary.

Jomsom (or more correctly *Dzongsam* or 'new fort') is primarily an administrative and commercial centre inhabited by government officials and merchants engaged in the distribution of goods brought by plane and by caravans of ponies and mules. The more interesting villages of this region are the Thakali settlements of Tukche and Marpha. From Jomsom an easy side trip may be made to the *gompa* at Thini, about an hour from Jomsom on the east bank of the Kali Gandaki.

Day 14

Jomsom

The Kali Gandaki/Thak Khola valley has been a major trade route for centuries. Until 1959, salt collected from salt-lakes in Tibet was exchanged for rice and barley from the middle hills region of Nepal. Wool, livestock and butter were also traded for sugar, tea, spices, tobacco and

Kalopani

manufactured goods from India; but the salt-grain trade dominated the economy. This trade has diminished not only because of the political and economic changes in Tibet, but also because Indian salt is now available throughout Nepal at a price much cheaper than Tibetan salt. Indian salt, from the sea, contains iodine. Many people in Nepal once suffered from disfiguring goitres caused by the total absence of iodine in their diet. Indian aid programmes financially assisted the distribution of sea salt in a successful program to prevent goitres — but the Tibetan salt trade has suffered because of the artificially low prices of Indian salt.

The Thakali people of the Kali Gandaki valley had a monopoly on the salt trade of this region. They are now turning to agriculture, tourism and other forms of trade for their livelihood. They are traditionally excellent businessmen and hoteliers and have created hotels, inns and other businesses throughout Nepal. Their religion is a mixture of Buddhism, Hinduism and ancient shamanistic and animistic cults, but they claim to be more Hindu than Buddhist. There are few *mani* walls or religious monuments along the Kali Gandaki, although there are large *gompas* in Tukche and Kobang. Despite their trade with Tibet, the Thakalis are not of Tibetan ancestry; they are related to the Tamangs, Gurungs and Magars.

From Jomsom the trail follows the river valley southward through Marpha, a village huddled behind a ridge for protection from the wind and dust. This is a large Thakali village, at 2665 metres elevation, that exhibits the typical architecture of flat roofs and narrow, paved alleys and passageways. The very limited rainfall in this region makes these flat roofs practical; they also serve as a drying place for grains and vegetables. The excellent hotels and small restaurants of Marpha provide a fine introduction to the Thakali system of inns, which extends from here to Pokhara. Marpha is a clean and pleasant village; there is an extensive drainage system that flows under the flagstone-paved street. Be sure to sample the local apple *rakshi*. There are impressive *kanis* at both ends of Marpha.

Across the river from Marpha is the village of Chaira, a Tibetan settlement with a carpet factory. Traders from Chaira often sit along the trail near Marpha selling their wares. Pause a minute along this part of the trail and observe the scenery — high snow peaks, brown and yellow cliffs, splashes of bright green irrigated fields and flat-roofed mud houses clustered here and there. Except for the height of the peaks, this country is almost identical to central Afghanistan; it is eerie to find such similarity in a place so distant both physically and culturally.

As the trail proceeds south, it passes an agricultural project established in 1966 by His Majesty's Government to introduce new fruits and vegetables into the region. It may be possible to purchase fresh vegetables and almonds here; local apple cider and fruit preserves are available in Marpha and Tukche, and so, of course, is apple *rakshi.* Further south is Tukche, once the most important Thakali village. Tukche ('Tuk' — grain and 'che' — flat place), elevation 2590 metres, was the meeting place where traders coming from Tibet and the upper Thak Khola valley with salt and wool bartered with traders carrying grain from the south. In Tukche the Thakali inn system has reached its highest level of development — private rooms, menus, room service and indoor toilets. There is even one Tukche hotel that has a branch in Kathmandu. The economic effect of the loss of the grain trade has not been entirely offset by tourism however; many people have moved out of Tukche. A walk along the back streets of the village, particularly close to the river, will reveal many abandoned and crumbling buildings behind the prosperous facade of the main street.

From Tukche there are two trails to choose from. Crossing the Kali Gandaki to the east bank on a series of small temporary bridges, a long but easy trail traverses the gravel bars on the riverbed, climbs over a wooded ridge, then crosses the Kali Gandaki on a large bridge where the river races through a narrow cleft. The west bank trail passes through the architecturally interesting villages of Khobang, also called Kanti (2560 metres), and Larjung (2560 metres), built with narrow alleyways and tunnels connecting houses with enclosed courtyards, a complex and picturesque system providing protection from the winds of the Kali Gandaki valley. This trail also provides access to the *gompa* just above Khobang. The best mountain views — of Dhaulagiri and Nilgiri (7061 metres) — along the Kali Gandaki are to be had on this stretch of trail. A trail to the Dhaulagiri icefall begins just south of Khobang and climbs up the south bank of the Ghatte Khola. This route was explored by Herzog's expedition in 1950 and abandoned because it was too dangerous. In 1969, seven members of the American

Dhaulagiri expedition were killed by an avalanche in this area. A side trip may be made to a meadow near the foot of the icefall at an elevation of about 4000 metres. It's a long uphill climb up steep grassy slopes, so it is wise to make an additional camp at Tal, a lake at about 3100 metres elevation above the village of Naurkot, and make a day trip to the icefall area, returning to Tal for the night.

From Larjung, the west bank trail climbs to Sokung (2590 metres) through pine, juniper and cypress forests. It then descends to cross the Kali Gandaki on a new suspension bridge (where it joins the east bank trail), climbs over a wooded ridge and crosses back again to the west bank just before Kalopani. A dramatic change in the vegetation — from dry, arid desert-like country to pine and conifer forests — occurs during the day's journey.

Kalopani (2560 metres) is another town that is prospering from the influx of trekkers. There are hotels here and even an enclosed campground among the white-washed houses.

Day 15

Kalopani

Tatopani

From Kalopani it is a 20-minute walk to Lete (2470 metres), a spread out town with several clusters of buildings. From Lete a trail leads across the Kali Gandaki and, after several days of rough climbing in bamboo jungle, it reaches the base camp used by Herzog's expedition in 1950 for the first ascent of Annapurna, at that time the highest mountain ever climbed. The base camp may also be reached by an equally difficult trail up the Miristi Khola from near Dana. Maurice Herzog's book *Annapurna* provides essential background reading for this portion of the trek down the Kali Gandaki.

The trail descends from Lete village to the Lete Khola. There are a few *bhattis* here, near the long suspension bridge. This bridge, as many in Nepal, has a steep ascent and descent on the approach, so there is an alternate trail that drops to the stream, crosses it on a log, and rejoins the trail on the opposite side. The trail descends steeply through forests to Ghasa, which has two settlements, at about 2000 metres elevation. This is the last Thakali village on the trek and the southernmost limit of Lama Buddhism in the valley. Here the vegetation changes from mountain types, such as pine and birch, to sub-tropical trees and shrubs, including stinging nettles and cannabis. Below Ghasa the trail crosses a suspension bridge at 1935 metres and then enters the steepest and narrowest part of the canyon. The trail here is cut through solid rock, and there is a short section that is a three-sided tunnel. Across the river there is a view of the old trail, now fallen into disrepair, that has an even longer and more spectacular stretch of cliffhanging trail. The trail descends to the river-bank, then climbs over a ridge to Kopchepani where a signboard (facing south) proclaims 'welcome to Mustang'. This is the southern boundary of the Mustang district — you have not been magically transported to Lo Monthang. The trail descends to the river again and crosses it on a wooden bridge where the river rushes through a steep rocky canyon, then ascends to the hamlet of Rukse Chhara (1550 metres), situated at the foot of a high and spectac-ular waterfall that tumbles into a series of cataracts near the village.

Staying on the west bank of the river, the trail descends to Dana, three separate settlements with elabor-ately carved windows and balconies, at 1400 metres. Most of the people of Dana are Magars; there are also a few Brahmins and Thakalis. The large peak across the valley is Annapurna South (7273 metres); the large village high on the hillside across the valley is Nerchang. From Dana the trail descends, passing through a small tunnel carved out of the rocky hillside, then descends further to Tatopani at 1180 metres. There is a police checkpost at the north-ern end of the village.

Tatopani means 'hot water' in Nepali; the village gains its name from the hot springs that occur near the river below the village. There is a choice of several bathing spots, including a 'municipal bath' with a cement-lined pool on the banks of the river at the southern end of the village. Tatopani also has many well-provisioned hotels, restaurants and shops, including a shop boasting a kerosene-powered refrigerator full of cold beer, cokes and orange soda. Many tourists making only a short trek come here from Pokhara and spend their time relaxing in the hot springs and enjoying the hospitality of this small village. Note that the total descent on this day is more than 1200 metres from Kalopani, but it is hardly notice-able (going downhill) because the gradient is so gentle.

Day 16

Today's climb is a long one of more than 1500 metres. A short distance downstream from Tatopani, the trail crosses the river on a large suspension bridge. This bridge

Tatopani

⬇

Ghorapani

appeared on the cover of Toni Hagen's *Nepal, The King-dom of the Himalayas*. The trail goes downstream a short distance past a few houses, then descends and crosses the Ghar Khola on a new suspension bridge before the climb begins in earnest. It is a steep climb of about 500 metres to the top of a rocky spur where a single house stands like a sentinel. From the spur the trail descends a bit to Ghara, a Magar village at 1705 metres. The going becomes easier as the trail becomes gentler, ascending gradually towards Sikha, another Magar village at 1980 metres. Sikha is large and prosperous with shops, a hotel, and a British Army training centre at its upper end. Above Sikha the trail crosses a huge landslide. Observe the way the slick mica soil has slid off the underlying rock. Passing Chitre at 2390 metres, the trail ascends in forests towards Ghorap-ani pass. There are some sheep *goths* and some pastures along the way, but generally the ascent is through rhod-odendron forests. The pass, called Deorali (which means 'pass'), is at 2834 metres elevation. There are some hotels, shops and a camping place here. It is well worth staying at the pass to see the spectacular panorama of Dhaulagiri I, Tukche, Nilgiri, Annapurna I, Annapurna South, Hiunchuli and Glacier Dome. An early morning excursion may be made to Poon hill (3193 metres), about an hour's climb, where a tower offers an even better unobstructed view of the high Himalaya. The settlement of Ghorapani itself, where there are the best hotels, is about 10 minutes below the pass at 2775 metres, but there is no view from here.

Ghorapani means 'horse water', and is no doubt a welcome watering stop for teams of horses, mules and ponies that carry loads between Pokhara and Jomsom. These picturesque caravans, with melodious bells that can be heard from great distances, and wondrous plumes and head-dresses on the lead horses, are reminiscent of ancient Tibet. Herded by Tibetan men who shout up and down the trail, they lend a unique touch to the Jomsom trek. The ponies also grind the trail into dust and sloppy mud with their tiny sharp hooves and frighten trekkers into jumping into the bushes as they careen downhill, but the colourful photographs and harmonious tinkle of bells almost make it worth the trouble.

Day 17

From Ghorapani the trail begins the long drop to the Modi Khola valley. The day begins with a steep descent

Ghorapani

Birethanti

through magnificent rhododendron forests, alongside a small sparkling clear stream, to the hamlet of Nayathanti at 2460 metres and Bahunthanti at 2250 metres. Continuing through forests, then through pastures and cultivated fields, the trail enters the large Magar village of Ulleri, 2070 metres. It continues its steep descent from Ulleri to the Bhurungdi Khola, which it crosses on a series of two bridges at 1580 metres. The trail then becomes more gentle, a welcome relief on the knees after the long descent from Ghorapani, and passes through the villages of Tirkhedunga at 1525 metres and Hille, 30 metres below. Both these villages, perched on the side of the canyon, have small hotels and restaurants, the better ones being in Tirkhedunga. The trail follows the Bhurungdi Khola valley, crossing the river to avoid a steep cliff, then recrosses it to continue down the north bank beside waterfalls and bamboo forests to the large village of Birethanti, situated on the banks of the Modi Khola at 1065 metres. This is a large and prosperous town with a winding street paved with large stones, and many well stocked shops, hotels and even sidewalk cafes at the far end of the village. A trail up the Modi Khola to Ghandrung begins at Birethanti just behind the last house of the village.

Day 18

Birethanti

Naudanda

The trail crosses the Modi Khola on a suspension bridge and, after passing a few houses alongside the river, begins a steep switchbacking ascent up a dusty trail to Chandrakot, perched on the end of a ridge at an elevation of 1550 metres. The views of Annapurna South and Macchapuchhare, the 'fish tail' mountain, are excellent from this point — except that Machhapuchhare looks more like the Matterhorn than a fish tail from this angle. You must go into the Annapurna Sanctuary, several days to the north, to see the mountain in its proper perspective — but that's another trek.

Following the ridge to Lumle at 1585 metres, the trail suddenly ascends a set of wide stone stairs. This is part of the British Gurkha Repatriation Programme in action, an experimental farm that introduces new vegetables into Nepal and trains retired Gurkha troops in the proper management and operation of farms. The largest part of this project is far above the trail on the hillside. It may be reached by a trail from Khare.

Climbing again, the trail crosses a ridge crest at Khare, a large village strung out along the trail at 1710 metres, then enters the Yamdi Khola valley and begins the final descent of the journey. Still following the ridge, the trail crosses a small pass and descends past a large school, a new hotel and several scattered houses to Naudanda (1430 metres), a large village with a police checkpost, school and several hotels varying from tiny *bhattis* to well developed, western-style hotels. Campers should consider the school yard or the ridge behind the village. The views of the entire Annapurna range in the morning make a night stop in Naudanda worth the sleepless night caused by barking dogs near a camp or a noisy hotel room in the middle of the village. To the south, there are excellent views of Phewa Tal (lake) and the 'city lights' of Pokhara.

Day 19

Naudanda

Pokhara

It's a quick zip down the excellent broad trail to the foot of the Yamdi Khola valley (or your first grind up a steep hill in the heat if you're reading this backwards). Two tea shops greet you in Phedi, situated at the foot of the hill where the flat valley begins at 1130 metres elevation. Crossing the river, the trail traverses rice fields, sometimes on good trails, but sometimes precariously across the tops of the dikes that provide water for the thirsty rice. The trail is particularly complex during rice growing season — early fall and late spring. From Suiket at 1125 metres you can cross straight across the fields (fine in winter), but in rice season, you should take a more circuitous route and follow a small canal near the north side of the valley along a trail that is usually drier. There is a rudimentary road as far as Phedi and two Russian-built jeeps ply the route from here to Pokhara several times a day. The fare is 10 rupees, and it's standing room only as the jeep lurches across bridges that don't exist and wallows in and out of mudholes. The service is unreliable, but if you are lucky enough to catch a ride, you can save some walking — although you did come here to walk, so a rough ride doesn't really serve much purpose.

Continuing through the pleasant village of Hyangja at 1070 metres, the trail begins to show signs of entering an industrially developed region. As the trail criss-crosses irrigation canals on wide stone slabs under huge shading trees, power lines slyly appear and the children are a little more persistent in their demands for candy, pens and money. Hyangja is a popular destination for those living in the fancy hotels in Pokhara who walk a few km out of town to get 'the feel of a trek'. Beyond Hyangja is the

Tibetan Camp, where a small hotel offers the last cup of tea on the trek. There is a carpet factory and a monastery here; a large retinue of Tibetan traders sell their wares alongside the trail. After crossing the Yamdi Khola, the road is suitable for buses and taxis. The paved road begins a few hundred meters beyond, near the Shining Hospital and a high school. Here at 1060 metres, it is possible to hire a taxi to the airport or bus stop in Pokhara, about three km distant, but it is more fun to walk through the long strung-out bazaar of Pokhara. Though the paved road is hard on feet accustomed to trails, it is all downhill.

Accommodation in Pokhara includes the fashionable and peaceful *Fish Tail Lodge* located on the lake. The western style *New Hotel Crystal*, the *Mount Annapurna Hotel* and the Tibetan owned *Himalayan Hotel*, where you have a choice of setting up your own tent or using their simple bungalows (and eating their good food), are situated across from the airport. You can also find excellent accommodation among the small hotels along the shore of Phewa Tal, or camp in the dirty and overcrowded campsite near the lake at about 900 metres elevation.

The return to Kathmandu may be made by bus or plane the following morning.

ANNAPURNA SANCTUARY

This section details the route to Annapurna Sanctuary, the site of the Annapurna South Face Base Camp. Though it is not a difficult trek, the route can become impassable because of snow and avalanches in winter. It is the only major trekking route in Nepal that has significant avalanche danger and it is imperative to inquire locally whether the trail is safe. Trekkers have died, and groups have been stranded in the Sanctuary for days, because of avalanches. The route provides an interesting variety of terrain, from lowland villages where rice is grown to outstanding high mountain views. The trek from Pokhara to Annapurna Base Camp and back may be made in as few as 10 or 11 days, but it is best to allow two weeks for this trek to fully appreciate the high altitude scenery. A diversion from Ghandrung to Ghorapani on the return route provides a view of Dhaulagiri from Poon Hill.

Day 1

Pokhara

Dhampus

From Pokhara there are several choices of routes to Ghandrung. The first is to follow the trail towards Jomsom through Naudanda to Chandrakot, then turn north up the Modi Khola Valley, descending and crossing the river on a small wooden bridge near the settlement of Sholebhati, then climbing towards Ghandrung. This route takes (by definition) three days to Ghandrung.

The second option descends from Chandrakot to Birethanti, then proceeds up the west bank of the Modi Khola all the way to Ghandrung. There is little to recommend this route over the first option, though it may be a good choice for a return route, as it offers the first cold beer (at Birethanti) sooner than the other options.

The third option, which is described here, requires two days to Ghandrung and is the most direct, though it involves a little more climbing than the other two choices. From Pokhara the trail begins near the Shining Hospital at the end of the paved road. See the last day of the Manang to Jomsom trek description for details of this portion. Passing by the Tibetan Camp and Hyangja, the trail leaves the Jomsom route at Suikhet. Turning north, the trail climbs the ridge above the Yamdi Khola valley, reaching the village of Astam, 1400 metres, at the top of the ridge. Following the ridge west, the trail passes by Hyengjakot and Dihal to Dhampus at 1800 metres.

Day 2

Dhampus

Ghandrung

From Dhampus the trail climbs continually to a pass at 2160 metres, then descends to Tolka, and a bit further to Midi. Here there are two *bhattis* and the first view of Annapurna South and the village of Ghandrung. The trail then contours to Landrung, 1650 metres, a large Gurung village situated above the Modi Khola. Along the trail it is likely that you will encounter people collecting money for schools. They will produce a ledger book showing the donations of other trekkers and enter your contribution into their records. They are legitimate, but it is an adult version of the creative begging that tourists have encouraged. From Landrung the trail descends steeply to the river, crossing it at an elevation of 1370 metres on an exciting log bridge. This is a temporary structure that replaced a sturdy bridge that was washed away during the 1980 monsoon. The trail then ascends steeply through cultivated fields, past a few scattered houses, on a seemingly endless set of stone stairs to Ghandrung, a huge Gurung village, at 1950 metres. This village is the second largest Gurung village in Nepal (the largest is Siklis), and is a confusing cluster of closely-spaced slate-roofed houses with neatly terraced fields situated both above and below the village. It is wonderfully easy to get lost in the maze of narrow alleyways while trying to get through the village. Fortunately, hotels and a camping spot (the village schoolhouse) are both located at the south end of the village, so they are easy to find on arrival. There are also *bhattis* and hotels of varying standard throughout the village. The people of this village are particularly friendly to foreigners, and the village headman, an ex-Gurkha who speaks good English, can often arrange for trekkers to witness a traditional Nepali or Gurung dance staged by the village children. He is such a successful impresario, and the demand from trekkers is so great, that he now charges Rs 200 or 250 to arrange a performance. The views of Annapurna South from Ghandrung are outstanding and Machhapuchhare, seen from here in its fish tail aspect, peeps over a forested ridge.

Day 3

Ghandrung

Chhomro

After winding its way through the village, the trail climbs towards a small creek, crosses it, and begins a climb among some huge rocks to a pass north-west of the village. It crosses the pass (2220 metres), where a few houses and a tea shop offer refreshment, but more often amusement, as the woman "bartender" here tells dirty jokes to passing porters. From the ridge, the trail descends steeply to some stone houses beside the Khumnu Khola, crosses the stream at 1770 metres, then climbs to the settlement of Khumnu on the north side of the valley. Climbing steeply, the trail regains the elevation lost from Ghandrung, then contours eastward out towards the Modi Khola, finally reaching a point about level with, and just north of, Ghandrung. Here the trail turns north up the Modi Khola valley and descends through forests to Chhomro at 1950 metres. This is the highest permanent Gurung settlement in the valley, but herders take sheep and goats to high pastures in the valley during the summer months. There is a good view up the canyon to the north-west of Annapurna South, which seems to tower above the village, and there are good views of Macchapuchhare ("machha — fish and "puchhare" — tail) across the valley. It is from this point and northwards that the reason for the name of this peak becomes apparent. Machhapuchhare was climbed to within 50 metres of its summit in 1957 by Wilfred Noyce and David Cox on one of the early expeditions in Nepal. The mountain is not now open to climbers, but a lower outlier to the south, Mardi Peak, elevation 5586 metres, is open to trekking parties.

Day 4

Leaving Chhomro, the trail descends and crosses the Chhomro Khola, then climbs out of the side valley in

Chhomro

Kuldi

which Chhomro is situated. Climbing high above the Modi Khola on its west bank, the trail passes through forests of rhododendron, oak and hemlock to a British sheep breeding project at Kuldi (2380 metres). A small stone rest house offers some shelter, or a camp may be made beyond in the bamboo forests. There is only one small camping place between here and Hinko, so it is best to make a short day today and make the long haul to Hinko the following day. It is a very tiring day, and impossible with porters, to try to reach Hinko in a single day from Chhomro. The bamboo forests beyond Kuldi are dense, though the trees are hacked down by the hundreds to make *dokos*, the woven baskets carried by porters, and mats for floors and roofs. In winter it is common to encounter snow anywhere from this point on.

Day 5

Kuldi

Hinko

The trail climbs steeply through bamboo forests, then through rhododendron and hemlock up the side of the canyon, occasionally dropping slightly to cross tributary streams, but generally climbing continuously. When there is snow, this stretch of trail is particularly difficult, because the bamboo lying hidden on the trail beneath the snow provides an excellent start to a slide downhill. At Doban, about two hours beyond Kuldi, there is a small bamboo hotel in a setting reminiscent of a Japanese watercolour painting. Hinko, at 3020 metres, is often called 'Hinko Cave' because a huge overhanging rock provides some protection above the only spot flat enough for camping on this side of the valley. There is no wood at Hinko or beyond, so fuel, whether wood, kerosene or gas, must be carried from below for the entire time that it is planned to stay in this region.

Day 6

Hinko

Annapurna Sanctuary

The trail crosses a ravine just beyond Hinko, then climbs through large boulders as the valley widens and becomes less steep. The "gates" to the sanctuary may be seen ahead, and they are soon passed at about 3570 metres. There are places to camp here, but it can be dangerous in winter and even in spring due to avalanches. Avalanches from Hiunchuli and Annapurna South, peaks which are above but unseen from this point, can come crashing into the valley with unbelievable speed and frequency. More than one party has been forced to retreat from the approach to the sanctuary because of deep snows and continual avalanches.

As the trail continues into the sanctuary, the valley widens and reaches a small stone hut at 4050 metres, built by the British sheep breeding project. Camp may be made near the hut or at any number of other sites in the area. There is a *bhatti* that sometimes operates at the Machhapuchhare Base Camp; it may or may not be open, depending on whether the innkeeper — and his supplies — have been able to reach the hotel through the avalanche area. From a camp in the sanctuary, it is possible to visit the base camp for the 1970 Annapurna South Face expedition. This climb, led by Chris Bonnington, was the most spectacular ascent of an 8000 metre peak, up the near-vertical South Face of Annapurna that towers above the sanctuary to the north-west.

A number of peaks accessible from this area are open to trekking parties, Tent Peak (5500 metres) offers a commanding 360-degree view of the entire sanctuary, and its higher neighbour Fluted Peak (6390 metres) offers some mountaineering challenges not found on Tent Peak. Hiunchuli (6441 metres) to the south is also open to trekking parties that have made prior application to the Nepal Mountaineering Association and paid the appropriate fee. All three of these peaks are significant mountaineering challenges and require skill, equipment and advance planning.

Western Nepal

Western Nepal is often described as "unexplored", but westerners have a bad habit of assuming that what is unknown to them is unknown to everyone. Western Nepal is densely populated by both Hindus and Buddhists and the countryside is criss-crossed by trails in all directions. It is remote and unknown from the western viewpoint because of its relative inaccessibility and distance from Kathmandu. Regular flights to Jumla and several other airstrips in the west greatly reduce this remoteness but will add considerably to the cost and logistics nightmares. A flight from Kathmandu to Jumla now costs about $100 each way if you are a foreigner. The flight operates twice a week and is heavily booked by local people who pay a lower fare. You could consider flying to Nepalgang, a hot Terai town, and trying for space on one of the frequent shuttle flights to Jumla.

Another factor that discourages trekkers in western Nepal is that many of the culturally and scenically interesting regions are closed to foreigners.

Many of the trails in the west continue to the north side of the Himalayan ranges of Nampa, Saipal and Kanjiroba, making it possible for trekkers to zip up easy trails along river valleys into Tibet — a practice that both the Nepalese and Chinese would like to discourage. Dolpo and Phoksumdo Lake to the east of Jumla are closed. Humla to the north-west of Jumla is restricted, as is the Mugu Karnarli Valley north of Mugu village. The map on the following pages show the regions of western Nepal closed to foreigners as of mid-1981.

JUMLA to RARA LAKE

Rara Lake, elevation 2980 metres, is the focal point of Lake Rara National Park and is a major destination for treks in western Nepal. The trek to Rara Lake is the most interesting trek that is currently open to foreign trekkers in the Karnarli Zone of western Nepal. The route is very much "off the beaten track" and affords glimpses of cultures and scenery much different from that in the rest of Nepal. Rara Lake itself is a clear high-altitude lake ringed with pine, spruce and juniper forests and snow-capped Himalayan peaks. In the winter there is often snow on the ridges surrounding the lake.

The trek to Rara is somewhat strenuous and tends to be expensive because both food and labour are scarce and overpriced in this part of Nepal. For those seeking an opportunity to experience solitude in the wilderness and who are able to overcome the logistical complications of the region, this trek may be the best choice. I have never made this trek; the following information was provided by Terence Walker, who has spent a lot of time in the region.

Day 1

Jumla

Uthugaon

It is a two hour flight by Twin Otter aircraft from Kathmandu to Jumla. If you manage to obtain a seat you still may not be able to take all your baggage even if you pay for the excess, because of the weight limitations of the aircraft. The alternatives are to try to find a seat on a charter flight arranged by a trekking company or by the National Parks office. If you have arranged your trek through an agent, they will no doubt use a charter flight, so you will have none of these hassles.

Jumla, elevation 2434 metres, is a large bazaar situated above the Tila River. There is a chronic food shortage in this region — most of the Nepalganj-Jumla shuttle flights are cargo flights that carry rice and other staples — so it is usually difficult to purchase enough food for a trek from Jumla bazaar. It is better to carry all your food from Kathmandu — if you can get it onto the plane. There are a few porters available in Jumla, but they are expensive, do not speak English, and are not particularly eager to leave their homes. The people throughout the region are

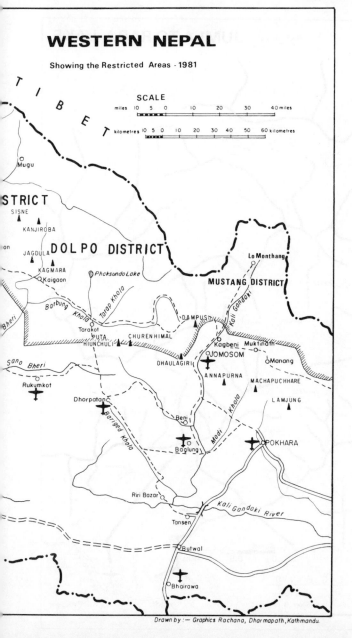

WESTERN NEPAL

Showing the Restricted Areas - 1981

SCALE

miles 10 5 0 10 20 30 40 miles

kilometres 10 5 0 10 20 30 40 50 60 kilometres

T I B E T

Mugu

...STRICT

SISNE

KANJIROBA

...on   JAGDULA   DOLPO DISTRICT

KAGMARA

Kaigaon   Phoksundo Lake

Lo Monthang

MUSTANG DISTRICT

Bheri   Barbung Khola   Tarap Khola

Tarakot   DAMPUS...

PUTA   CHURENHIMAL   Kagbeni Muktinath

HIUNCHULI   JOMOSOM

Sano Bheri   DHAULAGIRI   Manang

ANNAPURNA

Rukumkot   MACHAPUCHHARE

Dhorpatan   LAMJUNG

Barigad Khola   Beni   Modi Khola

Baglung   POKHARA

Riri Bazar   Kali Gandaki River

Tansen

Butwal

Bhairawa

Drawn by :— Graphics Rachana, Dharmapath, Kathmandu.

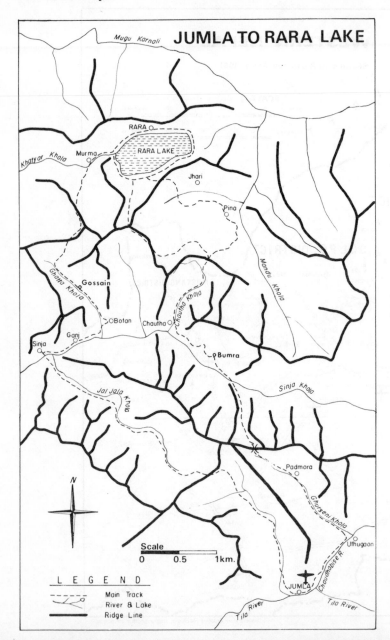

JUMLA TO RARA LAKE

L E G E N D

- - - - Main Track

River & Lake

━━━━ Ridge Line

Scale
0   0.5   1km.

Thakuris, a Chhetri caste that has the highest social, political and ritual status. Westerners, being considered low-caste by high-caste Hindus, are traditionally not welcome in Thakuri homes, so a trek in the Jumla region cannot be arranged as a "live off the land" trek.

From Jumla the trail to Rara follows the north bank of the Tila river, then turns north up the Chaudhabise River. The Jumla valley soon disappears behind a ridge as the trail follows the river, keeping fairly level, passing through fields and pine forests. This is a major trade route into Jumla bazaar and it is not uncommon to meet traders not only carrying goods, but also packing goods on horses and even goats. The first village to be encountered is Uthugaon, elevation 2531 metres; there is a good campsite near the school, across the river from the village.

Day 2

Uthugaon

Sinja Khola

From Uthugaon the trail begins an ascent up the Ghurseni Khola valley, beginning gently, but becoming steep as the climb continues. The canyon becomes very narrow with vertical cliffs on both sides as the trail ascends through a deep forest of pines, spruces and firs. At about 2900 metres elevation the large Chhetri town of Padmora, the last village in the valley, is reached. Above Padmora the logistics of the trek become more complex because of the limited water supply high on the ridge. Therefore, the day is a long one, continuing over the pass at 3400 metres and down to the Sinja Khola on the opposite side.

Near the pass is a small shepherd's camp where water may usually be found in the fall; this offers an alternate camp and makes a shorter day if water is available here. From the pass there are views of Patrasi Himal (6860 metres) and Jagdula Himal (5785 metres) to the east. The area near the pass is a rhododendron and birch forest where it is usually possible to spot the Impeyan or Danfay pheasant, the colourful national bird of Nepal. From the pass the descent is steep to the Sinja Khola, where a camp may be made at an elevation of 2700 metres, near a log bridge that spans the river.

Day 3

Sinja Khola

Chautha

The day begins with a casual walk along the river valley through forests and occasional fields of wheat and corn. The trail then crosses a stream and ascends very steeply for about 1½ hours to the village of Bumra, 2850 metres. From Bumra the trail meanders high above the river, then descends to a tributary stream, the Chautha Khola. Just across this stream is a small hotel in the tiny village of Chautha — but food and supplies may or may not be available here. In order to make the following day easier, it is best to continue an hour or more up the valley and make a camp in the forest alongside the stream.

Day 4

Chautha

⬇

Rara Lake

top of
second
pass
looking
up the
Mugu
Karnali

The climb up the Chautha Khola valley continues on through beautiful forests to a high meadow, then on to the Ghurchi Lagna pass at 3450 metres. From the pass there are spectacular views of the Mugu Karnarli river and snow peaks bordering on Tibet. There is a choice of trails from the pass. The easiest trail is the trade route that descends steeply from the pass to the village of Pina, 2400 metres. From Pina the trail contours above the village of Jhari, then climbs a 3000 metre high ridge above Rara Lake. It is a short descent to the lake where there is an abundance of excellent camping spots among the grassy meadows and juniper groves along the south shore of the lake.

The more scenic, but difficult, trail along the ridge begins from the Ghurchi Lagna pass, then traverses the ridge to the west. It climbs gradually through high meadows and forests, then becomes steeper as it heads towards the top of the ridge at an elevation of more than 4000 metres. From this ridge, Rara Lake appears like a giant crater with a high Himalayan backdrop. Continuing along the top of the ridge for 1½ hours, the trail finally reaches a large rock *chorten*, then drops towards Rara Lake through heavy pine and spruce forests until it reaches the grassy meadows on the shores of the lake. This is a difficult route and can be blocked by snow in the winter. The trail is not always obvious; a local guide is an asset on this route.

looking north-
east from the
drainage

Day 5

Rara Lake

Rara Lake, at 3062 metres elevation, is the largest lake in Nepal. It is almost 13 km around the lake, and a day devoted to making this circuit is well spent. Designated a National Park in 1975, the region offers a remoteness and wilderness experience unlike any other in Nepal. An entrance fee of Rs 60 is charged by the National Park office. There are a few park wardens' houses and the remnants of the now deserted village of Rara are on the north side of the lake, but otherwise it is an isolated region where birds, flowers and wildlife thrive. Among the large mammals in the region are Himalayan bear, Himalayan tahr, serow, goral, musk deer and red panda. The lake is also an important resting place for migrating waterfowl.

Day 6

Rara Lake

Gossain

It is possible to return to Jumla via the same route, but it is more interesting to make a circuit via a different trail. The first day from Rara Lake is long because, again, there are few water sources along the route. An early start is essential in order to reach Gossain in a single day. From the west end of Rara Lake the trail follows the Khatyar Khola south-west to the village of Murma. The trail crosses the river on a log bridge below the village, then climbs steeply to 3300 metres up the ridge at the south end of the lake. If the weather is clear, there is an excellent view of the western Himalaya from the top of this ridge. The trail stays high, then descends through forests to reach the Ghatta Khola and follows this stream towards Gossain at 3100 metres elevation. There are several excellent camping places along the stream both above and below Gossain.

Day 7

Gossain

Sinja

Today is a short walk (needed after yesterday's long day) down the Sinja Khola to the village of Sinja. Descending the Ghatta Khola past Botan, the trail turns west along the Sinja Khola, then follows the fertile valley through a very heavily populated region. This is a Brahmin and Chhetri area that was the capital of the Malla Kingdom in 1300 AD. The ruins of the old palace can be seen across the river from Sinja, 2400 metres elevation.

Day 8

Sinja

Jumla

It is possible to reach Jumla in a single day from Sinja, though there are camping places before Jumla that would allow a more leisurely two-day trip. From Sinja the trail goes back into uninhabited wilderness, meeting very few people. The deep forests along the way are very lush and abounding in wildlife. The trail climbs gradually, but continually, passing a large meadow en route to the pass at 3500 metres. The long descent from the pass to Jumla is through a forest of mystical-appearing birch trees draped

in Spanish moss.   There are many good campsites along
this stretch of trail if there is no rush to reach Jumla.

Other Destinations

As interesting, culturally enriching and historic as the major treks may be,
the possibility of visiting other regions should not be neglected. Although
there are restrictions involved with the issuance of trekking permits, and
some areas are still closed to foreigners, there are many places in Nepal
that are both fascinating and accessible. Many trekkers make the mistake
of varying their route by attempting a high pass (5500 to 6000 metres) only
to discover that they, their equipment, or other members of the party, are
totally unfit for the cold and high elevations. Often they will be forced to
turn back, severely altering their schedule, so that they fail to reach their
primary objectives. High passes should be attempted only after the major
goal of the trek has been achieved — usually on the return to Kathmandu.

The major trade routes are the shortest way to a particular destination
but if you will allow another few days it is possible to follow less direct, often parallel, routes through villages not even on the maps in areas less wes-
ternised than the primary trails. Agents who arrange treks are usually eager
to assist with such variants. The cost of the more unusual treks may be
slightly higher, but the opportunities and rewards will be greater.

There are a few other trekking destinations that are recommended and
promoted by agents. I have not described them here for several reasons.
Most importantly, I have not been to these regions and therefore have
no firsthand experience. The second reason is that they are either too
easy and not particularly interesting, as the Kathmandu-Pokhara route, or
they are too difficult for a first, or even a second trek, as the Tilicho Lake
or Makalu Base Camp route. The following data may be of interest in developing an understanding of these areas.

KATHMANDU-POKHARA
The trek from Kathmandu to Pokhara may be made as an easy nine or 10-
day trek from Trisuli Bazar to Begnas Tal, just outside of Pokhara. This is
the easiest trek in Nepal and has few uphill climbs of any significance. There
is an opportunity to visit Gorkha, to make side trips to Bara Pokhari, a high
altitude lake overlooking Manaslu, and to visit Siklis, the largest Gurung
village in Nepal. The views of the Himalaya are good on this trek, but the
route never actually gets into the high mountains.

ROLWALING
Rolwaling is the east-west valley below Gauri Shankar, just south of the Tibetan border. This region is isolated and interesting but most treks conclude

their visit to Rolwaling by crossing the 5755 metre Tesi Lapcha pass into Khumbu. I would suggest that any crossing of Tesi Lapcha be made from Khumbu into Rolwaling, not by visiting Rolwaling first. There are two reasons for this: well-equipped, willing porters are easier to get in Khumbu than in Rolwaling and in the event of altitude sickness there are better facilities for help if you make your retreat on the Khumbu side than if you make a retreat back to the isolated villages of Beding or Na in Rolwaling. A second way to visit this region would be to forgo Tesi Lapcha and go as far as Na, then retrace the route back to Kathmandu. Tesi Lapcha is particularly dangerous because of frequent rockfalls on its west side, and the icefall near the pass has changed in the past few years. The new route through the icefall is said to be technically difficult (requiring an axe and crampons) most of the time. Rolwaling is currently (1981) closed to trekkers.

MAKALU BASE CAMP

An outstanding trek in eastern Nepal may be made from either Dharan or Tumlingtar by walking north up the Arun River to Sedua and Num, then crossing 4110 metre Barun La into the upper Barun Khola valley for a close look at Makalu (8481 metres) and Chamlang (7319 metres). The route is not particularly difficult but it becomes a long trek because of the great dis-

tance up the Arun that must be covered. An even wilder trek may be put together by crossing Sherpani Col and West Col into the upper Hongu Basin. This trek has been attempted a few times by organised groups and has proved itself a most difficult and potentially dangerous trek. Better to travel from Lukla if you want to go into the upper Hongu Basin and the five lakes, Panch, Pokhari, situated there.

TILICHO LAKE

There is another pass south of Thorong La between Manang and Jomsom. From Manang, the trail goes on to the village of Khangsar, then becomes a goat trail scrambling over moraines to Tilicho Lake, situated at an elevation of 4120 metres, at the foot of 7132 metres high Tilicho Peak. Tilicho Lake is usually frozen (except when you decide to trust the ice and walk on it) and is depicted on Herzog's maps as the "great ice lake". From the lake, there are several alternative routes, including Meso Kanto pass at 5330 metres and another alternate pass a little further north. The trail is difficult and hard to find. One very experienced trekker described the trail as only a figment of someone's imagination — he claimed there was no trail at all. Thorong La is a good safe route between Manang and Jomsom; better to make a side trip to Tilicho Lake from Manang and not take all your equip-

Old Palace in
Gorkha

ment and porters on the Tilicho Lake trail. Sometimes there are army training exercises in the valley east of Jomsom and the route to Tilicho lake may be closed at this point. Inquire in Kathmandu and again in Manang before you make your plans. It might be possible to cross the pass and be turned back to Manang an hour before Jomsom.

JUGAL HIMAL

To the east of Kathmandu lies a chain of peaks called Jugal Himal, which includes Dorje Lakpa (6990 metres), Madiya (6800 metres) and Phurbi Chhyachu (6658 metres). From the south it is an easily-accessible region, although it requires a long uphill climb. From Dolalghat on the Kodari road there is a jeepable road to the large bazaar of Chautara (1410 metres). A trail from Chautara descends to the Balephi Khola, then follows a ridge to Bhairav Kund, a holy lake at 3500 metres elevation. A return may be made from here to Tatopani on the Kodari road, or a circuit may be made around the head of the Balephi Khola valley to Panch Pokhari, five lakes at an elevation of 3600 metres. From Panch Pokhari, trails lead to Tarke Gyang in Helambu, or back down the ridge to Panchkal on the Kodari road. This is a remote and unfrequented region, despite its proximity to Kathmandu.

Trekking in China

Trekking in China is administered and arranged by the Chinese Mountaineering Association under the same rules as those for mountaineering in China. The CMA makes all arrangements for a trek with the assistance of provincial mountaineering associations and local physical culture associations in remote villages near the mountains. The first few trekkers were allowed into China only in 1980 and the first groups were arranged in 1981. Because trekking is under the mountaineering rules, all treks currently must be near one of the peaks open for mountaineering. These peaks are:

Tibet:

Mt Qomolangma (Everest), 8848 metres

Mt Xixabangma (Shishapangma or Gosainthain), 8012 m

Xinjiang Province:

Mt Mustagata, 7546 metres

Mt Kongur, 7719 metres

Mt Kongur Tiubie, 7595 metres

Mt Bogda, 5445 metres

Sichuan Province:

Mt Gongga (Minyakonka), 7556 metres

Mt Siguniang, 6250 metres

Qinghai Province:

Mt Anyemaqen, 6282 metres

The regions open to trekkers span the country and include spectacular mountain scenery that varies from the plains of Tibet to the lush bamboo forests of Sichuan province and the open plains of Xinjiang. A trek in China offers a special opportunity to visit small communes in remote areas and to travel in places where few foreigners have ventured before. Tibet, because of its high altitude and inaccessibility, is still a difficult and potentially dangerous destination. The access to the other peaks is not as difficult, so treks in the other provinces of China are less expensive and are equally as interesting as a trek in Tibet.

Tourism and mountaineering is encouraged by China not only for the friendship that it develops between China and other countries, but also for the foreign exchange that it generates. The prices are high, though not unreasonably so, for staff, hotel accommodation, trekking arrangements and transport. All trekking must be arranged through a signed agreement with the CMA and all treks must be accompanied by a liaison officer and interpreter. It is these two factors that complicate the arrangements and drive the cost higher.

Almost always, the arrangements must be made in person in Beijing (Peking) by a representative of the trekking or mountaineering group. However, one may only travel to China at the invitation of a Chinese organisation — and that invitation is usually secured only through personal contact. The Chinese are very serious about developing friendship between individuals and countries, and are reluctant to make arrangements with anyone who they do not know personally. Thus, a trek or climb in China must be preceeded by a personal visit by one of the members of the trekking party. This becomes an additional expense of the trek that must be somehow divided amongst the trekkers.

An interpreter is a must — both according to the regulations and in fact — unless there is someone in the party that is fluent in Mandarin Chinese. Few officials and no village people speak any English; communication is impossible without an interpreter. A liaison officer is the CMA representative who takes responsibility for logistics, transport and personnel. The Chinese liaison officers who I have met are enthusiastic about their jobs and do quite well in expediting travel through remote country. A liaison officer in China is an important addition to any party heading for the mountains. Not only must the interpreter and liaison officer be paid, but they must be provided with accommodation and food — at the same rates that are charged for you — and with equipment, salary, travelling allowance and insurance. I was a bit shocked on my first visit to China to discover that we were paying for 4 people to stay in the hotel instead of only the 2 members of the trekking party. With much apology it was explained to me that this is how things work, and I suppose that it is reasonable way to ensure that these two people are always available if they are needed.

Distances are great in China and transportation is expensive. To reach any of the trekking areas, it is necessary to take a long domestic flight from Beijing and then drive several hundred kilometres in a chartered jeep, truck or bus at prices of $1 to as much as $5 a kilometre. Additionally, since the starting point for most treks is far from a city, it is necessary for the vehicles to wait at the roadhead during the trek — and a waiting fee is charged.

These factors make an individual trek in China an economic nightmare and a 'do it yourself' trek a total impossibility. The only sensible way to trek in China is to spread the expenses of the interpreter and liaison officer as well as the reconnaissance trip and the overhead of initial meetings with the CMA over as many people as possible. This then leads to the same 'complete arrangements' approach that I recommend for trekking in Nepal. In China, unlike Nepal, there is no other alternative. Many of the trekking agents listed in the appendix have China trekking programmes in addition to their Nepal treks. Prices are high because of the high initial cost of arrangements by the CMA and because the liaison officer, interpreter and trek leader are also charged at the same rate, so their expenses must be divided amongst the group members. In Tibet the prices become more than double those for treks in other parts of China because of the remoteness of this region. If you can find a way to afford prices of $170 to $250 per day plus airfare, a trek in China is an outstanding and worthwhile experience.

Part 4

Mountaineering in Nepal

Although this is a book about trekking, a short discussion on mountaineering in Nepal is appropriate. The first trekkers in Nepal were, of course, mountaineers who were either on their way to climb peaks, or were exploring routes up unclimbed peaks. There was furious mountaineering activity in Nepal from 1950 to the 1960s, with all the 8000 metre peaks being climbed.

By the early 1970s the emphasis had shifted to impossible feats like the south face of Annapurna and finally Everest South-West Face, both climbed by expeditions led by Chris Bonnington. The expeditions in the '60s and '70s were often well-equipped and sometimes lavish as governments, foundations, magazines, newspapers, film-makers, television producers and even private companies sponsored expeditions to higher and more spectacular peaks. Expeditions became big business and the climbers took the jobs with seriousness and dedication. It is not uncommon for trekkers to be refused admission into expedition base camps. The team members do not have time or energy to entertain tourists and there have also been incidents of trekkers pinching souvenirs from among the expensive and essential items that often lie around such camps.

In 1978 the Nepalese mountaineering regulations were changed in a manner that is consistent with current trends in mountaineering to allow small scale attempts on 18 peaks. No longer is it necessary to go through a long application process, to hire and equip a liaison officer, and to organise a huge assault on a major peak in order to try Himalayan mountaineering. The 18 peaks provide a great range of difficulty and are situated throughout Nepal. Any well qualified trekking group can attempt them.

There are three seasons for mountaineering in Nepal. The pre-monsoon season from April to early June was once the only season during which major peaks were attempted. In the '50s all the attempts were in the "lull before the storm" that occurs between the end of the winter winds and the beginning of the monsoon snow. The Swiss attempt on Mount Everest in 1952 was driven back by the terrific cold and high winds when they made an expedition in the fall season. It was not until 1973 that Everest was successfully climbed in the fall, though the fall, or post-monsoon, season of September and October is now a period of many successful expeditions. In 1979 the Ministry of Tourism established a season for winter mountaineering. It is bitterly cold at high elevations from November to February, but recent advances in equipment technology have allowed several teams to accomplish what was thought before to be impossible — a winter ascent of a Himalayan peak. Climbing in the monsoon, from June to August, is not practical.

Many trekking agents are organising expeditions to both large and small peaks in Nepal, and the ascent of a small peak (if a peak higher than any in North America can be presumed to be "small") is often included as an option to a trek. As regulations for climbing a small peak require an established liaison in Kathmandu (usually a trekking company), it is best to get in touch with a trekking agent in order to organise a climb in Nepal, rather than try to do the whole project on your own — though it is possible to organise a climb without any assistance if you have a good idea of what you need and where you are going. Before you consider climbing a "trekking peak", reread some books on Himalayan expeditions. The weather is often bad, and you can be forced to sit in your tent for days at a time. Usually a well-equipped base camp is necessary, and the ascent of a peak can require one or more high camps that must be established and stocked. Most peaks require a minimum of four days and it can take as much as three weeks for an ascent.

SMALL PEAKS

Climbing in Nepal is administered by two organisations. The Ministry of Tourism is responsible for major expeditions, and the Nepal Mountaineering Association issues permits for small peaks open to trekking groups. The type of climbing that would be of interest to most trekkers is encompassed by the regulations for small peaks. There is a minimum of formality, requiring only the payment of a fee and the preparation of a simple application. The rules require that the party be accompanied by a sardar who is registered with the Nepal Mountaineering Association, that the permission will be for an initial two week period (extendable another two weeks for an additional fee), that any Nepalese employed above base camp must be insured for Rs 75,000, and that all camps must be cleaned of trash at the conclusion of the climb. The fee is US$200 for peaks above 6100 metres and US$100 for peaks less than 6100 metres. The permit is valid for a period of one month and a group of up to ten persons. An extra US$5 per person is charged if the group exceeds ten climbers.

The peaks available to trekking groups under these regulations are:

Everest Region

Island Peak	6153 metres	20,188 feet	
Kwangde	6194 "	20,323 "	
Kusum Kangru	6369 "	20,897 "	
Lobouje East	6119 "	20,076 "	
Mehra Peak	5820 "	19,095 "	
Mera Peak	6431 "	21,100 "	
Pokhalde	5806 "	19,050 "	

Rowaling Region

Pharchamo	6282 "	20,611 "	
Ramdung	6021 "	19,755 "	

Mangang Region

Chulu East	6200	"	20,342	"
Chulu West	6630	"	21,753	"
Pisang	6091	"	19,985	"

Langtang Region

Ganga La Chuli	5846	"	19,180	"

Annapurna Region

Fluted Peak	6390	"	20,966	"
Hiunchuli	6337	"	20,792	"
Mardi Himal	5555	"	18,226	"
Tent Peak	5500	"	18,045	"

Ganesh Himal

Paldor Peak	5894	"	19,338	"

The peaks range from simple walk-ups like Mera Peak to reasonably difficult and dangerous peaks like Kusum Kangru. There is no comprehensive guide-book to these peaks, though a search of old Himalayan Journals and expedition books will turn up a lot of information.

MOUNTAINEERING EXPEDITIONS
The rules for mountaineering on major peaks require a minimum of six months advance application to the Ministry of Tourism, a liaison officer, a fee of as much as US$1000 depending on the elevation of the peak, and endorsement from the government or the national alpine club of the country organising the expedition. There are 87 peaks open for foreign expeditions and another 17 peaks open for joint Nepalese-foreign expeditions. Some peaks, such as Everest, are booked many years in advance, while others have very few expeditions. Further information is usually available through alpine clubs in your own country.

CLIMBS ON EVEREST
Mountaineering and trekking in Nepal has relied heavily on the progress and inspiration developed by various expeditions to Everest. Much of the attraction of Nepal in the early days resulted from the discovery that the highest peak in the world lay within the forbidden and isolated kingdom. Though it was named Mount Everest by the Survey of India in 1856 after Sir George Everest, retired Surveyor-General of India, the peak had been known by other names long before. The Nepalese call it Sagarmatha and the Sherpas call it Chomolungma. The Chinese now call it Qomolangma Feng. The history of attempts and successes on the mountain is one of the classics of mountaineering history.

1921 – British

The first expedition was a reconnaissance through Tibet from Darjeeling led by Lt Col C K Howard-Bury. They spent months mapping and exploring the Everest region and gave the first climbing school for Sherpas on the slopes leading to the North Col. Though it was not an actual attempt on the peak, they reached the North Col at a height of 7000 metres.

1922 – British

The first attempt on the mountain was led by Brig Gen C G Bruce. The expedition, as were all attempts until 1950, was made from the north after a long approach march across the plains of Tibet. The highest point reached was 8320 metres. Seven Sherpas were killed in an avalanche below the North Col.

1924 – British

Again Bruce led a team of British gentlemen in their tweed suits to Everest. They didn't have crampons and had a furious argument about whether the use of oxygen was "sporting". On this expedition George Leigh Mallory and Andrew Irvine climbed high on the mountain and never returned. Lt Col EF Norton reached 8565 metres without oxygen.

1933 – British

This expedition, under the leadership of Hugh Ruttledge reached a height of 8570 metres, just 275 metres short of the summit. Frank Smythe's book *Camp Six* is an excellent personal account of this expedition.

1934 – a solo attempt

Maurice Wilson flew alone in a small plane from England to India, then crossed Tibet to make a solo attempt on Everest. While usually dismissed as a crank, Wilson did accomplish a lot before he pushed himself too far and froze to death on the slopes below the North Col.

1935 – British

A name to become associated with Everest first came into prominence when Eric Shipton led a small expedition as far as the North Col.

1936 – British

Another British expedition led by Ruttledge only reached a point slightly above the North Col.

1938 – British

Another famous name associated with Everest came to the forefront when H W Tilman led a small expedition in which Eric Shipton reached almost 8300 metres.

1947 – a solo attempt

Earl Denman, a Canadian, disguised himself as a Tibetan monk, travelled to Everest and tried a solo attempt. He quit below the North Col and returned immediately to Darjeeling.

1950 – British

After the war, Tibet was closed, but Nepal had begun to open her borders. H W Tilman made a peripatetic trip all over Nepal, including a trek from Dharan to Namche Bazar. This was the first party of westerners to visit the Everest Region. They made the first "ascent" of Kala Pattar and walked to the foot of the Khumbu Icefall.

1951 — British
Eric Shipton led another reconnaissance, reached the Western Cwm at the top of the Khumbu Icefall, and proved that Everest could be climbed from the south.

1952 — Swiss
Leader Dr Wyss-Durant organised an effort in which Raymond Lambert and Tenzing Norgay reached a height of almost 8600 metres.

1952 — Swiss
Rushing to beat the British, the Swiss tried again in the fall of 1952 but cold and high winds drove them back from a point just above the South Col.

1953 — British success
The huge British expedition, led by John Hunt, succeeded in placing Edmund Hillary and Tenzing Norgay on the summit on 29 May 1953.

1956 — Swiss
Albert Eggler led an expedition that placed four climbers on the summit of Everest and also made the first ascent of Lhotse.

1960 — Indian
The first Indian expedition reached a height of 8625 metres but was forced to retreat because of bad weather.

1960 — Chinese
The first ascent from the north;

three members of this team reached the summit in the night.

1962 — Indian
The second Indian expedition also was unsuccessful, though they reached a height of 8700 metres.

1962 — an illegal attempt
Woodrow Wilson Sayre and three others obtained permission to climb Gyachung Kang, then crossed into Tibet and tried to climb Everest. They reached a point above the North Col before they returned.

1963 — American
The American Mount Everest Expedition, led by Normal Dyhrenfurth, was successful in placing six persons on the summit, including two by the unclimbed West Ridge.

1965 — Indian
Capt M S Kohli lead an Indian team that placed nine climbers on the summit of Everest.

1966-1968
Nepal was closed to mountaineers.

1969 — Japanese
The Japanese made a reconnaissance to look for a new route up the South Face of Everest.

1970 — Japanese
A 38-member Japanese team placed four climbers on the summit. This was the expedition that included the famous "ski descent" of Everest. Six Sherpas were killed in the Khumbu Icefall.

1971 — International
Norman Dhyrenfurth led an ambitious expedition with climbers from 13 nations attempting both the South-West Face and the West Ridge, finally retreating from a height of 8488 metres on the face route.

1971 — Argentine
An unsuccessful attempt led by H C Tolosa.

1972 - European
K M Herligkoffer led a team that attempted the South-West Face, reaching a height of 8300 metres.

1972 -- British South Face
An attempt on the South Face was led by Chris Bonnington.

1973 — Italian
The largest Everest expedition ever, under the leadership of Guido Monzino, placed eight climbers on the summit.

1973 — Japanese
Two members of a team led by Micheo Yuasa, reached the summit in the first successful ascent in the fall season. The ascent was via the traditional South Col route after the team made no progress on the South-West face.

1974 — Spanish
Financed by a Spanish battery company, the Spanish expedition was unsuccessful.

1974 — French
This expedition ended in disaster when an avalanche killed the leader and five sherpas.

1975 — Japanese
The Japanese Women's Everest Expedition was successful when Ms Junko Tabei and Sherpa Ang Tsering reached the summit.

1975 — Chinese
A few days after the Japanese success, a Chinese team placed nine persons, including a women, on the summit. The large survey tripod they erected is still on the top of Everest.

1975 — British South Face
Bonnington led, and Barclays Bank financed, an expedition that successfully climbed the difficult South-West Face of Everest.

1976 — British-Nepal Army
Two British members of a joint British-Nepal Army expedition reached the summit in the spring.

1976 — American
The American Bicentennial Everest Expedition, led by Phil Trimble, placed two members on the summit during the fall.

1977 -- New Zealand
A New Zealand expedition in the spring was stopped by bad weather and heavy snow.

1977 — South Korean
The fall attempt of the South Koreans, in which two climbers reached the summit, was the earliest fall success ever.

1978 — Austrian
In three separate teams, nine climbers reached the summit of Everest. Reinhold Messner and Peter Habler made the first ascent of the mountain without using oxygen.

1978 — German/French
Led by Dr Herrligkoffer and Pierre Mazeaud, this gigantic expedition placed 16 climbers on the summit via the South Col and made a live radio broadcast from the "roof of the world".

1979 — Yugoslav
Five climbers reached the summit via a new route — the West Ridge all the way from the Lho La. Ang Phu Sherpa fell and was killed during the descent.

1979 — Swabian
Another international group placed 13 climbers on the summit under the leadership of Gerhard Schmatz. Mrs Schmatz and Ray Genet died as a result of an overnight bivouac during the descent.

1980 — Polish winter expedition
The first winter ascent was made via the South Col after a long struggle. Two climbers reached the summit.

1980 — Polish
Another Polish expedition in the spring, with many of the same climbers as the winter expedition, pioneered a new route via the South Pillar, to the right of the British South Face route. The summit was reached by two climbers.

1980 — Basque
For the first time, two teams were allowed on the mountain simultaneously, and two climbers reached the summit via the traditional South Col route.

1980 — Japanese - from the North
A large and expensive expedition reached the summit by two different routes from Tibet. One climber reached the summit via the North-East Ridge and two climbers via the North Face.

1980 — Reinhold Messner — Solo
On August 20, Reinhold Messner made his second oxygenless ascent of Everest, this time from the Tibet side — and alone.

1980 — Nepal/Italian
A post-monsoon joint expedition of the Nepal Mountaineering Association and Club Alpino Italiano was forced back from the summit because of weather and logistic complications.

1981 — Japanese
A winter expedition was led by 1970 Everest summiter Naomi Uemura. It ended without success after reaching the South Col.

1981 — British
At the same time as the Japanese winter attempt, a British team led by Allan Rouse attempted the West Ridge, but was not successful.

1981 — Japanese
Meiji University sponsored a spring attempt led by Sinichi Nakajimi on the West Ridge.

Suggested Reading

There are hundreds of books on Nepal, Tibet and the Himalaya, some dating back to the 1800s. A trip to your local library will provide you with an armload of fascinating books. I have listed below some publications that I have found important and interesting; most are recent enough to be available in large libraries. Many of these books, and others not available in the west, can be purchased in Kathmandu.

Another good source of material on Nepal is the *National Geographic* Magazine. There have been about ten issues over the years that have had some material about Nepal and the Himalaya. Also look up copies of the *Himalayan Journal*, an annual publication of the Himalayan Club in Bombay, India.

NEPAL — THE LAND & ITS PEOPLE

Nepal — the Kingdom in the Himalayas: Toni Hagen, Kummerly & Frey, Berne, 1961 — a definitive documentation of the geology and people of Nepal; contains many fine photos. Hagen is working on a revised edition.

Mount Everest, the Formation, Population and Exploration of the Everest Region: Toni Hagen, G O Dyhrenfurth, C Von Furer Haimendorf and Erwin Schneider, Oxford University Press, London, 1963 — a shortened version of material in Hagen's book (above) combined with other works desciding in detail the Solu Khumbu region. Contains good maps.

The Sherpas of Nepal: C Von Furer Haimendorf, John Murry, London, 1964 — a rather dry anthropological study of the Sherpas of the Solu Khumbu region.

Himalayan Traders: C Von Furer Haimendorf, John Murray, London, 1975 — the sequel to Sherpas of Nepal, but more readable. A fascinating study of the change in trading patterns and culture among Himalayan peoples throughout Nepal.

Mustang — a lost Tibetan Kingdom: Michel Peissel, Collins & Harvill Press, London, 1968 — a description of the forbidden Mustang region north of Jomsom.

Nepal Himalaya: H W Tilman, Cambridge University Press, London, 1952 — a delightful book filled with Tilman's dry wit. It describes the first treks into Nepal in 1949 and 1950. The book is out of print and very hard to find; try a large library, it's impossible to buy a copy anywhere.

People of Nepal: Dor Bahadur Bista, Ratna Pustak Bhandar, Kathmandu, 1967 — an excellent overview of the various ethnic groups in Nepal, written by a Nepalese anthropologist.

The Festivals of Nepal: Mary M Anderson, George Allen & Unwin, London, 1971 — describes all of the important festivals of Nepal; contains a lot of background information about the Hindu religion.

High in the Thin Cold Air: Edmund Hillary & Desmond Doig, Doubleday, New York, 1962 — describes many of the projects undertaken by the Himalayan trust; also contains the story of a scientific examination of the Khumjung *yeti* skull.

Schoolhouse in the Clouds: Edmund Hillary, Penguin, London, 1968 — describes the construction of Khumjung school and other projects in Khumbu. Good background on where all those bridges, hospitals and schools came from.

The Kulunge Rai: Charles McDougal, Ratna Pustak Bhandar, Kathmandu, 1979 — anthropological studies of the Rais in the Hongu Valley, especially the village of Bung.

Vignettes of Nepal: Harka Gurung, Sajha Prakashan, Kathmandu, 1980 — personal accounts of treks throughout Nepal. Good historical and geological background is included. Many maps.

Mani Rimdu, Nepal: Mario Fantin, Toppan Co, Singapore, 1976 — colour photos and descriptions of the dances of the Mani Rimdu festival at Thyangboche Monastery.

NATURAL HISTORY

Birds of Nepal: Robert L Fleming Sr, Robert L Fleming Jr & Lain Bangdel, published by the authors, Kathmandu, 1976 — the definitive work on the hundreds of species of birds in Nepal. Contains many outstanding colour paintings of birds.

Forests of Nepal: J D A Stainton, John Murray, London, 1972 — if you're interested in trees, this is the book for you.

The Arun: Edward W Cronin, Jr, Houghton Mifflin Company, Boston, 1979 — a natural history of the Arun River Valley.

Stones of Silence: George B Schaller, Viking Press, New York, 1980 — a naturalists travels in Dolpo.

Himalayan Flowers and Trees: Dorothy Mierow & Tirtha Bahadur Shrestha, Sahayogi Press, Kathmandu, 1978 — the best available field guide to the plants of Nepal.

MOUNTAINEERING EXPEDITIONS — A MAJOR INFLUENCE OF WESTERNERS IN NEPAL

Americans on Everest: James Ramsey Ullman, J B Lippincott, Philadelphia, 1964 — the offical account of the 1963 American expedition.

The Moated Mountain: Showell Styles, Hurt & Blackett, London, 1955 — a very readable book about an expedition to Baudha peak; Styles makes fascinating cultural observations as he treks to the mountain.

Forerunners to Everest: Rene Dittert, Gabriel Chevalley & Raymond Lambert, trans by Malcolm Barnes; Harper & Row, New York, 1954 — a description of the two Swiss expeditions to Everest in 1952; includes a fine description of the approach march.

Annapurna: Maurice Herzog, Jonathan Cape, London, 1952 — a mountaineering classic that describes the first conquest of an 8000 metre peak. Contains a good description of the Annapurna region, including Manang, and a visit to Kathmandu in 1950.

Annapurna South Face: Christian Bonnington, Cassell, London, 1971 — the beginning of a new standard of mountaineering in Nepal and an excellent description of the problems of organising an expedition.

Faces of Everest: Major H P S Ahluwalia, Vikas, New Delhi, 1977 — an illustrated history of Everest by a summiter of the 1965 Indian expedition.

The Ascent of Rum Doodle: W E Bowman, Dark Peak, Sheffield, 1979 — a classic spoof of mountaineering books; good diversion after you have read a few expedition accounts that take themselves too seriously.

NEPALI LANGUAGE

Basic Gurkhali Grammar: M Meerendonk, Singapore, 1964 — one of the best introductory texts on Nepali, which the British Army calls Gurkhali. Written for the army, so it teaches a slightly weird military vocabulary.

Basic Gurkhali Dictionary: M Meerendonk, Singapore, 1960 — a handy pocket sized dictionary of the Nepali language. Quite useful once you understand the rudiments of the grammar.

Trekkers Pocket Pal: Summer Institute of Linguistics, Avalok, Kathmandu, 1977 — a handy phrase book for trekkers.

TIBET — A CULTURE THAT HAS INFLUENCED MUCH OF NEPAL

Tibet: Thubten Jigme Norbu & Colin Turnbull — an excellent account of the culture and religion of Tibet by the brother of the Dalai Lama.

The Secret War in Tibet: Michel Peissel — a one-sided description of the resistance of Khampa warriors against the Chinese takeover in Tibet; published in England as *Cavaliers of Kham.*

Seven Years in Tibet: Heinrich Harrer — the best-selling book describing Harrer's adventures in Tibet before the Chinese occupation; also contains commentary on Harrer's discussions with the Dalai Lama.

GUIDEBOOKS

Kathmandu & the Kingdom of Nepal: Prakash A Raj, Lonely Planet, Melbourne, 1980 — a complete guidebook to Nepal, written by an American educated Nepali, resident in Kathmandu.

Nepal Namaste: Robert Rieffel, Sahayogi Press, Kathmandu, 1978 — a good general guidebook written by a long-term resident of Kathmandu.

A Guide to Trekking in Nepal: Stephen Bezruchka, The Mountaineers, Seattle, 1981 — detailed information about how to organise a backpacking or live-off-the-land trek and many route descriptions.

Nepal Trekking Guidebooks: John L Hayes, Avalok, Kathmandu, 1976 — a series of three guidebooks describing trekking routes in Nepal. More self-guiding (though not complete) than the descriptions here.

Nepal Trekking: Christian Kleinert, Bergverlag Rudolf Rother, Munich, 1975 — a set of route descriptions in a fancy plastic cover that you can carry with you on your trek. Describes some very ambitious routes and schedules.

MEDICINE

Medicine for Mountaineering: James A Wilkerson, The Mountaineers, Seattle, 1975 — an outstanding reference book for the layman. Describes many of the medical problems typically encountered in Nepal. One copy should accompany every trekking party.

Mountain Medicine: Michael Ward, Crosby, Lockwood, Staples, London, 1975 — good background reading on cold and high altitude problems.

Where There Is No Doctor: David Werner, The Hesperian Foundation, Palo Alto, Calif, 1977 — a good laymen's medical guide with lots of application to Nepal.

Altitude Sickness: Peter Hackett, American Alpine Club, New York, 1979 — required reading for anyone who treks above 4000 metres.

Trekking Agents

It becomes difficult to prepare an up-to-date list of all trekking agents throughout the world because many new agents are springing up (and sometimes disappearing) every season. This list gives the addresses of most agents who specialise in trekking. It includes overseas offices of Nepalese companies, tour operators who form entire groups to Nepal, and agents who sell space on treks organised by others. The huge number of agents now selling trekking makes it difficult to make any judgement about the quality of service you may expect. From each of these agents you should be able to obtain any additional information you need about Nepal and trekking — most have staff who have trekked in Nepal. The list also concentrates on agents that have been organising treks in Nepal for several years — an indication that they know all the details necessary to organise your trek properly and that they are financially stable. All these agents offer a variety of treks and several choices of dates; most of them can also arrange your plane tickets to and from Nepal if you wish. Most will also allow you to book your trek and flights through your own local travel agent.

There are, however, a number of trekking agencies operated by people whose goal is a free trek in Nepal. Be careful and check out the financial and business background of an agent if you book a trek through a small agent at a bargain price. You may discover that your group is cancelled or that the price is increased at the last minute because the agent could not get the necessary number of people to make the trek economical.

AUSTRALIA & NEW ZEALAND

Adventure Travel Centre, First Floor, 28 Market St, Sydney, NSW 2000.
Adventure Travel, New Zealand, PO Box 6044, Napier, New Zealand.
Australian Himalayan Expeditions, 28-34 O'Connell St, Sydney, NSW 2000.
Ausventure, 860 Military Rd, PO Box 54, Mosman, NSW 2088.
Himalayan Journeys, c/o Travel Administration, 5th floor, 58 Pitt St. Sydney, NSW 2000.
Peregrine Expeditions, Suite 710, 343 Little Collins St, Melbourne, Vic 3000.
Venture Treks, 71 Evwlyn Rd, Howick, Aukland, New Zealand.

USA & CANADA

Adventure Centre, 5540 College Ave, Oakland, California 94618.

Folkways International Trekking, 14903 SE Linden Lane, Milwaukie, Oregon 97222.
Himalaya, Box 371, Oakland, California 94604.
Himalayan Journeys, PO Box 26731, San Francisco, California 94126.
Himalayan Rover Trek, PO Box 24382, Seattle, Washington 98124.
Himalayan Travel, PO Box 481, Greenwich, Connecticut 06830.
Journeys, PO Box 7545, Ann Arbor, Michigan 48107.
Mountain Travel, 1398 Solano Ave, Albany, California 94706.
Mountain Travel Canada, 737 Burley Drive, West Vancouver, BC V7T 1Z7.
Nature Expeditions International, 599 College Avenue, Palo Alto, California 94306.
Sobek Expeditions, PO Box 7007, Angels Camp, California 95222.
Wilderness Travel, 1760 Solano Ave, Berkeley, California 94707.
Wind Over Mountain, 925 University, Boulder, Colorado 80302.

UK

Exodus Expeditions, 167 Earls Court Rd, London SW5.
ExplorAsia, Blenheim House, Burnsall St, London SW3 5XS.
Himalayan Journeys, 17 Stanthorpe Road, Streatham, London SW16.
Sherpa Expeditions, 3 Bedford Road, London W4.
Thomas Cook Searcher Holidays, PO Box 36, Thorpe Wood, Peterborough.
WEXAS International, 45 Brompton Road, Knightsbridge, London SW3 1DE.

FRANCE

Club Mediteranee, Les Favrande, 7440 Chamonix.
Delta Voyages, 54 Rue des Ecoles, 75005 Paris.
Explorator, 16, Place de la Madeleine, 75008 Paris.
Nouvelles Frontieres, 37 rue Violet, 75015 Paris.

GERMANY

Dav, German Alpine Club.
Hauser Exkursionen, Neuhauser Strasse 1, 8000 Munchen 2.
Sporthaus Schuster, Rosenstrasse, 8000 Munchen 2.

SCANDANAVIA

Den Norsk Turistforening, Stortingsgaten 28, Oslo 1, Norway.
Norsk Rejsebureau, Frederiksberggade 10, 1459 Copenhagen K, Denmark.

SWITZERLAND

Arca Tour, Gartenstrasse 2, CH-6301 Zug.
ARTOU, 8, rue de Rive, CH-1204 Geneve.
Intertrek, Lehnstrasse, CH-9050 Apenzell.

ITALY
Trekking International, via GF Re 8, 10146 Torino.

JAPAN
Alpine Tour Service, 7F Kawashima Hoshin Bldg, 2-2, 2-chome, Shimbashi, Minato-ku, Tokyo.
Saiyu Riyoko, 1-1-17 Kouraku Bunkiyoku, Tokyo.

OTHER
International Travel Agency, PO Box 122, Airport PO, Dharan, Saudi Arabia.
Express Travel, Suite 27, Midland Plaza, M Adriatico St., Ermita, Manila Philippines.
Holland International, Suite 401, Far East Shopping Centre, 545 Orchard Road, Singapore 9.

Suggested Timetable

As soon as you decide you are going to Nepal:
  Begin your physical conditioning program.
  Reserve space on a trek with a trekking agent; send him the required deposit.
  Have a passport photo taken and get ten copies.
  Apply for your passport.

After your space on the trek has been confirmed:
  Begin a reading program about Nepal and the Himalaya.
  Get a thorough medical exam from your doctor. Have him complete the physician's certificate provided by the agent.
  Begin your series of immunisations.
  Start to accumulate your equipment.
  Write to the Nepalese embassy for a visa form.

Not later than two months before your departure date:
  Apply for your Nepalese visa.
  Confirm with your trekking agent that you will be travelling with a group — or present your agent with your final schedule for your alternate travel plan.
  Send additional payment, as required, to the agent.
  Secure baggage and accident insurance.

No later than one month before your departure date:
  Have your passport and visa in hand.

216 The Nepali Language

Complete your immunisations and have the certificate stamped by your local health office.

If you have not already done so, finish payment for trek and plane fare.

Obtain sufficient traveller's cheques from your bank.

Finish accumulating your equipment — check the weight you carry on plane (under 20 kg) and on the trek (under 15 kg).

The day you leave — at the airport:

Register your camera, lenses and tape recorder with the customs if they are new, this will ensure that you are not charged duty on them when you return home.

The Nepali Language

Nepali is the working tongue of Nepal and is understood by almost everyone in the country. Many ethnic groups have their own language, which they speak amongst themselves, using Nepali outside their own region. The Sherpas speak Sherpa, Nepali and some Tibetan. Nepali is the mother tongue of the Brahmins, Chhetris and Thakurs — the highest castes in Nepal. It belongs to the Indo-Aryan or Sanskrit family of languages. Its nearest relative today is Kumaoni (spoken in a region of north-west India). Nepali has much in common with Hindi, the official language of India, which has the same origins. It has also taken many words from Persian, through Hindustani.

Some useful words and phrases are listed below. Since Nepali, like Hindi, uses the Devanagari script, transliteration to Roman script was necessary.

Pronunciation:	a	is pronounced as in	ba*ll*oon
	ā	is pronounced as in	*fa*ther
	e	is pronounced as in	caf*e*
	i	is pronounced as in	r*i*m
	o	is pronounced as in	g*o*
	u	is pronounced as in	*cu*ckoo
	ai	is pronounced as in	ch*ai*se

Phrases

In Nepali the verb is placed at the end of a sentence. Grammatically, questions are identical to statements. The differentiation is made by the inflection of one's voice.

What is your name?	*Timro nām ke ho?*
My name is....	*Mero nām.......ho*
Is the trail steep?	*Bato ukālo chha?*
How are you?	*Tapailai kasto chha?*

Which trail goes to.....?	*Kun bāto......jānchha?*
Where is my tent?	*Mero tent kahān chha?*
The food is good?	*Khāna mitho chha?*
This river is cold	*Yo khola chiso chha*
What time is it?	*Kati bajyo?*
It is 5 o'clock	*Pānch bajyo*
What is this?	*Yo ke ho?*
It is cold today	*Āja jāro chha*
It is raining	*Pāni parchha*
That is OK	*Thik chha*
What is the name of this village?	*Yo gāunko nām ke ho?*
Where is a shop?	*Pasal kahān chha?*
Please give me a cup of tea	*Ek cup chiyā dinuhos*
It is enough	*Pugchha*
I don't know	*Thāhā chhaina*

Numbers

1	*ek*	11	*eghāra*	25	*pachchis*
2	*dui*	12	*bāhra*	30	*tis*
3	*tin*	13	*tehra*	40	*chālis*
4	*chār*	14	*chaudha*	50	*pachās*
5	*pānch*	15	*pandhra*	60	*sāthi*
6	*chha*	16	*sohra*	70	*sattari*
7	*sāt*	17	*satra*	80	*ashi*
8	*āth*	18	*athāra*	90	*nabbe*
9	*nau*	19	*unnāis*	100	*ek say*
10	*das*	20	*bis*	1000	*ek hajār*

hello, goodbye	*namaste*	food	*khānā*
thank you	*dhanyabād*	vegetable	*sāg*
bird	*charo*	water	*pāni*
water-buffalo	*bhainsi*	hot water	*tāto pāni*
chicken	*kukhoro*	cold water	*chiso pāni*
cow	*gāi*	hot	*tāto*
dog	*kukur*	hot (spicy)	*piro*
horse	*ghorā*	tasty	*mitho*
pig	*sungur*		
beer (local)	*chang* or *janr*	mountain	*parbat*
whisky (local)	*rākshi*	river (small)	*khola*
meat	*māsu*	river (large)	*nadi, kosi*
tea	*chiyā*	steep (uphill)	*ukālo*
bread	*roti*		
egg	*phul*	steep (downhill)	*orālo*

cold (weather)	*jāro*	happy	*khushi*
warm (weather)	*garam*	left	*bāyān*
trail	*bāto*	right	*dāhine*
		tired	*thākyo*
house	*ghar*	enough	*pugyo*
shop	*pasal*	yes (it is....)	*ho*
latrine	*charpi*	no (it is not....)	*hoina*
		this	*yo*
mother	*āmā*	that	*tyo*
father	*bābu*	mine	*mero*
son	*chhoro*	yours	*timro*
daughter	*chhori*	expensive	*mahango*
younger sister	*bahini*	cheap	*sasto*
younger brother	*bhāi*	big	*thulo*
elder sister	*didi*	small	*sano*
elder brother	*dāi*	maybe	*hola*
friend	*sāthi*	good	*rāmro*
		not good	*narāmro*
day	*din*	clean	*sāph*
morning	*bihāna*	dirty	*mailo*
night	*rāt*	heavy	*gahrungo*
today	*āja*	his, hers	*unro*
yesterday	*hijo*	here	*yahān*
tomorrow	*bholi*	there	*tyahān*
day-after-tomorrow	*parsi*	which	*kun*
		where	*kahān*

Lonely Planet travel guides

Africa on the Cheap
Australia — a travel survival kit
Burma — a travel survival kit
Central Asia on a Shoestring
Hong Kong, Macau & Canton
India — a travel survival kit
Israel & the Occupied Territories
Japan — a travel survival kit
Kashmir, Ladakh & Zanskar
Kathmandu & the Kingdom of Nepal
Malaysia, Singapore & Brunei
Mountaineering in Papua New Guinea
New Zealand — a travel survival kit
North-Easting Asia on a Shoestring
Pakistan — a travel survival kit
Papua New Guinea — a travel survival kit
The Philippines — a travel survival kit
South America on a Shoestring
South-East Asia on a Shoestring
Sri Lanka — a travel survival kit
Thailand — a travel survival kit
Tramping in New Zealand
Trekking in the Himalayas
USA West

WHERE TO FIND LONELY PLANET TRAVEL GUIDES

Lonely Planet travel guides are available around the world. If you can't find them ask your bookshop to order them from one of the distributors listed below. For countries not listed write to Lonely Planet in Australia.

Australia Lonely Planet Publications Pty Ltd, PO Box 88, South Yarra, Victoria 3141.
Canada Milestone Publications, Box 6006, Victoria, British Columbia, V8P 5L4.
Hong Kong The Book Society, GPO Box 7804, Hong Kong.
India UBS Distributors, 5 Ansari Rd, New Delhi.
Japan Intercontinental Marketing Corp, IPO Box 5056, Tokyo 100-31.
Malaysia MPH Distributors, 13, Jalan 13/6, Petaling Jaya, Selangor, Malaysia.
Nepal see India
Netherlands Nilsson & Lamm bv, Postbus 195, Pampuslaan 212, 1680 AD Weesp.
New Zealand Caveman Press, PO Box 1458, Dunedin.
Papua New Guinea Gordon & Gotch (PNG), PO Box 3395, Port Moresby.
Singapore MPH Distributors, 116-D JTC Factory Building, Lorong 3, Geylang Square, Singapore 1438.
Thailand Chalermnit, 1-2 Erawan Arcade, Bangkok.
UK Roger Lascelles, 16 Holland Park Gardens, London, W14 8DY.
USA (West) Bookpeople, 2940 Seventh St, Berkeley, CA 94710.
USA (East) Hippocrene Books, 171 Madison Ave, New York, NY 10016.
West Germany Buchvertrieb Gerda Schettler, Postfach 64, D-3415 Hattorf a H.

LONELY PLANET NEWSLETTER

We collect an enormous amount of information here at Lonely Planet. Apart from our research we also get a steady stream of letters from people out on the road — some of them are just one line on a postcard, others go on for pages. Plus we always have an ear to the ground for the latest on cheap airfares, new visa regulations, borders opening and closing. A lot of this information goes into our new editions or 'update supplements' in reprints. But we'd like to make better use of this information so we are now producing a quarterly newsletter packed full of the latest news from out on the road. It appears in February, May, August and November of each year. If you'd like an airmailed copy of the most recent newsletter just send us A$1.50 (A$1 within Australia) or A$5 (A$4 in Australia) for a year's subscription.